For
Barbara Nangaypa Dhamarrandji

Sorcerers and Healing Spirits

Sorcerers and Healing Spirits

Continuity and Change in an Aboriginal Medical System

Janice Reid

Australian National University Press
Canberra
1983

First published in Australia 1983
Printed in Australia for the Australian National University
Press, Canberra

©Janice Reid 1983

This book is copyright. Apart from any fair dealing for the purpose of study, research, criticism, or review, as permitted under the Copyright Act, no part may be reproduced by any process without written permission. Inquiries should be made to the publisher.

National Library of Australia
Cataloguing-in-Publication entry

Reid, Janice, 1947–.
    Sorcerers and healing spirits.
    Bibliography.
    Includes index.
    ISBN 0 7081 1768 6.
    [1]. Aborigines, Australian — Medicine.
    2. Yolngu (Australian people). 3. Healing —
    Religious aspects. I. Title.
    615.8'99

Library of Congress No. 82-71833

United Kingdom, Europe, Middle East, and Africa: Eurospan
3 Henrietta St, London WC2E 8LU, England

North America: Books Australia, 15601 SW 83rd Avenue, Miami, Florida 33157 USA

Japan: United Publishers Services Ltd, Tokyo

South-east Asia: Information Publications Pte Ltd, 24 New Industrial Road, Singapore, 1953

Acknowledgments

Throughout the fieldwork at Yirrkala, Northern Territory, on which this book is based, I was blessed with patient and caring Aboriginal teachers, friends and family. My gratitude to my adoptive sister Barbara (or Nangaypa) Dhamarrandji, her daughter Milminyina and others of my Yolngu family is beyond expression. I am also indebted to Daymbalipu Mununggurr, Dadaynga Marika, Galarrwuy Yunupingu, Gatjil Djerrkura and Gawirrin Gumana for their guidance and support in my work; Maypilama Gurruwiwi and all of my sisters for their patient help as co-workers and interpreters; Nininggurr Dhamarrandji, Nyapalilngu Dhamarrandji, Wandjuk Marika, Djewiny Ngurruwutthun, Dundiwuy and Gunapa Wanambi, Laklak Yunupingu and all of the health workers at Yirrkala for helping me to understand a little of Yolngu culture. I am grateful to members of the Yirrkala Town Council (now Dhanbul Council) and community elders for assisting me throughout my work and for giving me permission to undertake and publish this study. I hope they are justified in their often expressed wish that students, doctors, nurses and others who read this book will gain a greater understanding of and respect for Aboriginal culture. I also hope that while imposing an anthropological perspective on their world view, I have preserved its integrity and meaning.

I was very fortunate to have had the presence and friendship for some of the time in the field of other researchers. All were exceedingly generous in introducing me to those they knew could assist me in my work and in offering advice and information relevant to my study. Nancy Williams opened doors for me which otherwise would have remained closed and consistently gave me her time, energy, support and scholarly advice during fieldwork and writing. I am indebted to David Biernoff, Ian Dunlop, Frances Morphy, Howard Morphy and Neville White for their advice and material help both in and out of the field.

Many other people offered hospitality and assistance while I was at Yirrkala or on my way to or from the field: Maria Brandl, Max and Elizabeth Chalmers, Ed Garrison, Tom and Dulcie Gavranic, David Hordern, Stan and Jean Linco, Brian Reid, Lossa and Jonetani Rika, Joyce Ross, Barbara Tynan, Elizabeth Weiner and especially Torika and Samuela Vateitei.

In Sydney and Canberra I was supported and encouraged by many friends and colleagues. Russ Hausfeld helped me find a direction when I could only see dead ends and patiently read and gave detailed comments on many drafts of my work. Diane Barwick, Jeremy Beckett, Fay Chapman, Vicky Burbank, Jenny Guest, Raul Pertierra and David Turnbull also read earlier drafts of the manuscript and offered thoughtful critiques. Peter Lawrence commented most helpfully on my work and guided me to literature which was pertinent to my analysis. Paul Alexander, Diane Bell, Gillian Cowlishaw, Don Gardner and Fran Hausfeld all offered valuable advice. I am very grateful to each of them.

I also extend sincere thanks to academic staff and fellow students at Hawaii and Stanford Universities for invaluable discussions and tuition throughout my time there. In particular I am grateful to Clifford Barnett, and to George Collier, Jane Collier, Benjamin Paul, Renato Rosaldo and Dawn Ryan for their guidance and support *in situ* and in the field.

The study was funded by Stanford University, the National Science Foundation (USA), the National Health and Medical Research Council (under the program directed by John Cawte, Australian Transcultural Psychiatry) (1974-5), the Australian Institute of Aboriginal Studies (1978, 1979 and 1981) and the North Australian Research Unit (1981). My employers, the University of New South Wales (1974-7), the Cumberland College of Health Sciences (1978) and the Commonwealth Institute of Health at Sydney University (1979-) have facilitated my work in every way. I am particularly grateful to Robert Black for his help and encouragement. Thanks also go to the staff of the Commonwealth Institute of Health audio-visual department (including Patricia Moylan), administration and typing services and to Nola Johnson and Jaci Fischer of the University of New South Wales for their valued assistance.

Finally, my warm thanks go to my family and friends, especially Elizabeth Bryan, Susan Rao, Vikram Rao, Joan Reid, Keith Reid and Judith Strauch. Their unwavering support over the years has meant more to me than I can say.

Contents

Acknowledgments	v
Language conventions	ix
Introduction	xi
1. The Yolngu	1
2. The causes of affliction	32
3. *Marrnggitj:* the Yolngu healer	57
4. Sorcerer and healer: a matter of boundaries	79
5. The search for meaning	92
6. A semblance of change	119
Appendix: Questionnaire	157
References	159
Index	171

Illustrations

Maps

1. Arnhem Land   4
2. Yirrkala and its homeland centres   13

Tables

1. Causes suggested for hypothetical illnesses   122
2. Suggested treatments for hypothetical illnesses   123
3. The contemporary aetiological domain   147

Plates

1 The author with members of her Yolngu family during a day's hunting at Lom (Crocodile Creek) on the coast near Wallaby Beach   xv
2 Gove District hospital, Nhulunbuy   21
3 Health worker dressing an injury during morning clinic at Yirrkala health centre   22
4 Watching television at dusk at Galoro homeland centre   23
5 A *marrnggitj* (healer-diviner) of Yirrkala with his diagnostic and healing stones (*milirrk*)   59
6 A *bukulup* (*liyalupthun*) or washing ceremony held at the end of a funeral   80
7 Collecting the edible fruit and medicinal leaves of the tree *dhurrpinda* or *monydjuti* (*Buchanania obovata/arborescens*)   93

Language Conventions

All Aboriginal terms used in this book are in Gumatj, an Eastern Dhuwala dialect of the Yolngu language group (Morphy 1977). The orthography used here is similar to that devised by Beulah Lowe (Lowe n.d.) for Gupapuyngu, a Western Dhuwala dialect spoken in the Milingimbi area.

Yolngu words are printed in italics. Consonants are pronounced as in English, with the following exceptions:

Lamino–dental
th, dh, nh - t, d and n pronounced with tip of tongue between or pressed against teeth

Lamino–palatal
tj, dj, ny – tj similar to 'ch' as in 'church'
dj similar to 'j' as in 'job'
ny as in 'new'

Trill
rr – rolled r

Retroflexed
ṯ, ḏ, ṉ, ḻ, r – pronounced with tip of tongue bent back to touch roof of mouth

A glottal stop is represented thus: *Galiwin'ku*. 'Ng' is pronounced as in 'sing'.

Yolngu languages have a three-vowel system with a feature of length. Pronunciation of vowels varies according to context, but the following scheme provides an approximate guide for pronunciation of the Yolngu words used in this book.

Short
i (as in 'sit')
u (as in 'put')
a (as in 'cup')

Long
e (as in 'seen')
o (as in 'room')
ä (as in 'father')

British spelling conventions are used for English words.

Introduction

> . . . magic is a spurious system of natural law as well as a fallacious guide of conduct; it is a false science as well as an abortive art.
> Sir James Frazer, *The Golden Bough*, 1922, p. 11.

> . . . I consider the attempts to dismiss magic as a sort of false science, resting on a wrongful association of ideas, or on the omnipotence of words, a mistake of both fact and reason, as erroneous as the attempt to dismiss myth as a disease of language.
> W.E.H. Stanner, 'Religion, Totemism and Symbolism' (1962). *White Man Got No Dreaming, Essays 1938-1973*, 1979, p. 124.

At the end of 1968, the year after I graduated from university in Australia, I took a position as a science teacher at Kerevat, a secondary school on the island of New Britain in Papua New Guinea. Kerevat was a boarding school which took the best students from village primary schools all over the island. I was the school's 'sick mistress'. Every afternoon I dressed tropical ulcers, dosed malarial fevers and struggled with the diagnoses of other maladies. One night I was called to the girls' dormitory to see Anna. She had been vomiting all day, was refusing food and water and would not talk to any of her friends. She vomited all that night and the next day. Sleepless and somewhat frightened I decided to contact her parents and send her to hospital in the main town. When I went to see her two days later she was gone. The doctor told me that, although he could not discern any cause for her condition, she had gone downhill rapidly in hospital. He thought the illness might have a psychiatric basis. Finally Anna's parents had told him they wanted to take her back to her village, and he had discharged her not knowing whether she would live or die.

Two weeks later, bright-eyed and smiling, Anna came to tell me she was back at school. She never again mentioned her illness but her girl friends explained that the family's circle of magical protection had been breached by someone who bore a grudge against them, and that Anna had been the sorcerer's chosen victim. At home Anna's clan had employed counter-measures to remove the spell. These had worked and she had recovered.

I was fascinated. The notion that a malevolent person could wreak such harm, or that people believed it sufficiently to become dangerously ill, was the stuff of adventure movie matinees in Australia. But here, among the most delightful and down-to-earth people I had ever met, it was real. My interest never left me. Twelve years later, in 1981, I was reminiscing with Papua New Guinean friends who had been at the school then and were now in the highest echelons of the post-Independence government. Incidents at the school of this sort, they said, were but a few examples of the behaviour of spirits and sorcerers in their society. Even in the nation's capital, over 1000 kilometres from home, they were obliged to make sure that they were protected from the malicious magic of others.

In 1969, I relinquished my teaching career and went to America to study anthropology, first at the University of Hawaii and then at Stanford University. After the required coursework and examinations, I was ready to begin field research for my doctorate. In 1974, after returning to Australia and making one visit to the North, I wrote to the Aboriginal Council of Yirrkala, an Aboriginal community in north-east Arnhem Land, Northern Territory, asking for permission to come and work there. It was granted. The Yirrkala people, today called Yolngu, belong to the society which Lloyd Warner named the Murngin in his anthropological classic, *A Black Civilization*. This book, based on fieldwork among the Yolngu affiliated with Milingimbi mission in the period 1926-9, contains an elegant exposition of Murngin magic and medicine. It seemed an ideal foundation for my own study. The questions I hoped to answer were the same questions which had intrigued me since my days in Papua New Guinea. What is social life like in a community where sorcerers and spiritual healers are taken for granted? What are the understandings of sickness and death held by the Yolngu today? Are they still those which Warner recorded, or have they changed? How do a people almost fifty years removed in time from the Arnhem Land of Warner's day reconcile indigenous views of health and illness with the views of the dominant white Australian society?

My interests were not solely intellectual. Growing up in Australia I had, like most white Australians, never met an Aborigine. In the 1950s and 1960s their plight was either ignored or unknown by most city people. It was in colonial Papua New Guinea that I first encountered both the kindly paternalism and the bald racism of my own people. I was in America when the angry Aboriginal voice began to be heard in Australia demanding land, compensation and recognition. Not until I returned did I begin to appreciate the suffering and bitterness of many Aborigines and the pervasive and defensive dislike of Aborigines by other Australians. I was deeply angered. It seemed to me then that one of the things I was in a position to do was to use my work to help bridge the gulf between Aboriginal people and the often culturally-blinkered health services on which they depend. To this end I later wrote articles with Aboriginal co-workers on Yolngu views of health and the care of the sick (Reid 1979a; Reid and Dhamarrandji 1978; Reid and Gurruwiwi

1979; Reid and Mununggurr 1977; Reid, Yunupingu and Yunupingu 1978) and worked on a parliamentary enquiry into Aboriginal health. But as I learned more about the precursors of Aboriginal suffering I became less sanguine about the task of countering the profound inequities in service delivery. It was clear that the forces which perpetuate paternalism and racism are historical and political (Reid 1982) and do not yield readily to reason. The Aboriginal experience in Australia echoes in some ways that of Papua New Guinea, but its effects are far less tractable because, in Australia, colonialism has no end.

This is not to say that all health services to Aborigines are thoughtlessly ethnocentric. The health authorities of the Northern Territory, where this study was conducted, are amenable to flexibility and experimentation in Aboriginal health care. The Department of Health has employed Aboriginal healers, instituted an Aboriginal health worker training scheme, and initiated a program to collect and identify indigenous medicinal plants. The Departments of Aboriginal Affairs funded three independent medical services in central Australia which are based on the principles of community development and Aboriginal control. The new spirit of cultural accommodation in a few, but by no means all, areas of Australia reflects a similar shift world-wide towards recognition of indigenous healing resources and the importance of community involvement in health care (World Health Organization 1978). In Australia, the House of Representatives Standing Committee on Aboriginal Affairs recommended in its report on Aboriginal health (Australia 1979) that:

> *Aboriginal cultural beliefs and practices which affect their health and their use of health services such as their fear of hospitalisation, their attitudes to pain and surgery, the role of traditional healers and the differing needs and roles of Aboriginal men and women, be fully taken into account in the design and implementation of health care programs* (p. 74, original emphasis).

The Committee also maintained that:

> Aboriginal communities have the right to determine the type of health care service they require and to be involved at all levels in the design and management of curative and preventive community health programs (p. 111).

Despite all the flurries of activity on the front lines of Aboriginal health care and a heightened interest in the social dimensions of sickness and curing, when this study began in 1974 no other major study of an Aboriginal medical system in its contemporary setting had been undertaken. Valuable data on magic and Aboriginal healing were to be found in the ethnographies of such well known scholars as Catherine Berndt (1964), Ronald Berndt (1947, and, jointly, 1977), Cawte (1974), Eliade (1973), Elkin (1935a, 1975, 1977), Howitt (1886) and Spencer and Gillen (1899). The studies of the Aboriginal response to white domination available at that time suggested that Aborigines readily accept the outward trappings of Western society while retaining many of the fundamental values and religious beliefs of their own society (for instance, Calley 1955; Elkin 1935b; Reay 1949; R. Tonkinson 1974). However, there were no substantial analyses of the adaptation of medical beliefs and practices to the changes of the past two hundred years. There seemed ample room for a study which would take as its focus the impact of social change on the medical system of one community.

More recent studies have shown that the role of the Aboriginal doctor and indigenous concepts about sickness and curing are still an integral part of life in many Aboriginal communities (Bell 1980, 1982; Gray 1976, 1979; Elkin 1977; M. Tonkinson 1982; Tynan 1979). Even now, though, most people who work with Aborigines, including health personnel, are unaware of the complexity and theoretical elegance of contemporary Aboriginal medical systems. It is my hope that this study of one such system will not only be of interest to academic colleagues but helpful to doctors, nurses and others working in cross-cultural settings, most particularly in Aboriginal health care.

In the Field

I arrived at Yirrkala in 1974 suitably equipped. I was bearing my typewriter, notebooks, camera, modest clothes, camping gear, gifts and research proposal. My first priority was to find someone to work with – a teacher and friend who would introduce me to the community. She would preferably speak English, be about my age and well respected. I would choose her when I had surveyed the situation. Four days later I was told through an interpreter that a woman a good ten years older than me, whom I had never seen before and who spoke little English, would work with me. She would be my sister, her subsection my subsection, her family my family, her clan my clan, and my name Djinyupa (Plate 1). She would introduce me to my fathers, mothers, brothers, sisters, cousins, uncles, aunts, grandparents, children and grandchildren. I was to learn their names, the appropriate kinship terms of address and proper behaviour towards each person. I did not know whether to be grateful or indignant. I was certainly daunted at the prospect of

1 The author with members of her Yolngu family during a day's hunting at Lorn (Crocodile Creek) on the coast near Wallaby Beach

having to navigate through the intricacies of the complex Murngin system, one of the textbook systems of Aboriginal kinship. I soon found, though, that the Yolngu were not as confused as the anthropologists and knew exactly how to explain their social map to newly adopted outsiders.

But, if I soon gained a working knowledge of my Yolngu relationships, my best efforts to learn other Yolngu skills were never quite equal to the challenge. As an honorary Yolngu I simply did not excel. My fires went out. I never caught a mud crab. One native fruit tree looked the same as any other to me. In the time it took the women to find and break up a load of firewood I had gathered a few unwieldy logs which I could not keep on my head. The infants took one look at me and turned away in tears while their mothers tried to coax them to smile at me by telling them I was their mother or sister. I loathed spiders, a fear which kin found exasperating. Not so snakes. I thought I would save some face when I was bitten by a snake and stayed utterly calm – but no one else saw the snake and, even when I became very ill, would not believe me. I forgot who my distant brothers and sons-in-law were and embarrassed myself, them and my sister by speaking to them directly. My *faux pas* always elicited howls of recrimination from everyone present. I suspect most people liked me but thought I was socially as competent as a three-year-old.

The first three months were a stormy passage. No evidence of the black magic which Warner wrote about was immediately obvious. My first questions were met with polite evasion. The older people seemed not to want to talk about the subject and the young said they did not believe these things. There were no singularly wise and spiritual individuals who hastened to the bedsides of the sick to perform healing rituals. Most people went to the health centre when they got sick, or took aspirin or cough mixture.

When the nursing sister then at the health centre learned I was doing some research which related to health she perceived me as a threat and thereafter refused to let me use health records or visit the health centre. Some white staff were kindly and welcoming. Most were uneasy about my presence. One man told me I was in grave spiritual danger investigating 'witchdoctors' and the realm of magic. Another pointedly said that, when the last researcher who had lived at Yirrkala and daily entertained Aborigines in his house left, they had to burn the furniture.

Nor was life with Yolngu entirely straightforward. My family was ever attentive and helpful. But the confrontations with white authorities over the preceding decade had left their mark. Some of the younger and travelled leaders were as ambivalent as I about research in their community. Their attitudes, which found expression on one or two very difficult occasions, are captured in the words of one young man who told a committee of inquiry in 1974:

> anthropologists and archaeologists are upsetting
> Aboriginal people. I feel very strongly about this because
> I have seen a lot of people . . . studying Aboriginal
> people . . . [T]o some of us who have had some kind of
> education these kinds of actions and these kinds of
> treatments are being seen as an insult (Australia
> 1974a:525).

As time passed, though, I became more accepted and capable as a community member. I was more sensitive to the unspoken demands of different situations, remembered who my relatives were, could communicate in simple Gumatj, learned to dance at ceremonies, and recognised the tendrils of edible yams when I saw them. I found that the most active healer at Yirrkala, who bore little resemblance to the sage elder of my imaginings, was a close relative. Once my sister vouched for my sympathy and trustworthiness he willingly told me his life story and let me watch when he treated the sick. My extended family absorbed me into daily life and so I was privy to the ways in which they managed and conceptualised illness. People from other clans came to know who I was, offered to teach me the principles of Yolngu medical theory and practice, and included me in medical crises. I reciprocated as best I could. I paid people for the formal work they did with me, shared my own possessions and, when asked, acted as a go-between. I was often asked to obtain services and information from government and mission staff which people found trying and sometimes humiliating to seek for themselves.

My feelings as the time came to leave Yirrkala in late 1975 were confused. Fieldwork – that ritual extolled as the making of the anthropologist – was over. I was relieved to be quitting, for a time at least, the demanding roles of inquirer and novice community member. But I had gained a second family who clearly cared for me as much as I them. When I was at Yirrkala a few years later I mused out loud in a moment of doubt about my status in the family that perhaps not everyone in the clan was comfortable having me around. One of my sisters looked hurt and indignant. 'You're our adopted child', she said. 'You're accepted as one of the family. Father always greets you whenever you come back, doesn't he? He took you as one of his own'.

At the end of 1975 some daughters came for a holiday in Sydney and then went on to stay with my own parents (their 'grandparents') in Adelaide. When my Yolngu mother was very sick in 1978 the head of her clan rang and asked me to 'come home'. I was back again later in the year as an adviser to the federal parliamentary committee then conducting an inquiry into Aboriginal health. When my Yolngu mother and father died within weeks of one another in 1979 I returned for the month-long funerals. Later in the year my sister and others came south for a holiday. Again in late 1981 I visited and caught up on changes. These visits, the occasional letters and the telephone calls both to and from Yirrkala enabled me to keep abreast of events in the community. When I came to write a book and could look back over seven years, I felt I knew quite a bit about Yolngu views of health, illness and death.

But what, in reality, did I know? This was a question I asked myself often as I analysed my data. How was I to reconcile the contradictions in what I had been told? The puzzles were many. If a sister, for instance, told me one of our brothers died because a sorcerer from another town attacked him in error, a man from another clan said the same brother brought his death on himself when he failed to fulfil ritual obligations, a woman from yet another clan that his wife was having an affair and her lover worked sorcery on him, and a young cousin that he died of a heart attack, what was I to believe? The answer was crucial to my analysis for Yolngu place great emphasis on knowing the 'true story' about any important event. Further, if other non-Aborigines were to read my findings they would want to situate them in the Western domains of fact and interpretation.

When I witnessed a series of events myself I could rely on my own observations. But when people explained, taught, gossiped, speculated, told yarns and accused, it became clear that there were as many truths as there were people to tell them (cf. Jay [1969] who designates his own observations during fieldwork in Java 'actuality' and his informants' statements 'conception'). The reasons for this are twofold and have to do with the social context of explanation, and what it means 'to know' in Yolngu society.

First, what a person told me about an illness or death depended on the speaker's relationship to me, the event itself and the people involved. I was perceived as a member of a particular family and clan for some purposes, and as a non-Aborigine and outsider for others. The information a person volunteered was moulded not only by how he (or she) perceived me in relation to the event, but whether he was making an accusation, dispassionately relating the facts as he knew them, embellishing a story for the entertainment of others, or seeking to enhance his own reputation or diminish that of another person.

Second, what I was told depended on what I had a right to know and what the speaker had a right to say. As Stephen Harris (1977) found in his study of learning at Milingimbi, for Yolngu, knowledge is more subjective and related to status than that of Western society; it is not an objective, secular entity which is available to anyone. What one knows and can say depends on one's family and clan membership, birth order, marital status, child-bearing status, sex, authority and age. For instance, mature men are entitled to know and reveal the secret religious lore of their society to young men during sacred ceremonies. When men say women do not know about a ceremony they mean they have no right to pass on knowledge about it. Most mature women know a great deal and are consulted by men on the conduct of their clans' ceremonies. But because they have not observed the ceremony or performed it they do not know it in the Yolngu sense. Conversely, both men and women go to great lengths to preserve the fiction that men do not and may not know about 'women's business'. In reality married men are well acquainted with the facts about pregnancy, childbirth and menstruation.

Once I came to be regarded as a familiar and reliable person, I gained the right to know whatever I saw, whatever I was invited to take part in, or whatever most women in their late twenties would be told. That I was mature but single was a troublesome anomaly in a society in which women marry very young. For most purposes, though, I was afforded a status similar to that of my older sister, who had two adolescent children and was a woman of standing in political and ceremonial matters.

Because sorcery and healing are part of the public domain of knowledge, the only relevant matters I could not, in principle, know about were the ritual offences and conflicts which lay behind some sorcery accusations. In these situations men or women either said that this was a secret matter, or took me aside and told me the details on the understanding that I would keep them to myself and write about them only in the most general terms. In all, what I came to know after several years depended on my own observations, my structural position, my status in the eyes of others, and on their motivations for telling me about community affairs. From conversations, formal interviews, camp-fire stories and my records of actual illnesses or deaths I slowly gained a sense of the Yolngu view of death and suffering.

Interpretation

One major area of Yolngu concern emerged from this data on sickness and death: sorcery. An attack by a sorcerer was almost always cited as the cause of a life-threatening illness or death. The precipitating factors—such as a fight, a breach of the law or adultery — varied, but the means were, in most cases, the same. Because of its prominence as a cultural motif in medical crises sorcery became a major focus of the study.

(Before outlining this approach I should, for those who are unfamiliar with such studies, interpose an anthropological comment on sorcery.)

Several people have asked me whether sorcery works and whether I believe in it. The short answer is that anthropologists approach belief systems of all societies, including, ideally, their own, objectively. Only very rarely do they subscribe to the ideas they are investigating. An axiom of the ethnographic enterprise is that sorcery is not 'real' in any empirical sense, or, if it is performed (and it is usually very difficult to find out whether it is), it does not actually harm the intended victim. This raises a few problems. What about people who confess to sorcery and witchcraft accusations? Anthropologists would say that any claim that they have successfully worked sorcery is a social strategy or a kind of culturally conditioned wishful thinking. And what of the person who thinks he has been attacked by sorcery and, for no apparent medical reason, dies? — such deaths have sometimes been interpreted as a physiologically mediated response to stress (Cannon 1942).

Intellectually, I uphold the axiom of the discipline. A Yolngu would reasonably say this is my belief, for in the social laboratory I cannot easily prove that sorcery is not used to the desired effect. I did, however, learn to think in the idiom and to predict, much to the satisfaction of my teachers, the likely explanations of a death or serious illness. I also came to be able to appreciate the implications of a bare narrative or obliquely phrased opinion about a death.

Ultimately belief is the heritage of one's cultural tradition. I was brought up with one set of assumptions about the nature of reality, the Yolngu with another. Nevertheless, several years of steeping myself in Yolngu ideas and reflecting on the social and intellectual content of sorcery stories have left their mark. It was instructive to catch myself at low points in fieldwork, when I felt vulnerable, fleetingly entertaining the question, 'What if . . .?', and walking faster when alone on a dark path at night. My short answer to the question, 'Do you believe in sorcery?' is usually [with apologies to Evans-Pritchard], 'Not when I'm in Sydney'.

As fieldwork progressed it became clear that Yolngu beliefs about causality in illness are not illogical superstitions. By no means. Sickness, sorcery and social events are linked in a logical structure which is comparable to that of a Western scientific theory. Seeing Yolngu medical concepts in this way makes it possible to understand how people cope with disruptive changes and accommodate the results of these changes within the traditional explanatory framework.

Commonly sorcery and witchcraft beliefs have been viewed as mechanisms for ensuring social equilibrium and control; what Douglas (1970:xxv) calls a 'homeostatic control system'. Witchcraft and sorcery, it has been argued, function to maintain social order (for instance, Nadel 1952; Epstein 1967) or, when social tensions become insupportable, to facilitate fission (Macfarlane 1970; Marwick 1964, 1965; and Middleton 1960). This, the structural-functional approach, based predominantly on studies of African societies, has greatly enriched our understanding of the social contexts and structural correlates of witchcraft accusations and beliefs, but, as I have suggested elsewhere (Reid 1978), is of limited use in analysing adaptation and change in belief (see also Douglas 1970 and Packard 1980).[1]

For instance, some writers have taken the position that, as societies 'modernise' and people move to large towns, sorcery and witchcraft beliefs will proliferate as symptoms of the ensuing stress and social collapse (see for instance, Hughes and Hunter 1970:478; Swantz in Feierman 1979). Others (such as Frankenberg and Leeson 1976; Hammond-Tooke 1970, and Mitchell 1965) have found an

1. It is also difficult to apply the findings of these studies in the Australian context because they mostly derive from the settled, agricultural societies of Africa where witchcraft, not sorcery (Evans-Pritchard 1937; but see also Turner 1964) is the major idiom of adversity, and accusations generally occur within groups, not between them as in Australia.

apparent decrease in witchcraft accusations in urban settings. They suggest that in towns, where relations are impersonal and hostility can be openly expressed, witchcraft beliefs become redundant.

While changes in the nature of social relations do undoubtedly influence belief systems, the structural-functional studies do not adequately explain how. Why do witchcraft beliefs apparently increase in some places and decline in others? Why do some migrants continue to blame their misfortunes on witches or sorcerers and others to prefer ancestors or spirits? Without some understanding of the meaning of social changes for the people involved and of the processes by which they revise or discard traditional beliefs the influence of social change on epistemology cannot be satisfactorily explained. This requires that beliefs are treated as subjects of study in their own right and their logic and meaning for believers examined.

The notion that beliefs about witchcraft, sorcery or religion are internally logical and plausible is a position taken and elaborated by Robin Horton (1962, 1964, 1968, 1970) and others (such as the contributors to Wilson 1970, and to Horton and Finnegan 1973; Skorupski 1973; Cooper 1975 and Hallpike 1976). It is a theoretical stance variously called intellectualist, neo-Tylorian or literalist. Though the elements of this position are to be found in the writings of such early scholars as Frazer (1922) and Lévy-Bruhl (1922), intellectualists generally look to the British anthropologist Sir Edward Evans-Pritchard as the founding ancestor of their clan.

In his rich ethnography, *Witchcraft, Oracles and Magic Among the Azande* (1937), Evans-Pritchard analysed the beliefs which the Azande of Africa hold about the causes of misfortune and the ways in which they explain specific troubles. The Azande attribute many (though by no means all) accidents and illnesses to witchcraft. To find out who has caused a given misfortune they consult an oracle. Poison is administered to a chicken and the names of suspects are put. If the chicken dies the diviner and inquirer have their answer and can take the prescribed actions. For Evans-Pritchard witchcraft is a system of knowledge with its own internal coherence and plausibility. When a Zande consults an oracle he is, within the terms of his own understanding, behaving rationally. If a poison oracle appears to contradict itself this in no way disturbs a Zande's faith in its efficacy, for many situational explanations can be invoked for its failure. Evans-Pritchard called these secondary elaborations of belief. Among the Azande, he wrote, there is no incentive to agnosticism. Beliefs about the witchdoctor, witchcraft and the oracle all hang together because,

> In this web of belief every strand depends upon every other strand, and a Zande cannot get out of its meshes

because this is the only world he knows. The web is not an external structure in which he is enclosed. It is the texture of his thought and he cannot think that his thought is wrong. (1937:194-5).

Drawing on his own study of the Kalabari people of the Niger Delta and other studies of African thought, Horton (1970) takes the idea of the contextual rationality of African beliefs further and compares them with Western science. Both systems, he says, have an intellectual function and share a large number of characteristics. Both the African villager and the scientist, whatever the idiom which they use, are engaged in a quest for explanatory theory. This quest, for both

> is basically the quest for unity underlying diversity; for simplicity underlying apparent complexity; for order underlying apparent disorder; for regularity underlying apparent anomaly (1970:132).

The key difference between the two is not in their purposes or even the structure of their ideas, but that

> in traditional cultures there is no developed awareness of alternatives to the established body of theoretical tenets; whereas in scientifically oriented cultures, such an awareness is highly developed. It is this difference we refer to when we say that traditional cultures are 'closed' and scientifically oriented cultures 'open' (1970:153).

Others disagree. There is ample evidence in Thomas Kuhn's (1970) study of the structure of scientific revolutions that scientists are not the dispassionate seekers after truth, unencumbered by intellectual prejudices, which they are popularly imagined to be. Their thinking is invariably shaped by the dominant paradigms, and such paradigms are yielded only reluctantly long after contrary evidence has become available. The characterisation of Western science as open and unhampered by presupposition is also disputed by Barnes (1969, 1973), Gellner (1974:149-67); Marwick (1974) and Polanyi (in the chapter of his book entitled 'The Stability of Scientific Theories Against Experience', 1958). Scientific theories, these writers maintain, are protected against falsification in much the same way as Azande beliefs. Authority, trust and commitment play a significant part in the transmission of scientific beliefs, just as they do in the transmission of witchcraft beliefs. Barnes suggests that it is the social context of thinking. and particularly the greater differentiation of roles and institutions within Western society (including the scientific community), rather than how people think, that distinguishes scientists and villagers.

With all of these arguments, though, as persuasive as they may be, there is an apples and pears problem: the comparison of the scientist, a specialist in his community, with the ordinary villager. If one looks at the ordinary person in both societies the similarities in thought become even more striking. Both subscribe to their society's beliefs, not because they understand their rationale, but because they are a cultural inheritance, handed down by the 'accredited agents of tradition'. All people, in short, think in patterns of thought provided for them by the societies in which they live. Marwick (1973) says:

> I have often . . . thought how much more dramatic and, in a way, much more emotionally satisfying Cêwa [who are horticulturalists of West Central Africa] theories of disease causation must be compared with our germ theory, according to which disorders are attributed to invisible organisms, which, for all most of us laymen really know from personal experience or observation, may merely be spots in the eyes of the pathologist or, even worse, unseen believed entities conjured up in the imagination of some physician wielding an antibiotic of wide spectrum, who may not even establish their existence, let alone their identity, before he takes steps to destroy them . . . In many respects, therefore, our attitudes towards these authorities are essentially similar to those of non-literate tribesmen towards their tribal magicians, and we have little to be smug about (1973:67).

On the face of it, the intellectualist view of belief as theory, with its emphases on secondary elaboration, closed thought and internal rationality, is no more amenable to a study of change than the structural-functional approach. If we accept the notion of uncritical loyalty to beliefs, writes the philosopher Ernest Gellner,

> it means that within it there can be no syncretism, no doctrinal pluralism, no deep treason, no dramatic conversion or doctrinal oscillation, no holding of alternative belief-systems up one's sleeve, ready for the opportune moment of betrayal. Frankly, I do not believe this (1974:156).

The Yolngu, I found, in keeping with Gellner's position, are not the unreflective prisoners of their beliefs which the open/closed dichotomy suggests. Neither, in all likelihood are the Azande. As Evans-Pritchard himself says:

> [Azande] beliefs are not absolutely set but are variable and fluctuating to allow for different situations and to permit empirical observation and even doubts (1937:195).

In this study I have taken a qualified intellectualist position: that Yolngu medical beliefs do indeed have many of the attributes of a theory, but that Yolngu are willing and able to objectify their theory and reflect on it. There is considerable evidence in the literature on traditional societies that people hold a variety of attitudes towards the received truths of their culture – from pious conviction, to scepticism and even outright disbelief (Buxton 1973:327; Feierman 1981; Gluckman 1968; Radin 1927). Variability exists because beliefs are held by individuals and individuals think. And it is precisely this propensity of individuals – some more than others – to reflect upon their situation and to consider old understandings in the light of new events, that holds the key for explaining how beliefs (or rather believers) respond to innovation and change (cf. Ardener 1970; Bauer and Hinnant 1980; Packard 1980).

Belief, like action, is socially situated, socially reproduced and socially revised. The continuing value of beliefs for believers lies in their capacity to give meaning to social and natural phenomena. When social, political and economic relations change and when customary modes of social action no longer produce the desired ends, believers, like scientists, must either live with the anomalies or abandon or revise their models of reality. Thus, change in belief cannot be understood independently of the social transformations which precipitate doubt and dissonance.

This study is an attempt to situate Yolngu ideas about sickness and death in their social context and to explain shifts in these ideas in terms of the explanatory and strategic functions they serve. It also provides a perspective on Yolngu views of the changes in their society as refracted through their medical beliefs and explanations. In the first chapter, I outline the historical circumstances, political conflicts and social upheavals which have shaped life as it is at Yirrkala today. Against this background various aspects of Yolngu medical theory are described: its assumptions, its structure, its content, its role in the management of illness, its use and its modification in the contemporary setting.

Yolngu, it will be seen, are not closed to new conceptions of reality. Indeed they use and modify their ideas to cope with unfamiliar and often threatening changes. At the same time, though, the core of their medical belief system endures, for it is confirmed in

Yolngu minds by the events which are parading across the contemporary social stage. To query the existence of the central idea of sorcery and all that it represents would be to query the myriad links between human behaviour, social order, ritual practice and spiritual well-being — the complex of relationships on which, in Yolngu eyes, the continuity of their society depends.

1 The Yolngu

In 1968 the Aboriginal people living at Yirrkala in the Northern Territory brought a suit against the mining company, Nabalco Pty Ltd, and the Australian government. The 'Yirrkala case' was to become a celebrated part of Australia's social and legal history, for it was the first land rights suit heard in an Australian court of law. In that year Nabalco had commenced construction for a bauxite mining operation on land excised as a lease from the Arnhem Land Aboriginal Reserve. The land was part of the traditional estates of the Rirratjingu and Gumatj clans, whose members were then living at the Yirrkala Methodist mission. In 1963, shortly after the first leases were granted, the Yirrkala people had sent a bark petition to parliament protesting the violation of their rights and the lack of consultation. Though the petition attracted publicity and led to a parliamentary inquiry it in no way secured the assurances the Yirrkala clans were seeking. So, with the support of mission staff, consulting anthropologists and legal counsel the Aborigines took their case to the Supreme Court of the Northern Territory in Darwin. They sought declarations that they were entitled to occupy and enjoy the land free from interference, an injunction restraining Nabalco from mining the land, damages, and a finding that the mining ordinance was unlawful.

In 1971 the judge, Mr Justice Blackburn, handed down a 262 page judgment. In the judgment he cogently reviewed the evidence and legal precedents but concluded that, whatever the merits of their arguments, there was no basis in Australian law for recognising Yolngu title to the land. The Aboriginal system of law, he found, did not provide for any proprietary interest, and the doctrine of communal native title did not form part of the law of Australia. 'All prayers for relief', he wrote 'must be refused'.

The people of Yirrkala were stunned by this denial of rights that seemed to them beyond question. Their reaction is captured in a letter they wrote to the Prime Minister:

> [We] are deeply shocked at the result of the recent Court case. We cannot be satisfied with anything less than ownership of the land. The land and law, the sacred places, songs, dances and language were given to our ancestors by spirits Djangkawu and Barama. We are worried that without the land future generations could not maintain our culture. We gave permission for one mining company but we did not give away the land. The Australian law has said the land is not ours. This is not so. It might be right legally but morally it's wrong.

> The law must be changed. This place does not belong to white man. They only want it for the money they can make. They will destroy the plants, animal life and the culture of the people (*Identity*, 1, July 1971:9).

Largely in response to this case and the sympathy it aroused the newly elected Labor government appointed Mr Justice Woodward, who had been one of the barristers representing the plaintiffs in the Yirrkala case, as Aboriginal Land Rights Commissioner. His brief was to inquire into the most appropriate way of recognising the traditional rights of Aborigines in relation to land. His recommendations led to the drafting of the Aboriginal Land Rights (Northern Territory) Act 1976. The Act was debated and passed in Federal Parliament and proclaimed on Australia Day (26 January), 1977. The Act gave the Yolngu, and other groups living on Aboriginal reserves in the Northern Territory, freehold title to their land. Nabalco, which by this time had built a town and processing plant and begun mining within a few kilometres of Yirrkala, had agreed to pay royalties to a trust fund for the benefit of clans affected by the mining and Aborigines living elsewhere in the Territory. The Act did not entirely protect landowners against unwanted mining and development, but it was tangible recognition of the rights of the people who had lived on the land for more than 30,000 years.

The Yolngu response to the threats to their land which have dogged the community since the early 1960s has had its counterpart in every conflict with outsiders before and since. With each new challenge the Yolngu have explained, reasoned, protested, or fought. In words, symbols and actions they have defended the integrity of Yolngu culture while negotiating the compromises that the white Australian presence has demanded. Whether they have opposed or welcomed the changes, they have always seen themselves, not as hapless victims of an industrial state, but as competent planners and negotiators.

The reality is that Aboriginal society in north-east Arnhem Land is being irrevocably transformed by forces outside Yolngu control. But the Yolngu do not echo the lament of a native American who said to the anthropologist Alfred Kroeber, 'The cup of custom is broken and we can no longer drink of life'. Unlike most Aborigines elsewhere they were protected from the worst depredations of the early settlers – the epidemic disease, the abduction of children, the rape and racism – by their isolation. By the time white Australians took a serious economic interest in their land, policies and feelings towards Aborigines were, even if slowly, changing. It was no longer acceptable to massacre a tribe for the killing of one white man. Aborigines were no longer seen as barely human, the possessors of an impoverished culture or no culture at all.

Throughout the history of their contact with non-Aborigines, whether as friends or enemies, the Yolngu have faced the intruders as equals and have never been forced radically to revise their perception of the relationship. As the history of Yirrkala and the events which led to its establishment show, the Yolngu have resisted some changes, welcomed others, but always re-interpreted events to themselves and others in terms of the 'everness' of their society and culture. They have attempted, however embattled, to cast the new and intrusive in the mould of the familiar and thereby affirm the continuity and worth of their culture. The Yolngu of Yirrkala are engaged, like all Aborigines, in 'an obscure struggle with us, the essence of [which] is their wish to go their own way' (Stanner 1979a:60).

In order to appreciate the role and adaptation of medical belief in Yolngu life today one needs to be familiar with the nature of Yolngu social relations, the recent history of the far north-east of Arnhem Land and the Yolngu response to some of the critical events of the past fifty years. In the following pages Yolngu society and some of the precursors and dimensions of their struggle are described.

Clan and Land

The lands of the Yolngu[1] lie in eastern Arnhem Land, an area of Australia which is tropical and monsoonal (Map 1). The wet season usually breaks in October. Storm clouds gather, the humidity increases and torrential rains begin to fall. By late December the 'Wet' reaches its peak and continues until the end of March. Through April and May the rains abate and, from about June until October (the 'Dry') the weather is clear, the days warm or hot and the nights cool. The vegetation of the area varies from open bushland dominated by eucalypts and wide expanses of grassland in upland areas to coastal pockets of dense monsoonal forest and, in the estuarine environment, expanses of mangrove swamps.

Throughout Arnhem Land, except in some parts of the interior and towards the end of a particularly dry season, food is plentiful. In the rivers and sea are fish, edible molluscs, crustaceans, turtle and dugong. The waterholes and swamps teem with wildfowl such as goose, duck, tern and junglefowl. Eggs are plentiful in season. Meat is provided by emu, crocodile, kangaroo, wallaby, opposum, bandicoot, porcupine and reptiles. Seasonal vegetable foods include wild fruits, berries, nuts, yams, and corms of the spike rush. In the

1. The word 'Yolngu' means 'Aboriginal person' in the dialects of the Yolngu language. The Yolngu have also been called Murngin by Warner (1958), Wulamba by Berndt (1955) and Miwuyt by Shapiro (1969).

4 SORCERERS AND HEALING SPIRITS

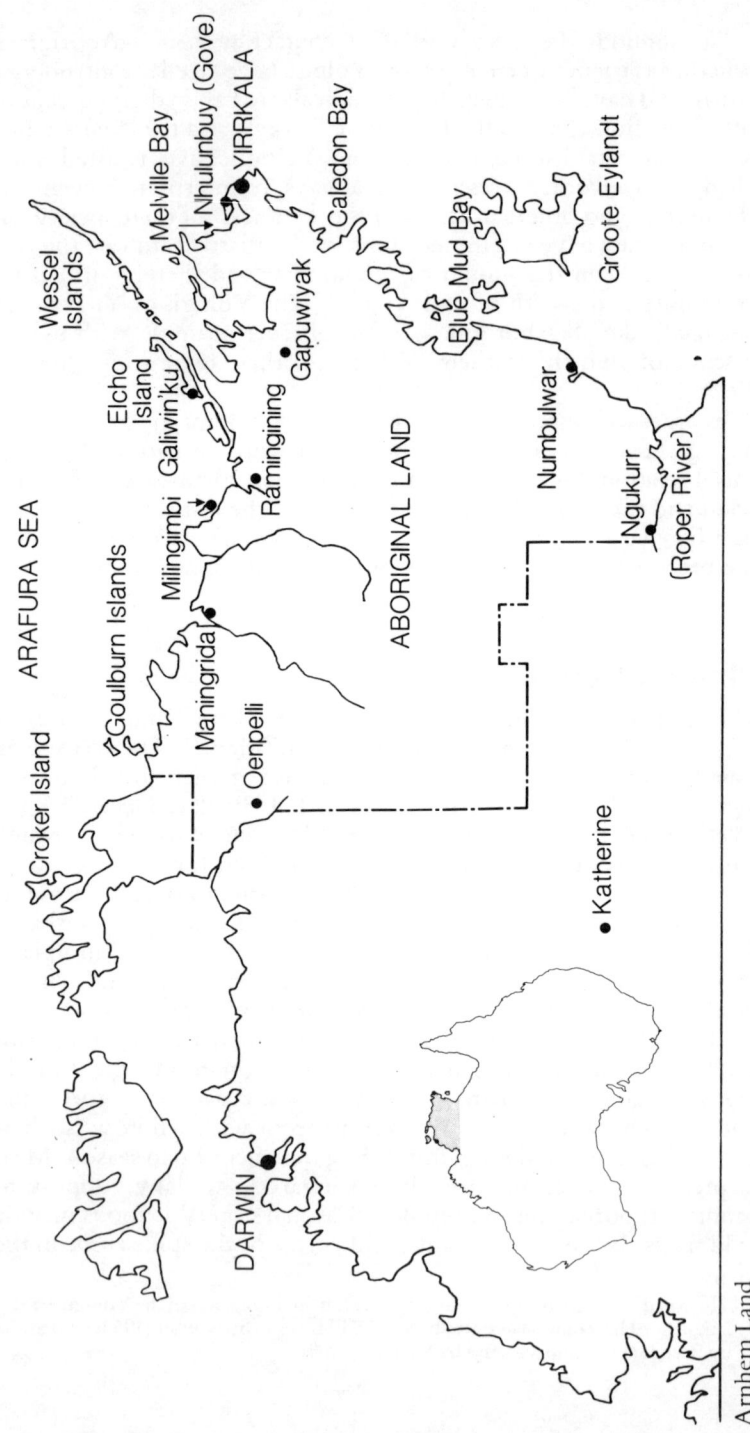

Arnhem Land

dry season such foods as turtle eggs and cycad palm nuts from which the 'bread', *ngäthu*, is made, are plentiful.

Accounts of ethnographers, historians[2] and older Yolngu people who recall pre-mission times provide a picture of the Yolngu before settlement. Before the establishment of the mission at Yirrkala the Yolngu were subsistence hunters, fishers and food collectors. They were semi-nomadic, moving and foraging in small groups of 40 to 50 people. Groups fluctuated in size with the availability of food resources and the shifting of families between related groups.

The roles of men and women within the society were distinct and complementary much as they are today. Before contact the women gathered vegetable foods and small animals or sea foods for their families while the men hunted larger game such as kangaroo, wallaby, fish, turtle and dugong. The contribution of the women to the daily food supply of the group was usually greater and more predictable than that of the men. In addition to collecting and preparing food the women made such articles as dilly bags and some ritual objects, took an active role in ceremonial activities and cared for the children. These activities continue to be a substantial part of a woman's responsibilities today. The men spend (now, as then) a greater part of their time and energies than do women in political and ritual activities such as mortuary and initiation ceremonies.

Everyone in Yolngu society is born into a specific clan, the clan of his or her father. The clan is a named group, the members of which are related through patrifiliation, speak a common dialect or *matha* and recognise one senior man as head. The head of a clan is usually the oldest in a line of brothers who inherits the position after his father's death. While there is only one named head, other senior men are also recognised as clan leaders.

The clan is corporate not only in membership but in its ownership of defined tracts of land. The boundaries, features and resources of the clan estates are said to have been created by the *wangarr*, the ancestral (or Dreamtime) beings. The *wangarr* gave each clan its *madayin* or sacred Law, consisting of the chants (*manikay*), dances (*bunggul*), sacred objects (*rangga*), paintings (*miny'tji*) and 'power', or secret names (*likan*). These beings are celebrated today in the poetic

---

2. There is a wealth of anthropological and historical literature on Yolngu society. In this chapter I have drawn on published material without specifically citing all sources. The works on the Yolngu which I have found especially valuable include those of Catherine Berndt (1971), Ronald Berndt (1955, 1964, 1965a, 1980) and their joint publications (1954), David Biernoff (1978), Wilbur Chaseling (1957), H.C. Coombs (1981), Stephen Harris (1977), Ian Keen (1977a), Campbell Macknight (1972, 1976), Frances Morphy (1977), Howard Morphy (1977a), Nicolas Peterson (1971), Neville White (1979), Warren Shapiro (1969, 1973, 1977), Lloyd Warner (1958) and Nancy Williams (1973, n.d., 1982). I have also been assisted by access to the Department of Aboriginal Affairs' files on Yirrkala held in its archives in Darwin.

chants and stylised dances performed at the religious ceremonies. The paintings and sacred objects are, in effect, title deeds to the land of each clan. In the mythology, some of the creator beings were transformed from human-like spirits into natural species or land forms. Others became the first human beings.

As Nancy Williams (n.d.:1-5; 1982) has written, land, for the Yolngu, is their most valued resource, a sacred endowment. The rights of ownership, use and occupation of land which were vested in the first ancestors of the clans and passed on to their descendants are precisely allocated and understood. They entail a complex set of responsibilities for the ritual and economic management of lands and their resources. The system of land tenure can accommodate demographic and seasonal vicissitudes as well as a range of human motivations and needs, including political ambition, economic advantage and religious vocation. It is a system based in law and buttressed by affection. The land is not only protected; it is cherished. Said one young man with great feeling when asked about his clan territory where a small community had just been established: 'It is the land of milk and honey!'

Each clan and thus each person belongs to one of two moieties, Dhuwa or Yirritja. These moieties are exogamous and so individuals marry someone from a clan of the opposite moiety. The marriage of preference is the matrilateral cross-cousin marriage of a man (*dhuway*) to a woman he calls *galay*. In the past and in some cases today a man had a future mother-in-law bestowed on him. Her daughters were thereby 'promised' to him. Marriages may be arranged, or contracts renegotiated later in life, but the son-in-law is expected to give gifts and food to his prospective parents-in-law as long as the arrangement exists. If the parents or daughter(s) break the contract he is entitled to substantial compensation.

Marriage was, and to some extent remains, polygynous. Girls married at puberty. Clan leaders in particular may have several wives and a large number of children. In many marriages the ideal of unilateral cross-cousin marriage is modified by several factors, such as the availability of women, economic considerations, and the determination of some young people to choose their own partners. Powerful older men could and did manipulate the system to their own advantage and marry women who either had been promised to someone else or were not strictly in the correct relationship for marriage.

Ian Keen (1977a) has argued that the inequable marriage system, which enabled older men to have several wives while 25- or 30-year-old men had none, was maintained by the religious system. A basic division in the society exists between those who have been initiated into the totemic mysteries and those (women of child-bearing age and young boys) who have not. (Older women are privy to much sacred knowledge but do not participate in the secret part of sacred rituals.) Religious knowledge is imparted to the men in stages. The rites of revelation (which include the display of secret carved and painted ritual objects) and instruction into the sacred knowledge of the clan begin with a boy's circumcision at the age of six or seven and continue throughout his adult life. The ritual and mythical knowledge gradually imparted in this way and with it access to supernatural power and sanctions is the property of the senior men.

It has been suggested by several ethnographers that the authority which their control of greatly valued secret knowledge conferred enabled the older men to thwart attempts by young men to circumvent the promise system, and so maintain a polygynous regime. Some women, of course, took lovers, but children so conceived were regarded as the children of their husbands and, in courting married women, the young men also courted the danger of severe punishment if their affairs were found out.

Peace and Conflict

Before white domination clans came together not only at times of peaceful ceremonial activity and joint economic enterprise but in times of conflict. Warner (1958) has described how, while the clan was the basic unit of solidarity, the ties of kinship, with their attendant obligations, duties, rights and privileges, tended to enlarge disputes to include other, allied, clans. By the same token, crosscutting ties of loyalty and blood limited conflict. Those clans which had divided loyalties in any fight often acted as peacemakers. A further powerful force in promoting peace and co-operation was the totemic ceremonies which drew together large numbers of clans. During these religious gatherings fighting and any infraction of the law was considered a direct insult to the totemic emblem and therefore to the clan. A tension existed in which warfare tended to undermine solidarity between clans, and ceremony to draw clans together in mutual endeavour.

Relations within the clan are, ideally, marked by co-operation, mutual support, reciprocal obligation, respect and affection. Warner maintained that, within the clan, 'no violent conflict ever takes place, no matter how much cause is given. Members may quarrel, but for clansmen to fight one another would be considered an unnatural act in Murngin society and it never occurs' (1958:17). He emphasised such obligations as the responsibility of a brother to respond to his sister's requests for help and to maintain an interest in her welfare, the identification of all clan members with the totemic well on the clan's land from which the spirits of people come and to which they go after death, the ritual solidarity of the males of the clan, the norm of mutual help between brothers, sisterly affection, parental care and family pride.

While it is true that fighting and hostility within a clan is very strongly discouraged and most major conflicts occur between clans or blocks of allied clans, the clans at Yirrkala today are not untouched by serious internal quarrels, anger or jealousy. It seems unlikely that relations were always as amicable in precontact times as Warner portrayed them. As Hiatt (1965) has shown for the Gidjingali of north-central Arnhem Land grievances can and do arise within groups. Many of the issues which cause animosity today would have been pertinent before mission times. There is, for instance, potential competition between real or classificatory brothers for women. Younger brothers may find themselves unable to marry because older brothers, in the same structural relationship to marriageable women, have prior rights. They may also compete for political or religious authority, even when the seniority of one is clear. Said one senior man of Yirrkala: 'Brothers always fight'.

While sisters are ideally close friends, the older sisters helping to rear and teach the younger, they are also correctly related for marriage to the same men. Some co-wives, often sisters, are affectionate and supportive of each other. Others are not. Conflict can occur when a girl joins a polygynous family as a new wife. Her co-wives may be jealous and she may resent being given the routine chores because of her junior status and having little say in the affairs of the family. On the other hand, it should be said that some older wives welcome a junior wife to help them with the work for the family.

Conflict is managed in several ways. (These are described in detail by Williams [1973]). A person can choose to air a grievance with a public display of anger, pacing back and forth in the camp, inveighing against those who have done him (or her) wrong, haranguing the audience with a recitation of his complaints and rallying support for his case. Disputes between close relatives are often taken to a family meeting or clan moot. Alternatively, the aggrieved may decide to show how angry he or she is by leaving and going to another hearth, camp or community for a time. Violence, of course — a fight with or without weapons — is always an option, though every attempt is made to prevent it through persuasion and conciliation.

When disputes do flare up, or the law is broken, a range of sanctions can be brought into play. Physical sanctions — a beating or a spearing — are still invoked, but within the limitations on violence imposed by Australian law. Other sanctions are restitutive; for instance, the payment of money or other goods as compensation for the breach of a betrothal or marriage contract. Temporary exile is an effective way of punishing an offender, protecting him or her from retaliation, and providing the emotional distance needed for negotiation of a settlement. Exiled offenders usually go to live with kin elsewhere.

The Yolngu are not averse to the excitement of a fight, but everyone recognises that violence begets violence, that resentments and disputes are bound to arise in their small community, and that it is to the advantage of all for conflict to be resolved peacefully. One is reminded living in a Yolngu community of the observation of the anthropologist, Elizabeth Colson, who wrote of the Tonga of Africa:

> I once took for granted the surface amiability of present Tonga community life but seventeen years of following the members of certain Gwembe Tonga villages have given me a better grasp of their involvement with each other. I now look around at a neighborhood gathering and wonder at the tough-minded determination that keeps hostilities from surfacing and disturbing the business of living (1974:44).

Trade and Invasion

Prior to the exploration of the Arnhem Land coast by Dutch and English, the only recorded visitors to the shores of this region of the continent were people of Malay descent from the Celebes (now called Sulawesi). The Malay traders, commonly known as Macassans, are known to have started sailing to the area in the early eighteenth century to harvest trepang (*bêche-de-mer* or seaslug), tortoise shell, pearl shell, sandalwood, and timber. When Matthew Flinders mapped the Australian coast at the turn of the nineteenth century (1803) he found at least 60 praus in the area, carrying a total of about 1200 crew members.

The Macassans spent many months camped around the coast of Arnhem Land. Though an occasional dispute or fight occurred, their relations with Aborigines were reportedly generally friendly and both groups enjoyed an exchange of goods and services. The legacy of the Macassan presence includes some Malay words (such as *rrupiya* for money, and *balanda* for a white person), the dugout wood canoe and items of glass, metal implements, cloth, the ubiquitous long-stemmed Macassan pipe, tobacco, alcohol and foreign foods. Yolngu incorporated into their ceremonies new songs, carvings, dances and other items depicting aspects of the Macassan culture. There was also some intermarriage and a few Aborigines returned on boats to Macassar to visit and, rarely, to stay in the Celebes. The Macassans, though, were transient and their influence on Yolngu culture appears to have been superficial. Their greatest impact was in the things they brought and bartered. The land-based economic and ideological foundations of Yolngu culture were little affected.

Flinders' visit in 1803 is the first known by a European. He was not impressed by the residents. When he landed in Caledon Bay some Yolngu stole an axe. He captured a man to hold as a hostage against the return of the axe but his ploy was unsuccessful. He finally released the man and sailed on, writing in his diary,

> I have some hope that those who may follow us will not be robbed, at least with so much effrontery; and at the same time, that the inhabitants of Caledon Bay will not avoid, but be desirous of further communications with Europeans (1814:213).

Desirous or not, white Australians were to intrude increasingly into the Yolngu world. In the late nineteenth and early twentieth centuries small parties of gold prospectors and explorers made brief forays into eastern Arnhem Land. One or two unsuccessful attempts were made to set up cattle stations. There are accounts, both Yolngu and non-Aboriginal, of skirmishes and killings. In one unequal conflict in 1875, typical of hostile contacts between Aborigines and settlers throughout Australia, Aborigines at Blue Mud Bay killed two white men of the Walker expedition. Forty of their number were massacred in retaliation (Macknight 1982). Yolngu living today tell stories of the apparently indiscriminate shootings of uncles, fathers, and other relatives which probably occurred between about 1915 and 1930 at Caledon Bay, Trial Bay and Gangan. The head of the people of the Dhalwangu clan, a man of indeterminate but considerable old age, was already in his twenties when a party of white men and 'black trackers' (Aboriginal police aides, probably from Roper River to the south) descended on his people at Gangan to the south of Yirrkala and opened fire on the small band, killing at least eight of his kin and wounding others. But, though their horses and weaponry gave them tactical superiority, white men were not the sole aggressors. Yolngu viewed them as strangers on their land who, unlike the Macassans, did not respect norms of reciprocity and mutual assistance. Whether to counter the growing threats to their sovereignty or to possess their tobacco, implements and food, Yolngu engaged in sporadic guerilla attacks on the intruders.

One of these attacks was to have results which cut deep into the heart of their society. By 1907 the Australian authorities had prohibited the visits of the Macassans. The niche they vacated was quickly taken by Japanese fishermen. In September of 1932, Aborigines at Caledon Bay set upon the crew of one fishing boat with whom relations had deteriorated (by Yolngu report because of their interference with women and exploitative use of Yolngu labour), killed five and looted their vessel. In 1933 a police constable, one of a party sent to investigate, was killed and two months later two white beachcombers were murdered. When the news of these killings reached Darwin there was talk of a police punitive expedition, but the protests of people in southern Australia prevailed. Instead the Anglican church organised the Arnhem Land Peace Expedition to contact the Yolngu involved and talk the killers into giving themselves up. With the help of Fred Gray, a trepanger who had been working in the area when the massacre occurred, they located the culprits and brought them to Darwin for trial. After protracted and, for the defendants, traumatic legal battles and a period in prison they were released. One, Dhäkiyarr, disappeared mysteriously before he could be taken home. Rumours said he had been killed by other Aborigines or the police. The others were returned to their people and, when I began this study in 1974, several of them were old men living at Yirrkala with their families.

Largely in response to these incidents, the Methodist Missionary Society decided to establish a mission for the Yolngu of the northeast. In 1934 the Reverend Wilbur Chaseling and his wife selected for the new settlement a portion of the northern coastline which, despite an exposed anchorage and poor soil, was well supplied with fresh water and provided an elevated building site on the small cliffs and hills near the beach. Shortly after their arrival, small groups of Aborigines came to settle, more or less permanently, at the mission. At least part of the attraction of the mission was the medical treatment, processed food, material goods and opportunities for wage labour it offered. For groups under threat it also provided protection from attack by other hostile clans. Chaseling (personal communication) estimates that there were between 50 and 100 people living at Yirrkala within a year of its establishment. Many continued to go out hunting, fishing and foraging for days or weeks at a time but then returned to camp for a time at the mission.

During World War II about 5000 Australian and American servicemen (the former being men of land- and sea-based squadrons of the Royal Australian Air Force) were stationed not far from the mission. Their base was Gove, named after a serviceman who lost his life on active duty in the Northern Territory. When not out flying the servicemen lived in self-contained camps and had little contact with Aborigines living at the mission, although the gardens established by the missionaries and cultivated with Aboriginal help supplied much of their fresh fruit and vegetables. The large airstrip which the Air Force cleared from bush is still the site of the airport.

It was during the war years that the first samples of the ferric orange-red soil of Gove Peninsula with its distinctive bauxite nodules were sent south for analysis. The first systematic geological survey of the area was conducted in 1952. By the early 1960s it had become clear to the Yolngu and to mission staff that a major mining venture was being proposed. In 1963 they made their first move to counter the threat by sending a bark petition to Federal Parliament in Canberra.

In 1968 an area was excised from the Arnhem Land Aboriginal Reserve as a mining lease in an agreement between Nabalco and the Australian government. The northern boundaries of the lease are less than one kilometre from Yirrkala. Throughout the three years from 1969 until 1971 when the Yolngu were arguing their case for land ownership in the Supreme Court of Darwin, construction was underway on the town of Nhulunbuy, the mine site, and a conveyor belt to the processing plant and loading wharfs at Melville Bay. Some work started at the mine in 1971, but in 1972 Nhulunbuy and the plant were officially opened. Nhulunbuy is a modern town of 4000 people with all the requisite facilities – a primary and high school, shopping centre, hotel, sporting facilities, and a hospital serving the entire north-east region. Charter flights and regular air services connect Nhulunbuy, and therefore Yirrkala, with Aboriginal communities in other parts of Arnhem Land, Darwin and southern cities.

Yolngu mainly come to town either to drink at the hotel or to shop. There are always a few Yirrkala residents in hospital and, if they are very sick, relatives camping in the patches of bush nearby. In general the mine does not employ Aborigines directly. Its labour force primarily consists of men and their families from 'down south' and single migrant men from southern Mediterranean countries and the Middle East. However, during the construction phase Yirrkala Brickworks, based in and employing people from Yirrkala community, made and supplied all the bricks needed for the town and plant. The company was envisaged as both an employer and training ground for Aborigines and a means of involving the community in economic development in the area. Now called Yirrkala Business Enterprises (YBE), the company has been contracted by Nabalco and the government to unload the supply barges, mow the lawns and collect the garbage in Nhulunbuy and work at the plant's waste mud ponds. It has recently taken over a bus service, car rental franchise, seafood enterprise and concrete batching operation. YBE is a large business with, as a government officer put it, 'a voice in the town', which provides piecemeal or permanent work for Yolngu men who want it.

Homelands Movement

At the same time as the town and mine facilities were being built,

Yolngu families and clans were talking about leaving Yirrkala. In the early 1970s Aboriginal groups throughout Australia who had long been living on settlements began to leave and, as some put it, 'go home' to their own lands. The movement was spontaneous and, from the point of view of ambivalent white missionaries and government officers, unplanned. Many Aborigines had wanted to move for several decades but were discouraged by government and missions and were afraid of being deprived of basic services if they left the settlements. With a change in government, greater availability of funds for Aboriginal initiatives and the new federal policy of self-determination, the invisible walls that kept people from leaving began to break down.

The decentralisation movement was fuelled by the stresses of settlement life, the alcoholism, the waywardness of the young as Aboriginal forms of social control were destroyed by non-Aborigines in power, the poor health, the threats posed to land by mining and pastoral companies and simply a homesickness akin to that of refugees displaced from their home country. By the end of the decade there were fifty-two outstations, or homeland centres as

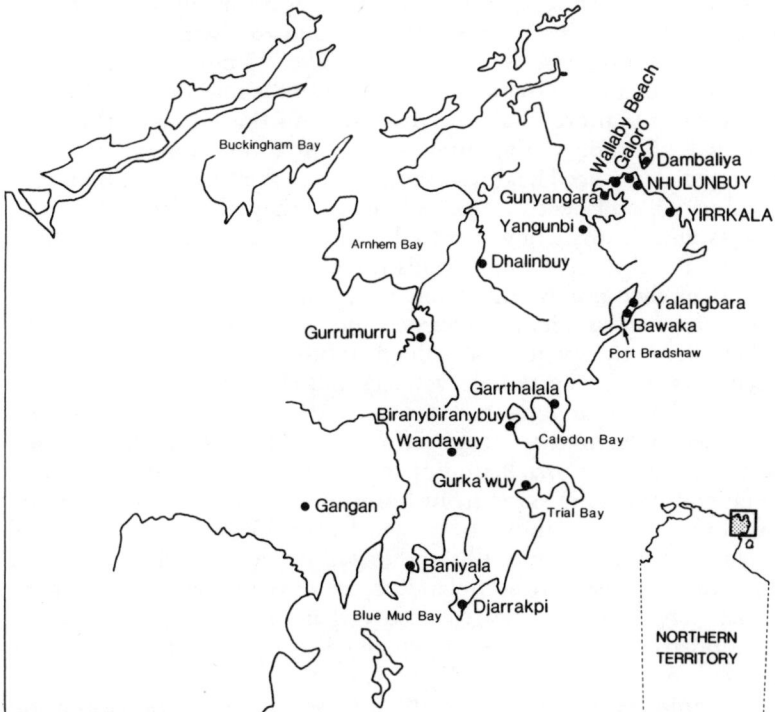

Yirrkala and its homeland centres

Yolngu prefer to call them, in north-east Arnhem Land alone. They are associated with the five major Yolngu communities, Yirrkala, Galiwin'ku, Gapuwiyak, Milingimbi and Ramingining.

Since Yirrkala was founded some extended families have come and gone from their own territories. Among these was the clan group headed by Wonggu, the Djapu patriarch whose father was killed in one of the early massacres and who, with his many wives and children, continued to live at Caledon Bay until shortly before his death in 1958. The mission at Galiwin'ku, Elcho Island, in the person of the flying missionary, Reverend Shepherdson, had always supported groups living in the bush. However, in 1973 and 1974 a concerted outmigration began. By 1975 eleven small communities totalling about 250 people had been established up to 150 kilometres from Yirrkala. By 1981 there were sixteen homeland centres (Map 2). These look to Yirrkala as a resource base for food, medical care, the marketing of art and craft, mechanical and building advice and other needs. The Community Development Office co-ordinates assistance to homeland centres and advises leaders on projects such as small fishing enterprises and gardens.

Some of the critics of the decentralisation movement have found it ironical, unromantic, or simply wrong that Aborigines should want both to move away from settlements and to have access to basic white Australian goods and services. The Yolngu, though, never envisaged that the movement would mean the rejection of all things Western any more than moving into Yirrkala meant they had rejected all things Yolngu. Their aspirations and needs have changed. They need health services because they are sicker than they used to be, and because, like all people, they are afraid of serious illness and death. They want education because they know their children will need Western skills to cope with the invaders and to face their changing world. They want store food because they like it and because it supplements hunted and gathered food in lean times. They want money for the valued goods it can buy such as tape recorders, two-way radios, vehicles and clothes.

Long before anyone had yet moved, the Village Council (as recorded in the minutes of a meeting on 10 April 1970), was thinking about commercial marketing of art and craft, fish, buffalo, tortoise shell and crocodile skins from homeland centres, and considering seeking loans to buy four-wheel-drive vehicles, start small businesses, set up windmills and install freezers. There was talk of investing royalties in homeland centre development. At the same time, parents were keen to ensure that the children's education continued and that Yirrkala remained a viable community. The aspirations of those leaving Yirrkala for their own lands in the early 1970s are captured in the words of Gawirrin Gumana, pastor and former chairman of the Council, whose father is head of the

Dhalwangu clan. One Dhalwangu homeland centre is Gangan. He was talking in 1974, shortly after it had been established.

> Talk about Gangan started a long time ago — before land rights and before Nhulunbuy. I was thinking about my tribal lands when I was in hospital in Darwin [in 1947] because my family was scattered in different settlements. I felt sorry for my people.
> Since the Court came to Darwin about land rights, this made me think more clearly. I was fighting not only for Yirrkala but for my own land. So I talked to my own people about going to Gangan — we talked and talked. First we made a road [in 1973]. Then we built an airstrip by hand with three axes, four shovels and two picks. Seven men and six ladies worked at it and it took us two and a half months. When the pilot landed in January 1974 he said it was a good strip. On September 14, 1974, we moved there.
> Other groups are moving out too because of the township [Nhulunbuy]. I feel it pulls people away so that they lose their culture and mix with European culture. Some parts of it are bad like drinking, stealing and gambling. The school, the hospital and work are good for people.
> I saved my pension money and money from bark paintings and my brothers contributed money. With that and the government's [financial assistance] we bought a long wheel base Landrover. We have the airstrip and garden. Next we are thinking of making a bush school. In 1975 we will build a real school. We'll have two Aboriginal teachers [both of whom have completed first year of high school]. We are building houses little by little. At the moment we have eight [corrugated-iron and bush timber frame] houses. Later we'll make a playground and basketball court. Young people will be employed in the office operating the radio, but we're also thinking of running cattle since we have plenty of water and grass. We may get a sawmill since there is also plenty of timber.
> We've had no diarrhoea or other illnesses since being there – no flu or bad colds. I think the fresh spring water may contribute to this. Our food consists of fish, waterlily, sugarbag [wild honey], wild yams, kangaroo, emu, goanna, blue tongued lizard, blanket lizard, freshwater turtles, flour, Uncle Toby's Oats, Cornflakes, Weetbix, rice, sugar, tea, syrup, jam and tobacco.

We are thinking of putting a notice at the turnoff saying 'No Entry'. If Europeans want to come to Ganga̱n they must send a message. If the answer is 'no', that's it. Those people who want to come and go are not helping. The only Europeans who can come are the mission people for preaching and clearing the road and building. There are too many voices from too many government departments who want things and ask things. I say, 'No, no, no', to government, church and strangers. I don't want people to come and try to tell us what to do. We have to practise [this way of life] and learn by ourselves.

As this account so clearly shows, the homeland centre movement is an attempt by Aborigines to assert their rights of ownership of their land and to determine the style of life which they wish to adopt without interference by non-Aborigines. In 1981, of the 1050 Aborigines affiliated with Yirrkala, 350 were living on homeland centres. Ganga̱n, with 50 residents, had become one of the most active and viable. It had eight houses, a wash-block, a windmill, pump, pipes and tank, a garden, tractor and plough, vehicle, airstrip, two-way radio, and a second-hand electric generator which the clan bought cheaply. Young people were providing basic medical care and running a small school supervised by a visiting teacher from Yirrkala.

Most homeland centres wax and wane in size as people come and go from Yirrkala for various reasons: the death of a venerated leader which requires that the land be vacated until it can be ritually opened again, the sickness of a family member who needs medical care, the onset of the wet season which renders some airstrips and all roads unserviceable, the lack of a school, disenchantment (particularly among some young people) with life in the bush and a desire to spend some time at Yirrkala or at the hotel in town, a salaried job at Yirrkala, a visit to see relatives, a call to attend a ceremony, the failure of a radio, and so on. Homeland centres do not cease to exist because people are away; when circumstances permit people go back again.

Yirrkala

Although only 20 kilometres from Nhulunbuy and the facilities it offers, Yirrkala itself is a small self-contained town. In 1974 there were about 800 Aborigines living at Yirrkala and its affiliated homeland centres, and 80 non-Aborigines at the settlement. By 1981 the population of Aborigines was approximately 1050 and of non-Aborigines 100. Clustered in one area of the settlement are the offices of Community Development, the Dhanbul Association (and Council), the Yirrkala Arts and Crafts shop and the general store. A short distance away is a modern health centre, the pre-school, a fast food outlet, an oval and basketball court. On the edge of the settlement are the new and well-equipped primary and post-primary school buildings. The Dhanbul Community Association is an all-Aboriginal incorporated and elected body which oversees the disbursement of royalties and other funds, considers and instigates action on town management matters, acts on requests for permits from outsiders to visit and deals with a range of other community issues.

The income from royalties has risen with the mine's production and with changes in the arrangements for payment. Until 1979 the Aboriginals Benefit Trust Account returned to Yirrkala 10 per cent of the total royalties paid by Nabalco and the remaining 90 per cent was distributed to Aboriginal groups elsewhere in the Northern Territory. The ABTA now returns 30 per cent to the clans at Yirrkala which is divided between the Dhanbul Association for investment or the use (as approved by the Council) of the community as a whole, and the major land owners, the Gumatj Association. In 1981 the total royalty payment by Nabalco was almost $1,000,000 of which 30 per cent went to Yirrkala. The landowning clans also receive substantial lease rental monies for the use of sites on their land.

There are more employment opportunities at Yirrkala than in more remote communities. A small number of Aborigines work in government offices in Nhulunbuy (three in 1981) and Yirrkala Business Enterprises has a substantial workforce. Men and women are also employed at Yirrkala as 'security orderlies', and on the work teams which do the plumbing, painting, building and general maintenance. Other Yolngu work at the store, the health centre, the office and the school. In all about one hundred Yolngu have full-time employment. Some of those who are not employed are eligible for supporting (single) mothers' benefits, old age, widow or invalid pensions, or child endowment (family allowance) payments. In 1981, 80 people in the community were receiving pensions. The mission took the position, which still has majority support from the Council, that unemployment benefits should not be claimed by anyone in the community and consequently no-one at Yirrkala receives the 'dole'.

The Arnhem Land Progress Association store is a major non-profit enterprise which sells a wide range of fresh and packaged foods and which, despite competition with Woolworths in Nhulunbuy, had an estimated $580,000 turnover in the 1981-82 financial year. The art and craft store is also a major source of revenue for community members who make and sell woven bags and baskets, bark paintings and carvings. By 1981 its annual turnover was approximately $150,000, generated by craft purchased from homeland centre and settlement residents for sale at the store, or to galleries and shops in southern Australian cities or overseas.

The primary and post-primary schools had an enrolment of 220 children in 1980, about two-thirds of whom were regular attenders. The school has staff engaged in adult education and literacy work (including the production of school texts in local dialects) as well as in classroom teaching. Some children go on to high school at Nhulunbuy, but few graduate. By 1975 only two girls had finished high school, but several young people had been to Bible College in Brisbane or to short courses in community development and administration in Sydney and Adelaide. Some have since attained positions of distinction outside Yirrkala, most notably Galarrwuy Yunupingu who was chairman of the Northern Land Council during its negotiations over uranium mining on Aboriginal land in western Arnhem Land. Gatjil Djerrkura, also of Yirrkala, is deputy chairman of the federal Aboriginal Development Commission. In late 1981 he also became the Department of Aboriginal Affairs area officer based in Nhulunbuy and responsible for the eastern Arnhem Land region, the first Yolngu to hold such a position.

All Yolngu at Yirrkala have western-style accommodation. The types and quality of housing at Yirrkala cover a wide range. Along the cliffs overlooking the sea and to the south of the store are areas of comfortable and well appointed two- and three-bedroom houses. Until the mid-1970s only non-Aboriginal staff lived in these houses – teachers, a mechanic, an electrician, an accountant, horticulturalists, pilots, community development officers, a plumber, a builder, the store manager, the art and craft adviser and so on. By 1981 a few were occupied by Yolngu, either prominent community leaders or individuals employed by the government (school, health centre) and their families. The houses of the Aboriginal camps as they are called, range from the old, corrugated-iron, unserviced dwellings at Beach Camp to the very basic two- or three-room houses (asbestos sheeting walls on a cement base with iron roof) of Top Camp and Balnguma Road (including Galpu Road) camp. Most of these have electricity, reticulated water and toilets, though a 1977 survey by health centre staff showed that many of the toilets and taps were not functioning. These camps are socially and spatially distinct. Each represents a group of clans or lineages which came from neighbouring areas of Arnhem Land to settle at the mission and who have close ties with each other.

The houses in the camps are in varying states of repair. Many are missing flywire, glass louvres and parts of walls. Insects — flies, cockroaches and, in the wet season when water tends to stand in certain areas, mosquitoes — abound inside and outside. Most of the houses provide a place to store belongings and to sleep when it is raining. Most people prefer to sleep, sit, talk and cook outside in the dry, warm months of the year. The number of people actually living in or around each house varies, but can be as low as two or as high as fifteen.

Health and Medical Services

The crowded sleeping arrangements in wet weather, the taps and toilets which only work intermittently or leak constantly, the lack of a consistently safe water supply or adequate storage facilities for food and the defecation of children on wet ground around the houses (see, N.T. Dept. Health 1977-8: 288-90) all combine to cause or exacerbate the diseases which most trouble the community: respiratory tract infections, gastro-intestinal disease, parasite infestations (especially hookworm) and the attendant anaemia, eye infections, and skin diseases such as scabies and impetigo.

It is difficult to draw a health profile of Yirrkala which is epidemiologically sound. Daily clinic attendance figures indicate the types of illnesses for which people seek treatment but, since they often do not come or bring their children to the health centre when they are sick (particularly if they think the illness will pass) the figures do not reveal the dimensions of community morbidity. During its inquiry into the 'Present Conditions of Yirrkala People' (Australia 1974b) the House of Representatives Standing Committee on Aboriginal Affairs took evidence from medical staff who had worked in the community and concluded that the health status of the children was 'lamentable'. The report referred in particular to surveys which found that a third of the under-fives weighed less than 80 per cent of the standard weight for age, a third suffered from chronic ear disease and a fifth from anaemia.

It is probably safe to say that the health status of the Yolngu is similar to that of other Aboriginal communities in the Northern Territory (see Moodie 1973). The infant mortality rate throughout the Territory is four times the national average. The National Trachoma and Eye Health Program's impressive health survey of Aboriginal and non-Aboriginal people throughout Australia found that at Yirrkala, 36 per cent of the 161 Aborigines under 21 years of age seen had trachoma (whereas only one of the 16 non-Aborigines seen were affected) and 20 per cent had ear infections (whereas no non-Aborigines had) (NTEHP 1977). Yirrkala figures for other conditions were not tabulated separately but, for all the communities of the Top End of the Territory which includes Yirrkala, 47 per cent of Aboriginal children had a nasal discharge (compared with 5 per cent of non-Aboriginal children), and 18 per cent of Aboriginal children had a skin disease such as scabies and impetigo (whereas in non-Aborigines the prevalence was negligible) (NTEHP 1980).

There is very little data on the health or demography of the Yolngu in the early years of Yirrkala mission. Methodist mission staff started keeping medical and birth records in the late 1950s. Milliken (1974) has analysed the data available to 1973 and shown an exceptionally high average natural rate of increase (4.1 per cent per annum) and a lower life expectancy and higher infant mortality rate than for the Australian population as a whole. The first missionaries found the Yolngu fit, wiry and generally healthy, but the only other early indication we have of health status is a 1947 survey of dietary patterns of people living at Port Bradshaw (McArthur 1960) which suggests that their diet was adequate and nutritionally well-balanced (see also Cook 1970).

Though we lack comparative base-line data there is little doubt that the Yolngu, like Aborigines everywhere, have suffered a profound dislocation in their lifestyle as a result of settling at the mission. Today their health is affected by crowding, poor sanitation, a diminished diet, alcoholism, heavy smoking of pipes and cigarettes, inadequate spacing of births and unaccustomedly large families (Reid and Gurruwiwi 1979), and the stresses of living with large numbers of people, many of whom are not close relatives and may be unfriendly. In addition to those diseases related to the physical living environment, the Yolngu, though more fortunate in diet and health than some Aboriginal groups, are increasingly afflicted by diabetes, cardiovascular disease, chest complaints, and urogenital diseases. Children displaced too early from the breast show signs of malnutrition. Some adults suffer the psychological disturbances brought on by social and familial stress. Finally a small number of adults is still being treated for leprosy and tuberculosis.

For almost 40 years Western health care was provided to the people of Yirrkala by mission staff. The first clinics at Yirrkala were conducted by the Reverend Chaseling. Clinics were held in a corner of the only building on the mission, a corrugated-iron shed. It was, he recalls, mostly a matter of 'eucalyptus above the belt and epsom salts below the belt'. Nevertheless he had considerable initial success in treating such endemic conditions as yaws and was able to avert epidemics of introduced diseases (such as influenza) by insisting that residents leave the settlement and that shelters be burned when serious infectious illness was introduced. According to Chaseling the people were enthusiastic in their acceptance of Western medical treatment. In his opinion it was one of the main factors which drew people to Yirrkala.

Until responsibility for the health services passed from mission to government and the hospital in Nhulunbuy was built, a small hospital at the settlement was staffed by nursing sisters employed by the mission who, with the help of Aboriginal women, provided a wide range of medical and other services. A doctor in Darwin, 650 kilometres away, could be consulted twice a day by radio and he visited every one or two months. When necessary, patients were evacuated to Darwin Hospital by air.

Since late 1971 inpatient care has been available from the large hospital at Nhulunbuy which serves the residents of Nhulunbuy and the Aborigines living on the settlements of eastern Arnhem Land and on Groote Eylandt (Plate 2). In 1975 a new health centre was opened

2 Gove District hospital, Nhulunbuy

at Yirrkala. In 1974-5 it was staffed by an average of four female Aboriginal health workers and a white nursing sister who commuted daily from Nhulunbuy. Later a male health worker joined the team. The health workers have generally completed primary school and some post-primary schooling. They learn most skills in the course of their work. All have attended short courses conducted by the Department of Health. During the 1970s the health workers assumed increasing responsibility for the services of the health centre until, in 1981, Yirrkala was one of the first communities in the Northern Territory to have its nursing sister withdrawn so they could take over the running of the centre (see, Yirrkala Health Workers, 1982). The health workers conduct daily

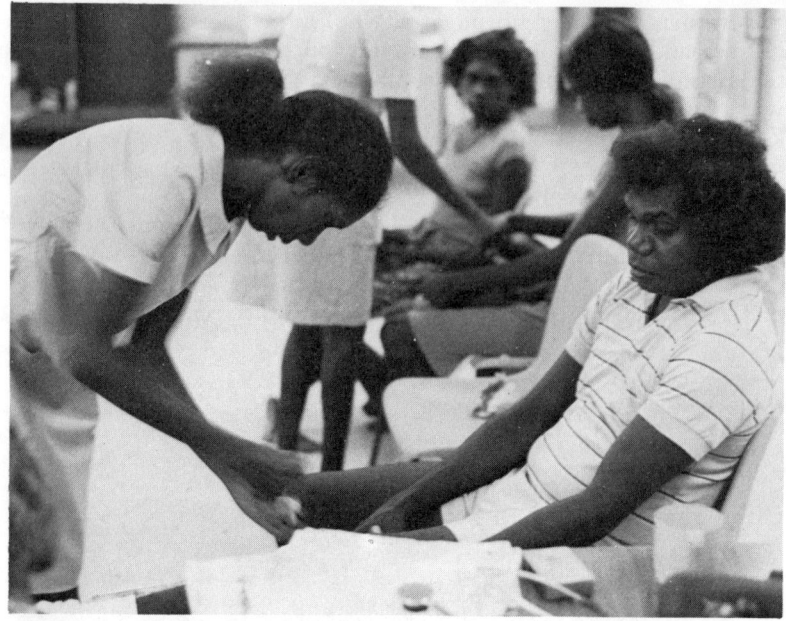

3 Health worker dressing an injury during morning clinic at Yirrkala health centre

clinics (Plate 3), consulting when advice is needed with medical or nursing staff in town. They are on rotating duty each night and weekend, referring cases when necessary to Nhulunbuy Hospital. They also make regular visits by air to homeland centres. Since at least 1974 regional medical officers have made a succession of attempts to start a health worker training program for the homeland centres, all of which have blossomed and faded. In early 1982 a program was again being mooted.

The school, health centre, store, council, mining town – all manifestations of the white Australian presence – have become an integral part of life at Yirrkala. Children of school age do not remember a time when there were no miners. People under thirty were not born when the war brought thousands of servicemen to the peninsula. Only the elderly can recall the days before the mission. Most people, though, are realistic. For all its strains and problems, settled living has brought facilities and an ease of access to necessities (such as food) which, like white Australians, Yolngu enjoy. It is a truism that Aborigines enthusiastically adopt Western technology and absorb it into their cultural repertoire. Two-way radios and four-wheel-drive vehicles are now a *sine qua non* of homeland centre life. But, at the same time, distinctively Yolngu traditions and mores are observed (albeit with adaptations to small town living: Reid 1979b) and, if threatened, defended. People still hunt, perform ceremonies, cherish their land, marry according to custom, and politic and dispute over matters Yolngu. Western culture, wherever possible, is pressed into the service of Yolngu wants, sometimes at a pace that can be disconcerting to the returning anthropologist:

> When I went back to Yirrkala at the end of 1981 I hired a car, an extravagance hitherto beyond my means. Feeling somewhat apologetic about this display of affluence, I set off to find my family who were said to be at a lagoon collecting *rakay* (the corms of the spike rush), fresh water tortoises, and wild eggs. When I arrived the women were expertly gutting a large goanna which they had just caught to cook on a bed of coals. I was welcomed with gifts of its delicious, barbecued liver, some tortoise meat and *rakay*.
> At dusk we packed people and food into my car and drove to a new homeland centre on the coast a few kilometres from Nhulunbuy which I had never seen. The homeland centre consisted of a cluster of large two room tents in a hollow behind a long white beach and

4 Watching television at dusk at Galoro homeland centre

beside a large grove of casuarina trees. As the goanna was being carved up and partitioned onto paper-bark for the various family groups a new Range Rover drove in, dwarfing my car. The clan leader to whom it belonged and who had just finished the day's work at Yirrkala, welcomed me and then went to a small shelter and started a generator. The spotlights on top of the aerial belonging to the two-way radio came on, flooding the area in light. Hearing the generator the children rushed up from the beach and pulled the covers off a colour television set! (Plate 4). As we ate our goanna meat we watched the evening's ABC programmes, beamed since 1980 by satellite from Sydney. Late in the evening, tired and not a little culture shocked, I unrolled my sleeping bag and turned in. I finally went to sleep to the shrieks of delight from the children at the antics of Jacques Tati in a replay of 'Mon Oncle'.

Resistance and Response

Televisions, radios and cars are part of the highly visible face of change at Yirrkala and are innovations which people have welcomed and incorporated. But behind the material trappings of daily life are changes which have been sources of contention, deliberation and concern. The most obvious is the mine. The Yolngu reaction to this threat to their land was outlined at the beginning of the chapter. However, the mine and mission have brought other changes which are less easily controlled by Yolngu and threaten their perception that they have a firm hand in shaping the direction of contemporary social processes. During the 1970s there were many challenges and equally many Yolngu strategies for meeting them. In concluding this discussion of the social history of the community two of the most pressing issues – alcohol and Australian law – are discussed, both to illustrate how Yolngu are responding to new problems, and to provide a background to the descriptions of sorcery and conflict which follow.

Characteristically, the Yolngu strategy in dealing with unwanted changes has been to resist if possible, compromise if not, but always to uphold in negotiations the value of Yolngu culture, their dignity as human beings, and their right to govern themselves. In all confrontations they have endeavoured to speak with a single voice, with the internal compromises this has required. In the land rights case, for instance, perceiving that the court would be unable to understand or deal with flux and dispute in the ownership of land they achieved a masterly consensus on the presentation of evidence for their claims. A similar consensus has been reached on the argument of their case for Yolngu jurisdiction over certain breaches of the law. On alcohol and its management, however, the community is divided.

The Yolngu experience of alcohol before the establishment of the mine was limited. The Macassans brought with them on their annual voyages relatively small amounts of *arak*, an alcoholic Indonesian beverage, and brandy (Macknight 1972) which would have provided modestly for their own needs and occasionally for some Yolngu helpers. The mission allowed no alcohol into the community. Before 1964 Australian Aborigines were not, in any case, legally permitted to drink. Some men may have obtained beer from the troops during the war but the earliest recorded incident is referred to in a heated letter from the mission to the Welfare Branch in Darwin in 1961 complaining that a man from a surveying camp had supplied three Yolngu men with methylated spirits. After 1968, when construction started and more employment was available for Yolngu, the men began to drink at the construction camp.

When, in the early 1970s, the leaders at Yirrkala realised that alcohol would be freely available from the bars and bottle shop of a hotel to be built in Nhulunbuy they retained a lawyer to contest the hotel's application for a publican's permit. They were agreeable to the sale of liquor at a restaurant and workers' club but adamant that it should not be sold publicly. The Yolngu leaders, however, lost the case and with it the first round of the battle to prevent the access of community members to alcohol. The core of regular drinkers who often camp and drink at the beach near the hotel grew and, by 1974, included some women. As the number of drinkers has increased so have the associated social problems. Intoxication leads to fights and family violence, to the loosening of tongues, the revelation of ritual secrets, and to the resurrection of old grievances. The nominal peace which exists in the community is jarred and disrupted by the disturbances caused by drunken men. Drinking drains from the community money normally used for subsistence needs. The hotel also acts as a magnet to the young men of settlements as far away as Maningrida and Groote Eylandt, some of whom the people of Yirrkala regard as untrustworthy and dangerous strangers.

A circular written by the Council chairman to the police and other authorities in 1978 gave the names of 100 male and 20 female heavy drinkers (of 155 men and 170 women over the age of 15 years in the community). It was prefaced by the comments:

> I am writing on behalf on my community'. . .
> concerning those who are bad behaviour and badly
> drunk and who disturb people and make people frighten.
> They should not speak the names of dead persons . . .
> this makes people wild . . .

> Young people are also not allowed to say the sacred name in the public area where women and children can hear . . . When a person arrives home . . . he talks without reason, swearing . . . The [obscene] word he uses for the female should not be used by drunk persons . . .
>
> Our men who are drinking all the time . . . are fighting with others from families and other clans . . . If one clan is against another clan, playing with his wife, or fighting then the two clans would sit and make agreement to send those two men away as their punishment . . .
>
> Sometimes a person is blamed when someone dies . . . This blaming causes a lot of problems . . . This blaming goes on for years and years and years, and in the past people have been blaming and killing each other . . .
>
> Are we going to keep sending our children away to Darwin Jail or can we make our own rules and regulations for our Community? . . . We can send them to Homeland Centre or give them hard bond or fine at Yirrkala. We could give them hard work to do rather than European Law coming to Yolngu people to stand on our shoulder and push us down.

When it became obvious that drinking could not be banned, Yolngu leaders were faced with the problem of regulating access and coping with the problems it caused. Over the past decade the Council and clan leaders who are opposed to drinking have negotiated various informal agreements with the hotel proprietor. These include closing the Aboriginal bar (which, by agreement with the Council is the only bar open to Yolngu) and stopping bottle sales during certain hours, during funerals or when men are drunk or fighting. The separate bar and restricted hours have been vocally opposed by some young men who say the arrangements are discriminatory. During a large funeral in 1979 young men of one clan were not allowed to buy liquor without a written permit from the clan head. No permits were forthcoming until the most important part of the ceremony had finished. However, at the same time, a prominent man of another clan and his brothers were openly flouting the arrangement by drinking and distributing beer at the ceremony. The clan head decided to change his tactics and, in 1980 during another funeral, himself organised the purchase and supply of beer. This move was widely criticised by the non-drinkers and did not, as hoped, prevent drunkenness and fights. In 1981 he was still struggling with the problem.

The Yolngu security orderlies are expected to police the laws that regulate bringing alcohol into the community. But they are generally thwarted by the dimensions of the task and daunted by the prospect of tackling large parties of men. When it was realised that the orderlies could not stem the flow, two places on the beach outside the Yirrkala town boundaries were designated 'wet' areas, but many of the drinkers continued to bring beer home. More girls began to drink and fraternise with non-Aboriginal men in the town, and several cases of car theft and breaking and entering by Yolngu men were reported. The Council seriously considered having the hotel closed to Aborigines and building a wet canteen at Yirrkala which would sell rations of beer (for instance, two cans per person per day) to residents. This plan is opposed by the women in particular.

In 1979 the Northern Territory Liquor Commission was established and empowered to issue liquor licences and declare certain areas restricted. At a 1980 hearing in Yirrkala those present were divided. The Council, non-drinking leaders and most women wanted the entire region, with the exception of Nhulunbuy and its recreation areas, declared dry to whites and Yolngu. The leader of the opposing clan refused to accept the right of others to make rules for his people and homeland centre. Taking into account all views the Commissioner decreed that an area within a 2 kilometre radius of the Yirrkala town centre would be dry and a notice to this effect was erected on the road into the community. However, though the taxi company had been instructed not to bring any drinking men or alcohol further than the notice and was assiduous in observing this rule, alcohol was still finding its way into Yirrkala in 1981.

In dealing with the consequences of drinking, Yolngu leaders face another problem: how to acknowledge the right of the police and courts to intervene without entirely ceding their own authority. If Yolngu are drunk and incompetent the police usually detain them in prison overnight. If they resist arrest, are involved in a fight, or otherwise cause offence they are committed for trial when the magistrate from Darwin makes his regular visit. The Yolngu recognise the right of police to arrest disorderly drinkers and sometimes seek their help in taking away drinkers who disrupt funerals. During court hearings sympathetic magistrates have taken advice from leaders or Yolngu community workers on the most appropriate sentences. One option besides imprisonment or a fine has been to place offenders on good behaviour bonds and to send them to their clan's homeland centre, where alcohol is banned, for specified periods of time.

The issue of jurisdiction over Yirrkala people who have broken the law – Yolngu or Australian – has troubled the community for many years. The trial and imprisonment of the killers of the Japanese at Caledon Bay was unequivocal evidence for the Yolngu of the force and encroachment of Australian law. In 1939, the anthropologist Donald Thomson, who was commissioned by the government to report on the situation in north-east Arnhem Land wrote that, 'Among these natives even the old men are themselves handicapped in these circumstances: they are now afraid to carry out their own legal codes in the presence of white man's authority, and the culprit thereby escapes the penalties of the laws of both the black man and the white' (1939:6). In her detailed study of the subject at Yirrkala from 1969 to 1971, Williams (1973) found that the Yolngu were attempting to assert and legitimise their jurisdiction over a wide range of wrongs. These they categorised as 'little troubles', as opposed to 'big troubles' such as murder and serious assault. Little troubles, they maintained, should be theirs to investigate and punish. From 1975 onwards several discussions were held to determine whether a court-house and cells could be built at Yirrkala and Aboriginal Justices of the Peace designated to hear certain cases. Progress has been slow but the Yolngu have been consistent and clear in their demands. Yirrkala's submission to the Law Reform Commission proposed the formation of a second community council consisting of two leaders chosen from each clan which would nominate police orderlies, convene courts, make rules, advise magistrates and oversee sentences. Punishment would be carried out by clan and family. All decisions, in the Yolngu manner, would be by consensus. The new council's brief would be to enforce a specified set of rules, namely:

(a) It is wrong to do anything which will or could, or is intended to harm another person.
(b) It is wrong to take or damage anything which belongs to somebody else.
(c) It is wrong to go where people have a right to be by themselves.
(d) It is wrong to do anything which will cause great noise or violence and will make other members of the community frightened or unhappy.
(e) It is wrong to behave outside the community in a way which will offend members of other communities or will cause trouble with them.
(f) It is wrong to do anything forbidden by Aboriginal law and tradition or to do anything which will make that law weak.
(g) It is wrong not to do those things which Aboriginal law or tradition says should be done.
(h) It is wrong to do anything forbidden by Balanda (white Australian) law. (LRC 1980:70).

Among the offences which fall within these categories and which Yolngu have said they want to deal with themselves are fighting, using threatening or insulting language, spreading false stories, disturbing the peace, drunkenness, damaging property, calling out the names of the dead, making sexual allusions to the living, offences relating to sorcery, minor stealing, petrol sniffing, failing to observe obligations such as looking after children and old people and refusing to marry a betrothed or deserting a spouse.

The Garma Council, comprised of clan elders and nominated members, was constituted in 1979 to deal with these issues of law and order. It is also responsible for matters affecting the land (mining, leases, prospecting) and clan relations. At the beginning of 1982 its role in legal matters had not yet been officially defined, but its members were still pressing for concrete recognition of their authority.

In seeking to hold fast to their land and be given the right to govern themselves it is probably true, as Berndt (1978-9:294) has said, that the Yolngu 'don't really know what they are up against'. Some of them, though, have a good idea. They know their land and their culture are under threat and they are worried. In the words of Galarrwuy Yunupingu of Yirrkala:

> The land is my foundation. I stand, live and perform as long as I have something firm and hard to stand on. If there is a flood on my land I will have to swim and all Gumatj clan will have to swim, but not for long, we will surely perish, then we will be just like thousands of other people whose lands have been stolen away from them. We will be the lowest people in the world, because you have broken down my back-bone, taken away my arts, history and foundation. You have left me with nothing (quoted in Cole 1979:149).

For the Yolngu of Yirrkala, as for Aborigines elsewhere the central issues are those of control and autonomy. They have responded to Australian law by attempting to articulate its principles with those of their own legal system in such a way that the integrity of their own jurisdiction is not only maintained but given further legitimacy. In a similar way Yolngu have sometimes used their bark paintings to convey to white Australians the worth of Yolngu culture and the significance of their land in the hope of securing a greater measure of autonomy (Morphy forthcoming). These struggles are probably being replicated in medical, legal or other arenas all over Australia. Until recently, though, non-Aborigines have had little knowledge and therefore little appreciation of Aboriginal strategies for cultural and political survival.

Fred Myers (1980), for instance, provides a valuable explication of the untiring attempts of the Pintupi of Yayayi to reach a satisfactory accommodation with the white 'bosses' by extending their own model of social relations to their interactions with whites. Diane Bell's study of the Kaititj women of Warrabri (1980, 1982) provides an illuminating perspective on women's attempts to preserve their image of themselves as competent nurturers and healers in a world which is rapidly crumbling. Bell argues that the performance of women's Dreaming ceremonies, which subsume a set of healing songs and rituals, provides an interweaving of past and present, creating an illusion of stasis and supporting the women's perception that they are capable members of their society. The believed relationships between social harmony and health are being threatened on the one hand, but asserted on the other. Each of these studies bears witness to the Aboriginal determination to give meaning to the present, and to preserve local autonomy in the face of profound threats to their world.

Though their control has been eroded by alien domination, the Yolngu continue to oppose unsought changes with eloquent determination. Where opposition is unfruitful they redefine situations to minimise their sense of being manipulated and maximise the sense of their own authority. Since they are not permitted to deal with all breaches of the law, they have defined a category of offences which they believe to be singularly their own business and likely to be seen as such by non-Aborigines. Since alcohol cannot be banned altogether the leaders are attempting to control access through indigenous channels of authority and to decry drunkenness in terms of the damage it causes to Yolngu institutions. Change is cloaked in the idiom of continuity. Compromise is masked by the rhetoric of control.

The Yolngu approach to illness and death, which is the subject of this book, can be seen in one sense as an extension of their approach to other serious concerns. The way the people of the community explain illness and death not only enables them to express their fears about the unsettling events which impinge on their lives, but to assert jurisdiction over their management. Granted jurisdiction (which is not always the case) the Yolngu can logically request help from the authorities on their own terms and reserve the right to deal with both the illness or death and its consequences. This approach is underpinned by a body of thought about the causes of physical suffering; a theory of human affliction. This theory is coherent and satisfying to the Yolngu and has not in their minds been surpassed by any alternatives Westerners have to offer. For this reason Yolngu explanations still command, at some level, the allegiance of everyone in the community and so constitute a shared understanding which has intellectual, emotional and strategic value. The following chapters describe the theory and its other face, spiritual healing. The concluding chapters deal with the theory's use in daily life and the way it has been adapted to explain illness and death in contemporary Yirrkala and to give meaning to some of the most troubling consequences of settlement.

2 The Causes of Affliction

Serious illness or injury and the suffering which accompanies them present a continual threat to the members of any society. They threaten the sick person with the loss of his (or her) social identity and with failure to meet obligations or fulfil personal aspirations. They also force him to confront his own mortality. For those who love or depend on the sick person, illness brings the sorrow of watching him suffer, the disruption to daily life of caring for him, the temporary loss of a productive member of the family and the fear that he might die.

It is rare in any society to find people who are able to accept incapacitating illness, injury or death as caprices of nature and not question why they or members of their families should be afflicted. Human beings abhor inexplicable suffering. In order to explain and cope with serious misfortune, each society has evolved sets of ideas and practices which can be invoked to explain the cause of an illness or death and help cope with its ramifications.

This chapter explores the set of causal beliefs on which the people of Yirrkala draw to explain the origin of life-threatening illness and the causes of deaths in the community. When talking about serious illness, the Yolngu specify its cause at two different levels: the 'proximate' cause (such as a sorcerer or spirit) and the 'ultimate' cause (such as the conflict, breach of a religious or social law, jealousy or spite which motivated the sorcerer or spirit). When a sorcerer or spirit is involved, the link between the ultimate cause and illness is indirect. It is mediated by a human or supernatural agent. When a sorcerer or spirit is not involved (when, for instance, a man becomes ill simply because he trespassed in a dangerous area), the link is direct. One of the functions of the Yolngu healer, or *marrnggitj*, is to divine the identity of the sorcerer and to use his power to right the physiological damage the sorcerer has caused.

Yolngu ideas about the cause and treatment of serious sickness rest on one assumption; that humans have the capacity to mobilise and to control the power which exists in the universe and are themselves vulnerable to attacks by others using that power (cf. Glick 1967). In Yolngu thought power is derived from the spirits, the invisible beings who live in and beyond the tangible world. There are several types of spirits, all of which figure in accounts of sorcery and healing. First, there are the spirits of dead people. Warner (1958:445-7) maintains that each person has two souls. One is the true soul or *birrimbirr* which originates in the totemic water-hole on the land of the clan and which after death returns there. According to Warner,

The soul, the totemic spirit, the Wongar or totemic ancestors, are all expressions of the fundamental sacred essence, the ultimate symbol of which is the totemic well, which is the repository of all the individual items which have been or will be incarnate in man or his religious objects (1958:447).

The other human spirit is the *mokuy* or *ngänuk*. After death it leaves a man's body and goes into the bush. It is a bad spirit, a ghost, and can be dangerous to the living. In pictures it is always depicted possessing a body but looking ugly and unpleasant. It is the *mokuy* which appears and terrifies men in remote places or which haunts them. It is also the *mokuy* which attacks a man and makes him insane.

The concepts of *birrimbirr* and *mokuy* are today not as clearly differentiated as Warner's description suggests. Their use varies with context and speaker. The terms may, in fact, refer to two aspects of the same spirit – the *birrimbirr*, benign, and the *mokuy*, hostile and dangerous. Morphy (1977a:114) suggests that *birrimbirr* is a complex concept referring to that aspect of a person's spiritual existence that comes from the ancestral spirit beings and to the animating spirit effective in a person's conception. It is probably always true to say that *mokuy* are non-living, immediate and threatening (especially just after a person has died). A *birrimbirr* is the spirit of a dead person which has already been repatriated by ritual to the land of the dead. Yolngu explain *birrimbirr* and *mokuy* variably, rather as a diverse group of white Australians might describe ghosts, spirits and souls (Keen 1977a:43; Williams n.d.:1.26-1.29).

A second category of spirits is the *wangarr* (or *wongar*) beings who are the mythological ancestors, the creator beings of the Dreamtime whose deeds are described in the myth and song cycles of the clans. Those of the *wangarr* said still to be inhabiting sacred sites on clan lands today are not dangerous unless offended. They are an integral part of the beliefs that validate a group's corporate identity and its ownership of a given estate. Third, there are the spirits, sometimes called *djamarrkuli* (children) or *manggata* which sometimes become the spirit familiars of the *marrnggitj*. These are neither spirits of the dead nor connected with the totemic realm.

Power can be obtained from any of these spirits. For the sorcerer, especially the malevolent *galka*, power usually comes from the spirits of the dead and for the *marrnggitj* either from these or the *manggata*. When a *galka* kills a man he often keeps his blood in order to harness the power associated with the victim's spirit. Thus killing both makes the *galka* powerful and helps him to kill again. Other individuals who wish to harm people by means of sorcery often obtain relics from sacred Dreaming places or draw the image of the victim in these places, invoking the power of the associated totemic ancestors to make their harmful deeds effective. A *marrnggitj* usually gains his power when accosted by spirits of the dead or *manggata*. These spirits either give him powerful objects or adopt him and work with him. A child *marrnggitj* described in Chapter 3 received his powers from the ancestral spirits of his clan who gave him special stones and aided him in his healing. He also had *djamarrkuli,* some of which reside in his special stones.

Ordinary people who are neither healers nor sorcerers may also, sometimes unintentionally, mobilise power. Men, in particular, have potential access to the power inherent in sacred objects (*rangga*) and sacred places. One man explained his personal power, which he has occasionally invoked to heal family members, in the following terms:

> My own power is from my mother's Dreaming, the Octopus Dreaming. The Octopus is really an Aborigine from a very long time ago [that is, a *wangarr* or totemic being] . . . When I concentrate hard I can bring up [mobilise] this power from the Octopus . . . when I do the Octopus dance . . . I can feel the power filling me. It is a personal power.
>
> It can be passed down as my father's [as well as mother's] was to me when he died, or from mother to daughter. These Octopus beings . . . protect me with this power. When two people tried to hurt me by pointing the bone the power told me it was going to happen . . . I can prevent any evil attacks. The *marrnggitj*'s power for healing has the same name. It is called *ganydjarr* or *mirritjal*.

Warner (1958:236) uses the term *dal* to describe an object which is either hard or strong or which is strong because of its magical properties, primarily because of its relationship with the totem or with death. Both classes, he writes, those of the totem and of the dead, belong to the 'inside' or sacred world. Both ritual and magic are channels by which the power associated with them can be correctly expressed in the world of the profane. Thomson (1975) maintains that, when used to refer to anything ritually strong or dangerous, *dal* should be qualified by the term *märr*. *Märr*, he states, refers to the spiritual power which emanates directly from the ancestral cultural heroes and which makes a dead body dangerous. It has 'religious totemic or supernatural implications'. Morphy (1977a) provides a fine analysis of the use of sacred paintings in ceremonial contexts to summon, release and direct this ancestral power, *märr*, to serve a variety of human ends: to direct the soul of a dead person towards the realm of *wangarr* beings, to renew the fertility of the land, or to release conception spirits.

When I questioned the speaker quoted above about his use of the terms *ganydjarr* (which is usually used to mean strong or powerful) and *mirritjal*, he explained that *ganydjarr* can be used in several contexts. It can refer to the power of a *marrnggitj*, to the power of a motor boat or car or to personal power such as his own. It is, he said, like the power which Jesus (though He came down to earth like an ordinary man) was given by His Father in heaven.

The power utilised by both sorcerers and healers is ultimately from the same source. This power is morally neutral. It is not the nature of the power a *marrnggitj* possesses which distinguishes him from a sorcerer but the choice which he makes about how he will use it. For the *marrnggitj* living at Yirrkala this power is held in trust. People believe they use it to heal and to protect others. While the potential for its use to harm people exists, *marrnggitj* and their families vigorously deny that they work sorcery, even on enemies, and they become offended and angry if anyone suggests such a possibility. The sorcerer, on the other hand, using one of the various techniques described below, activates power to kill. He is the antithesis of the *marrnggitj* and symbolises all the dangers the flesh is heir to.

Sorcery

The most feared of sorcerers are *galka*.[1] They are real human beings, almost always men, who have acquired the power and training to kill by stealth. Theirs is the domain of destructive magic causing sickness, injury and death. The powers and activities of *galka* are described in detail by Warner (1958:194-206). The accounts of the ways in which *galka* attack, immobilise and operate on their victims were given to him both by ordinary people and by a self-confessed *galka* who claimed to have killed several people. Warner writes:

> Among all the clans . . . there is a profound belief in magic. The effects of its power are twofold: it can harm and destroy, or it can benefit and cure . . . The 'black' magician [sorcerer] can injure or kill his victim, and the 'white' magician can cure him or restore his lost faculties. All deaths, sicknesses, certain types of bad luck, and, in general, all those occasions on which the individual is seriously out of adjustment with his community, physically, mentally, or socially, are looked upon as the effects of black magic . . .

1. The term *galka* is commonly used to refer to one or several sorcerers and to refer to the technique of sorcery itself (thus, one *galka*; several *galka*; *galka*, a deadly form of sorcery.)

Occasionally when a very old person dies the
diagnosis is, 'It was nothing, just old age'; but this is
very rare (1958:193).

Descriptions of the *galka* and his work were also recorded by Webb (n.d.) who was the founding missionary at Milingimbi and by Thomson (1961), who was in eastern Arnhem Land in 1935-7 and 1942-3. According to Webb, '[t]he '*ragalk*' [another term for *galka*] is a killer and in every death, no matter what may be the immediate cause, his activity is suspected' (n.d.:2.4). Thomson writes:

In Arnhem Land the belief is held that the death of any
person in full possession of his social personality is due, not to
what the white man terms 'natural causes' but to the act of an
enemy, often a person who is believed to bear a grudge, real
or imaginary, against the deceased. Even death from sickness
or drowning, from attack by shark or crocodile, and
especially from snake bite, is not regarded as the primary
cause, but merely the agent used by an enemy, or by a *ragalk*
whose aid he has enlisted, to bring this about. The only
exception to the belief about natural death is extreme old age,
when, in the words of one of my informants, the people say
'time belong him now' – his time is spent, he has lived his life
(1961:99).

Children of Yirrkala begin to learn of the dangers and deeds of *galka* (or *djanggitj*, as they are also called) as soon as they are able to understand what is said to them. An eighteen-month-old child will cringe in fear when teased with the threat of a *galka*. One of the first words a child learns is *galka* or *galkanha*. Like the bogeyman of Western society his name is called to tease and frighten young children and to deter adventurous toddlers from straying too far from the camp. Second only to *galka* as a means of disciplining, controlling or frightening young children are the threats of *bapi*! (snake) and *Ngapaki*! (European!). In a child's mind *galka* are ubiquitous. A three-year-old from Yirrkala who was holidaying with her family in Sydney ventured outside one night and came back a few moments later to announce, wide eyed and in earnest, that she had seen two *galka* out there. Asked what they looked like she gestured 'big ones' and insisted that all present stay inside and lock the doors.

Whereas many adolescents and adults are reluctant to speak about sorcery of any kind to a non-Aborigine, the younger children are uninhibited and enthusiastic in their descriptions of the activities of *galka*. A ten-year-old girl, for instance, described an attack on her mother at a homeland centre:

One night two *galka* came to the house where my mother was sleeping. One jumped onto the verandah and one crept up from behind the house. They forced three plastic bags down her throat. She was taken to Gurrumurru [a homeland centre] in the clan truck to see [the female *marrnggitj*] who massaged her stomach and used her children [spirit familiars] to take out the plastic bags. She then threw them in a tin of water.

Although children and adults have some knowledge of the way in which a *galka* attacks and kills his victim, few people say they know how a person becomes a *galka*. Most people of the community claim that no one at Yirrkala 'knows *galka*' and that *galka* are always strangers who travel long distances from communities to the south and west to seek out and kill the people of Yirrkala. (Both Warner (1958) and Thomson (1961) state that *galka* abound in tribes or clans to the south and west of Murngin country. Warner, as mentioned, actually met self-confessed *galka* and recorded accounts of their killings [1958:197-206].) The accounts which Yolngu give of the techniques of the *galka* are based either on personal experience as a supposed victim or the stories of others and are supplemented by their own observations of the deaths and serious illnesses of relatives.

The accounts of attacks by *galka* given by community members and those recorded by Thomson (1961), Warner (1958) and Webb (n.d.), typically have four phases. First of all the *galka* either waylays his victim in a secluded place or draws him there. Second, he puts the victim to sleep, cuts his body open, removes or mutilates his organs and drains away his blood. Third, he induces amnesia in his victim to ensure that he is either unable to remember or unable to tell anything about the attack. Fourth, the victim dies, usually within hours or days of returning home. The first of the accounts given below, in which each of the four stages is present, was given by a clan leader and senior man of the community to explain how a *galka* kills his victim. The second was given by a forty-year-old woman who claimed to have been attacked by a *galka* and survived.

Attack by *Galka*: The 'Ideal' Case

Galka people live inland from here, around Katherine, Daly River, and Alice Springs. Maningrida and Milingimbi have also become *galka* places now because, with Balanda living there, they are afraid to fight with spears because they know they'll go to gaol, so they fight secretly.

Galka come from a long way away and hunt in the night for their victims. They are real people. A *galka* finds a person and makes him [or her] unconscious. He then cuts the person's throat near the larynx, takes out something and replaces it with grass to stop the bleeding. Or he may make a cut and go in under the rib cage, poking his hand through and squeezing the liver to make it soft. Sometimes his hand goes up through the anus and rectum and he pierces the heart in several places with small needles so the blood flows everywhere.

For these operations the *galka* uses steel wire or a very sharp [miniature] shovel-nosed spear. While the person is unconscious he allows the blood to flow into a paperbark container which he seals at both ends and then hides in a short, hollow log. This he also seals and buries in a hole as deep as his upper arm. Here the blood grows in the image of something alive – like a bird, or emu, crocodile, snake or shark. This is bad blood called *wulä* or *mundi* which may be used for killing people or for good luck in hunting. It is the spirit in the blood that grows into the likeness of one of these animals.

After he has injured the man in this way the *galka* may say to him, 'When you go back to camp you'll be alive for only two days and a crocodile (or snake or shark) will get you'. The *galka* will force the man to go where he wants then send the animal to get him. He sometimes says 'When you go back to camp you'll cause great trouble with your wife and your relatives will hit you with a spear and you'll die straight away'. Sometimes the man just gets very sick at home and dies quickly.

Before he lets the man go, the *galka* heats a piece of steel in the fire and puts it on the wound to seal it. It will be almost impossible to see where the cut was made. It will be like a faint scar. Occasionally, if there are two *galka*, one will hit the person with leaves to make him wake up after the operation, while the other sits up in a tree. The victim wakes, looks up, and sees the *galka* sitting above him. The *galka* asks, 'Who hit you?' Angrily his victim replies, 'It must have been you', and attempts to spear him. The *galka*, however, jumps from the tree and stops him. He then instructs him, 'Go home that way' and indicates the direction. After the man has walked fifty yards, the *galka* jumps out of the bushes ahead of him and shouts, 'Whe-a-a-ay!' The victim is so frightened that his body becomes like that of a dead man or a spirit – just bones, no eyes or flesh. Then his skin reverts to that of an Aborigine and he walks on. Again the *galka* will run ahead and hide and, when he sees the man coming, jump out again. The man's skin will become purple with fear, and then go black again. Again the *galka* repeats this and the next time the man turns white and becomes a skeleton. Seeing this the *galka* thinks, 'Good, I've done well'. By the time the person returns to camp his skin is black again and he has forgotten what happened to him because the *galka* placed a special dillybag [containing magical objects] against his forehead. After a few hours or days at home the victim will be killed in a fight or accident or become very sick and die.

Attack by Galka: The story of a forty-year-old woman

This happened to me when my oldest child was small [approximately 1960]. I walked with my mother, brother's wife and sisters from Yirrkala to Waraminya to go hunting. When we arrived there I went off with my brother's wife to get *gangguri* and *yukuwa* [wild yams] at the billabong. However, we became separated and I walked on unknowingly towards two men who were hiding in the tall grass. Ahead of me I saw a tree with tendrils of the *yukuwa* twined around it. One *galka*, a Yirritja man of the — clan, was hiding behind that tree. His accomplice was a man of the Dhuwa moiety and — clan. While I was looking at the *yukuwa* leaves, the first man speared me with a shovel-nosed spear at the side of my left breast. The spear went right into my chest. I fell to the ground and he then got special leaves which he put over my eyes to make me blind. I called out for my mother. When he heard me, the Dhuwa man said to the Yirritja, 'Why have you speared her? She looks like — 's child'. But I was blind and lying on the ground.

They dug a hole in the sand in order to make a fire, the smoke of which could not be seen from a distance. The Dhuwa man sent the Yirritja man to look for the beetle, *bo<u>d</u>uk*, and then healed the wound the Yirritja man had made by putting his woomera in the fire, heating it and applying it to the wound. He then used the *bo<u>d</u>uk* to bite the edges of the wound together.

They had caught the blood which flowed from the wound in a paperbark container. If they had buried it to use for *wu<u>l</u>ä* I would have died. But the Dhuwa man, realising they had attacked the wrong person by mistake, threw it into the billabong so I would not die.

After this the Dhuwa man put dillybags against my head so that it cleared and I could open my eyes. 'Who are these men?', I thought. The Dhuwa man said, 'I'm Gamarrang [subsection]. You're well now.' I said, 'I know you two very well'. They still live at Elcho Island. I was wild and told them, 'When I get home I'm going to tell my mother and father.' Then I walked away. When I had gone about 20 yards I turned back because they had stopped me with their dillybags. They were now up in a tree. I started walking again. Fifty yards away I turned back and they were still there. They were using the power of the dillybag on me to stop me telling anyone about them. As I walked back to the billabong where my mother and the girls were, I thought, 'I'm going to tell them about it.' But when I arrived I'd forgotten all about it and didn't tell anyone.

From that place we went to Banambarrnga where we camped and fished. The *galka* were still following us. I wasn't well, so my mother told me to go back to the mission. I refused. I wanted to go with them. The next day, however, I felt sore inside, and my chest became bad. That day the others collected yams and shellfish but I didn't get any. I was so sick I thought I was going to die. I couldn't stand. I started to pray. I couldn't eat and drink much. Some of the others went back to Yirrkala to tell everyone the news that I was very sick. My father went and told the nursing sister who gave them a stretcher. The girls came back to get me and father waited with the others for me near the mission.

When we all reached Yirrkala the sister felt for my pulse, but it was gone. She told my father, 'She's very sick. But don't worry. She'll recover'. She gave me an injection, and after two days sent me to Darwin Hospital [650 kilometres away by air]. I spent two months altogether in hospital in Darwin and Yirrkala. But I still wasn't well. The pills and injections didn't really help me.

After I returned from Darwin I saw [the female healer] who came over from Gurrumurru. She massaged my chest and head with water and pulled a wire [a *galka*'s weapon] out of my chest. After that I was well. I wasn't sick any more. I gave her payment of material, dresses, tobacco, blankets, a necklace, two knives, a tomahawk and some money. It was after she cured me that I could remember what had happened to me.

I'm not sure why the *galka* attacked me. Maybe it was something to do with *madayin* [sacred, secret] trouble. They may have been looking for my cousin who had found some *wulä* [dried blood] made in the image of a kangaroo, broken a piece off and given it to a missionary to send to a museum. For this they were going to kill him.

The fear of *galka* prevents most people from hunting or travelling alone. While out hunting men and women will stay within earshot (preferably within sight) of one another. They will almost never stray alone from the immediate vicinity of the camp at night. Everyone is potentially vulnerable, even, some believe, white Australians. On one occasion I decided to walk alone along the main road back to Yirrkala from the nearby town of Nhulunbuy and was stopped by Aboriginal friends coming into town by car. A close friend among them was extremely angry and chided me in a loud voice for risking my life in an area inhabited by *galka*. She insisted that I accompany them back to Nhulunbuy and refused to talk to me for the rest of the day. Notwithstanding this incident, several people said that white Australians are immune from *galka* attack. They have a light skin and different blood (unsuitable for *wulā*). In addition, they are not involved in the fights, quarrels and ritual life which provide the motives for attacks by *galka*.

Few people know, or will say, how *galka* acquire the ability and power to carry out their work. One man, a ritual leader and church member at Yirrkala, suggested that their special knowledge and power, their 'cleverness', comes from their association with other *galka*, with death and with the spirits of the dead:

> How does the man make himself a *galka*? He may sleep at the grave or get the blood of a dead man. *Marrnggitj* [healers] get their power from the dead man's blood and have *manggata* [spirit familiars] in their dillybag. [This is the only instance in which I was told that the power of a *marrnggitj* could derive from the blood of a dead man. It is likely (as Warner (1958:237) mentions) that any *marrnggitj* who possesses this relic (described by Warner as 'a kind of resin') would have obtained it by trade or purchase.]
>
> If a man wants to be a magic man he keeps the bone or blood of the dead man and goes to sleep and the spirit of the dead man comes to him and says, 'Follow me and do this or that magic thing. Take this dillybag for keeping *manggata* which I will give you'. The dead body is the spirit. A medicine man learns from the body of a dead man and the spirit follows him and tells him what to do – to murder someone with magic things or to take blood from someone or to find out about sickness caused by another *galka* or to help people by healing their sicknesses. This is what the *marrnggitj* does. A man can use the dead man to be a *marrnggitj* or *galka*.
>
> If you want to be clever you keep the spirit of the man in your dillybag. It will give you power. The spirit

may say, 'What do you want? To kill someone?' You reply, 'Yes, I do'. 'OK', it will say 'I'll give you power to be a number one *galka*. If you ask to be a *marrnggitj* you will be. You can't ask to learn both sides, only one'.

In addition to the methods employed by the *galka*, there are several other types of sorcery. Whereas *galka* are almost always said to be strangers to the people of Yirrkala, it is believed that these techniques are used by ordinary people both inside and outside Yirrkala. The descriptions which follow are of the most commonly cited techniques. There are as many minor variations of each technique as there are individuals willing to talk about them. Those below are combinations of several descriptions, all of which correspond in basic detail.

Most frequently mentioned is the *manggimanggi*, a pointed object such as a bone taken from a dead man's forearm which is sharpened and threaded at one end with a string. It may also be a stingray barb or hard ironwood point. The *manggimanggi* may be rubbed with the blood (*wuḻä*), or skin or decayed flesh of a dead man and left in the sun all day to strengthen it. The string is wound around the upper part of the arm and the muscles flexed so the blood flows into the arm. The bone is pointed towards the victim. Sometimes the sorcerer sings a special song or spell while he points. Suddenly there is a kick in the arm, like that of a gun being fired, which tells the murderer he has hit his victim.

When the murderer goes home, he puts the point in a dry, preferably hot, place so the victim will die. *Manggimanggi* sickness is said to take one to three weeks to kill the victim, longer than *galka* sickness.

Biyi', or image magic is believed to kill a person's spirit. The sorcerer draws a picture of the victim or writes his name on a sacred place or tree (such as that of the Snake Dreaming) on land belonging to his own clan, or land which he has a right (by birth or marriage) to enter and use. The sorcerer then calls out his name and the parts of his body: 'This is so and so. I'm drawing your eye, your chin, your nose, mouth, leg, arm . . .' This man will then be very sick after one or two years.

Alternatively, a man can take a small powerful dillybag and hit the blanket or bed of a person he wishes to harm, or strike the place in the sand where he has been sitting. After a while the victim will become sick. If the drawing is at the Snake Dreaming place a snake will grow inside the man's body. Otherwise the man may suffer from a sore inside his body which gets bigger and bigger. *Biyi'* causes a serious, long lasting sickness which nothing can help.

Burrpuy means the spoiling or rotting of the body. (The term *burrpuy* is also used to refer to leprosy and it is said that this technique of sorcery can also be used to cause leprosy.) There are several ways of carrying out *burrpuy*. After a man has walked along the sand the sorcerer may follow, singing a dangerous song and piercing his footprints with a spear as he goes. He may also use a red-hot wire. This person will be well for two or three months until the sickness comes through his feet, his two legs swell and become very hot, he sweats and loses body moisture. The sickness moves up to his lungs and spoils them and his blood becomes black. Shortly thereafter he will die. The man who killed him will be safe because no one has any way of knowing who he was.

Alternatively, when the victim goes to the toilet someone may take his excrement and put it in the fire. His stomach will blow up like a football. Occasionally a person may take another's soiled clothes or underpants – particularly those soiled by his sweat or urine – make a fire inside a hollow log, put these inside and seal it. The victim's body will swell until the flesh inside is soft. When the skin is touched it leaves an impression. The victim is hot. He can't bear clothes. He will soon die.

This technique was implicated in the death of an older woman in the community, whose skirt and underpants, it was said, were stolen and buried with hot rocks in sand. She subsequently became ill and a large sore appeared on her buttocks. Two *marrnggitj* visited her but could not help because, they said, her clothes had burned away completely. Variations of this technique, as with others, are mentioned from other parts of Australia. Dr Betty Meehan was told at Maningrida that a person's underpants could be stuffed into the exhaust pipe of a car and the car started with the same effect. The possessions of early European settlers in Australia afforded a host of new materials and places for the sorcerer's activities, including the kitchen chimneys of the sheep stations, unrivalled places for subjecting clothing to intense heat (Reynolds, 1981:43).

A person is especially vulnerable if a sorcerer finds the wet patch where he has urinated. For this form of sorcery, called *barrakbarrak*, a sorcerer takes a sharpened piece of hardwood or animal bone to which bark string has been attached using natural tar. This is stabbed into the wet patch left behind when someone has urinated and left there. After several months that person will contract a sickness of the lower abdomen which will slowly spread to the lungs and chest, finally causing death. The sorcerer can also scoop up some of the wet sand, seal it in a bottle and bury it until the sand dries out. The victim will be unable to pass urine – only blood.

Nyira, or the singing of a spell, can be used to cause a violent electrical storm called *raminydji* or to make someone ill. The sorcerer 'sings' the food which the victim is about to eat ensuring that he will be taken ill when he does so. Alternatively he may lie down near his victim, pretending to be asleep and in the middle of the night sing dangerous songs towards him, blowing in his direction as he does so.

Finally, *mawiya* is a poison which is added to a victim's food and which is made by grinding old dogs' faeces and bones together.

Sorcerers today are also believed to take advantage of Western goods to improve their arsenal of secret weapons. The mother of an infant who had been critically ill with meningitis told me that the child had been attacked accidentally by several young men who were actually trying to hurt her. The men had placed a *manggimanggi* in a flash-light, aimed it at the woman from a distance and flashed it several times. The *manggimanggi* flew out and hit her child by mistake. Placing aspirin or battery acid in a man's drink are both said to be techniques used by sorcerers to harm their victims at Nhulunbuy hotel. One of the Yolngu healers (*marrnggitj*) of Yirrkala (see Chapter 3) possesses a bullet which he says he extracted from a patient, and which has been emptied and filled with paper. This, he claims, can be fired silently from a rifle by a sorcerer at his victim to cause a fatal illness.

These techniques of sorcery – *galka, manggimanggi, biyi', burrpuy, barrakbarrak, nyira, mawiya* and those employing European artefacts – are considered to be the causes of many serious illnesses and of almost all, if not all, deaths. No inquiry into the aetiology of an illness or reason for a death, though, stops here. While every effort is made to find out the proximate cause of an illness or death it is equally important to know why the attack took place at all. Every attack is presumed to have a reason, an ultimate cause, if only the malice of the sorcerer. Those reasons most frequently mentioned are discussed in the following section.

The Ultimate Causes of Illness and Death

The reasons given for the use of sorcery centre on conflicts between individuals and groups and on breaches of social and sacred laws which cannot go unpunished or unavenged.

Everyone in the community takes great care not to commit a *religious transgression*. According to one of the ritual leaders of Yirrkala, 'If a man goes against the Law [the body of religious knowledge and restrictions] without permission he'll be dead in one to three months' time'. While speaking to me with the tape recorder on he explained that he had to be careful only to tape discussions about secular matters because, 'If I say the wrong [sacred or secret] things on this cassette the old people may say, "No", and send a message to a *galka* to kill me. In one or three months I might really get sick'.

If a woman accidentally or deliberately goes to a sacred place or views sacred objects normally seen only by initiated men she will, it is generally assumed, be speared or be attacked by a *galka*. Similarly, if a young and uninitiated man watches a sacred ceremony, eats *dhuyu* (sanctified) food or goes into a forbidden area he also may be killed.

Throughout Arnhem Land *reciprocal ritual and economic obligations* exist between various clans and individuals. Failure to meet these obligations is considered sufficient cause for retribution. One of the senior men of Yirrkala described a situation which existed between the people of a clan living at Maningrida, a settlement approximately 300 kilometres to the west, and those of a Yirrkala clan:

> The people of Maningrida sent a ritual string and feather headdress to a man at Yirrkala who should have given it to the people of [another Yirrkala clan]. They in turn would have lengthened and returned it. But he kept it himself. In the wet season Maningrida sent a message to Yirrkala asking where it was. The people of the clan to whom it should have gone replied that they did not have it and did not know where it was. So the Maningrida people said they would send a *galka* to kill someone of that clan. They did this, and the tracks of the horse which the *galka* rode were seen in the area in which their victim died.

When the sharing of royalty payments was renegotiated in 1979 and royalties were paid directly to landowners for the first time, conflicting claims on the payments arose. Among those who considered that they had a right to a share of the royalties were men who were the sons or husbands of women of the landowning group (that is, men of the *waku* or sisters' sons' clans). When the infant daughter of the head of one of the landowning clans died, a senior man of an affinal clan told me the cause was sorcery. (According to the doctor it was dehydration and septicaemia.) Men of one of the *waku* clans, he said, had given sacred objects to the child's father expecting to receive a share of the payments as a reciprocal gift ('about $10,000', the speaker said). When the money was not forthcoming they 'got the child'. 'This', he added, as if it were to be expected, 'is the Yolngu custom'.

The *theft of ritual objects, sacred songs, myths, paintings or land* are often given as legitimate reasons for seeking revenge by sorcery. The theft of a sacred object (*rangga*), some important personal possession, ritual songs (*manikay*), paintings (*miny'tji*), myths or land will lead to open hostilities or to revenge 'in the secret way'. An older woman at Yirrkala recounted that, when some young men from Yirrkala visited Maningrida, one of them stole a dillybag which belonged to a *galka* and contained his powerful objects. When a message came on the 'skeds' (daily outpost radio sessions) asking for its return, the young man's mother attempted to make another but was unable to duplicate it. The young man did not return the bag and a *galka* therefore came and secretly killed a man at Yirrkala. Similarly, when a young boy died in a car accident near Yirrkala in 1976 at least one explanation given for his death was that the young driver had deliberately killed him (by physical or magical means) because the dead boy's clan had illegally used the sacred paintings of the driver's clan.

Personal grievances arising out of *broken marriage contracts, adultery and love affairs* provide abundant motives for presumed attacks by sorcery at Yirrkala as they do in other Aboriginal communities (Hiatt 1965; McKnight 1981). At Yirrkala today the relationships of young men and women who are not correctly related for marriage, the refusal of some to marry the partner chosen for them and the affairs of married and single people are nagging strains in the mesh of community relationships. (For a psychiatric perspective on these issues, see Eastwell 1974.) The actual causes of friction are several. A young woman, for instance, may resist marrying an older man or one who already has a wife or wives. (There is good reason to suppose that this was also a problem in pre-contact times.) The preference for monogamous marriages is now quite strong, at least among women. When I asked 41 women of the community how many wives a man should have, 32 said one and nine said two or more. (There was no effect of age on their answers; older and younger women were equally divided.) Some women say they want to marry a spouse of their own choice, though always, they emphasise, someone correctly related for marriage. The abrogation of a bethrothal contract invariably leads to quarrels within and between clans. Whether an agreement is enforced or a compromise worked out there are usually some people whose interests are neglected and who remain resentful.

The pressures on young and old have been increased by the interference of white staff in problems that Yolngu regard as their own business. Mission and government staff, of course, have never been happy about polygamy and what some refer to as child marriages. Generally, they have not been heavy-handed in their opposition but their influence has still been felt. In 1967 a meeting of the Aboriginal leaders from several Arnhem Land Methodist missions declared that girls born after that date should not be promised. Most parents, though, expect that their children will marry someone in the correct relationship and marriage contracts are still, quietly, being arranged.

The strains inherent in the marriage system and exacerbated by life in a densely settled community often surface as fights and quarrels.

One young woman, for instance, suggested that the terminal illness of a man of the community was caused by his daughter's boyfriend, a man from a distant settlement, who was angry about her father's opposition to their relationship. A man of the community whose brother was suffering from a painful urinary complaint explained to the attending doctor (in a clear allusion to its cause) that if a man did not take good care of his first wife she might work sorcery on him. During a familial attempt at conciliation between two brothers, the younger of whom had been seeing the older brother's 'promise', the latter warned his young brother that he might 'receive a dangerous thing' if he did not terminate the relationship. Later, when he learned that his unmarried sister was pregnant by one of the brothers of his errant 'promise' he was doubly angry and extended his veiled threats both to his 'promise' and to her mother and father. (This dispute and attempts at conciliation are detailed in Williams 1973:103-24.)

Murder is a *prima facie* cause for revenge. If a man dies unexpectedly or is openly killed, certain categories of kin are expected to avenge the death. Theoretically the fathers or brothers of the deceased will ask men who are sister's sons or husbands (*waku*) of the deceased to avenge the death. If they decline or fail, other members of a clan of the opposite moiety will be approached to exact revenge (Williams 1973:164). Revenge may be taken openly and the murderer attacked with a spear or knife, or those nominated may seek the services of a *galka* or work sorcery on the murderer themselves.

Jealousy (and the often associated activity, *gossip*) is one of the motives most frequently cited for a sorcery attack. When a senior man became seriously ill at Galiwin'ku, his sister's husband suggested that people there might be jealous of this man because of his influential position in a legal battle for copyright on all traditional paintings. (By this means it was hoped to prevent their indiscriminate commercial use on items such as teatowels and tablecloths.)

If a man acquires special status, he has reason to fear those who might resent his good fortune or superior abilities. A clan leader who was enthusiastically describing the progress of his homeland centre and plans for the future qualified his expression of hope that it would be of a 'high standard', saying 'I would like to make myself a high person, but if I do people might be jealous and complain.' Another clan leader said that he feared for his young son who had healing powers. The boy's father believed others who were jealous of his son's abilities might try to kill the boy. The adult male *marrnggitj* at Yirrkala expressed similar fears for himself but said that no one could actually kill him because his spirit familiars would warn him of the approach of any assailant. This *marrnggitj* said he refused an offer from a sympathetic doctor to go and work at a hospital because he feared that other (white) doctors might become jealous of his powers and try to kill him.

In 1977 I was told by a man from north-east Arnhem Land who was visiting Sydney that the female *marrnggitj* who lives at Gurrumurru homeland centre was ill. The doctor from Nhulunbuy diagnosed a heart attack. Two other people who lived there had now become *marrnggitj*. When I asked what had caused this woman's heart attack, his answer was allegorical. 'Think', he said, 'of three pearl divers. One of them is a much better diver than the others. One day, when they are out diving together the two less competent divers cut the air hose of the third. Why?' I suggested they might be jealous of him. He nodded meaningfully and said that *all* people – Europeans, Chinese, Japanese and Aborigines – are like that.

These, then, are some of the main offences and conflicts which are said to constitute provocation for the use of sorcery. Ideally, sorcery is only perpetrated on someone who deserves punishment. In fact, many of those who believe they have been victims of sorcery, such as the woman above who was attacked by a *galka* near Yirrkala, disavow any personal responsibility for an attack. They attribute it to the malice of the sorcerer, say it was a case of mistaken identity or believe they were attacked because of a relative's wrong-doing.

Most people assume that anyone from a distant settlement or hostile group may attack a person from Yirrkala. For this reason strangers are feared and avoided. A woman expressed great distress when some visitors arrived from Groote Eylandt, an island to the south, fearing they would attack her or others at Yirrkala. A senior clan leader refused to allow central Australian Aborigines and a Torres Strait Islander to visit Yirrkala when they came to assist in a linguistic program. The white Australians on the team were, on the other hand, given permission to work there. This man was also particularly worried by the influx of unrelated strangers to drink at the hotel in Nhulunbuy:

> When the Maningrida people were here our people were nervous and wouldn't walk in the night. When they landed at the airport they told some people they had come to kill us. When they heard this some of our people were very angry and went to the pub looking for them. They fought with bottles, wood and fists and Yirrkala men finally threw the Maningrida men into the billabong . . .
>
> When I heard this I went and saw the solicitor and asked him to speak to the police about it. This is our town. Their towns [for drinking] are Oenpelli and

Darwin. But the cyclone hit Darwin so now they come
here. They want to steal our sacred things. That's why
they have come to kill us.

As this statement indicates, accusations and suspicions of sorcery
focus, on the whole, on distant or unrelated people. Sorcery, as
McKnight observed of the Lardil of Mornington Island, is a
xenophobic concept (1981:41). *Galka* are almost invariably said to be
strangers from the west or south. As I drove through the outskirts of
Nhulunbuy one day my passengers pointed to an area of bush and
said a *galka* lived there. He had recently stolen the clothes and rifle of
a young Yirrkala man who was working in town as a police aide.
The man later found some of his belongings scattered through the
area. Asked how they could be sure the thief was a *galka*, they
replied, 'Because we didn't recognise his footprints'. The only
indication that anyone at Yirrkala 'knows *galka*' came from a young
man who claimed that the leader of an allied clan had asked him if he
wanted to learn how to be a *galka*. He demurred when told that he
would have to kill someone in order to qualify.

Despite the fact that several techniques of sorcery require access to
a victim's clothes or excreta, and are therefore easily performed by a
sorcerer in a close relationship to his victim, accusations involving
the members of a sick person's clan or allied clans are rare (but not
unknown as the threats of the aggrieved man against his brother,
'promise' and her family above indicate). The rarity of such
accusations reflects in part their serious implications. When a young
woman started to tell me that her aunt's swollen and infected arm
was considered the work (*burrpuy*) of a woman who was involved
with the sufferer's husband, her mother told her sharply to be quiet.
Gossip is considered most offensive, especially by the person who is
its target. Moreover, were such a speculation to reach the ears of the
accused it would cause serious trouble. The low frequency of
accusations within groups or between allied groups is due, first, to a
generalised fear of strangers, second, to social pressures
discouraging open discussion of intra-community suspicions and,
third, to the strong sentiments that close relatives should not fight.

Dreaming Places, Rituals and Spirits

Although most ritual or religious offences are said to be punished by
human agencies, such as *galka* or other sorcerers, illnesses are
occasionally attributed directly to breaches of certain prohibitions or
laws of behaviour.

Within the territories of the clans of eastern Arnhem Land are several *powerful and sacred areas*.² These areas are associated with the *wangarr* or mythical figures of the Dreamtime. Dangerous objects from these *wangarr* places can be collected and used by individuals to cause or, occasionally, cure sickness. A person who visits either the octopus *wangarr* or flying fox *wangarr* in the Wessel Islands to the north-west of Yirrkala can collect a stone or wood which he grinds up or burns to ashes in a fire. Either of these poisons will kill a person when put in his food. Powder of an octopus rock placed in a man's drink will cause an octopus to grow inside him producing vomiting and diarrhoea. Similarly if someone breaks a branch off a tree in the *djirang'* (boils) dreaming place and says, 'Go to Yirrkala', everyone there will contract boils.

During 1974 there was an epidemic of diarrhoea at Yirrkala. Everyone fell ill, including the dogs. It was said to have been caused by someone who had cooked a dangerous nut (called *gurrunggurr*) of the Warramirri Dreaming to the west. The west wind carried the smoke to Yirrkala bringing with it the sickness. The smoke of the *gurrunggurr* is so powerful that it may also kill all the fish and shellfish in an area (see also Webb n.d.: 129, 133, 206).

Certain *wangarr* places are dangerous in and of themselves. Anyone who trespasses in these areas, whether by choice or ignorance, is likely to be stricken with illness. If, for instance, a man walks through a certain *wangarr* place called Yingapungapu (Morphy 1977b) he will lose his strength and the bones in his legs and arms will break. It is also possible to contract leprosy as a result of entering such an area. A woman at Yirrkala is said to be 'weak-kneed' because she persistently collected shellfish at a location close to a dangerous *wangarr* place.

Another category of places which are considered dangerous are *wänung* places. Near Port Bradshaw, to the south of Yirrkala, there is a *wänung* place, a Fire Dreaming place. A trespasser in this area will automatically suffer from broken bones and sores inside his body. If he spears an animal in such a place, he and those who eat it will become ill. An old and senior man of a clan of the Yirritja moiety recalled the consequences of a foray into a *wänung* area in the 1930s.

> When I was out hunting kangaroo in Yirritja country I came to a special rock and got the *wänung* sickness. It is a *madayin* [sacred] place. If someone goes there his leg breaks and he gets sickness like *burrpuy* [leprosy]. A

---

2. A more detailed discussion of safe and dangerous places in eastern Arnhem Land is given in a paper by Biernoff (1978). He describes the classification of localities in terms of safety and danger, the differential access to these localities based on a person's social identity, the transformation in a locality's nature, and the transformation of an individual's view of sacred and dangerous as a result of increased knowledge, ritual power and understanding.

marrnggitj [now deceased] treated me and Mr Chaseling gave me an injection.

Several *wärral* places also exist near Port Bradshaw and in the Wessel Islands. These are jungle areas where all the trees and flowers are said to be red. In both these and the *wänung* places it is dangerous to pick up a stone or dig or to chop into a tree; the offender and his family will become ill. However, should a man wish to punish a community he can take sand from this area, toss it in the air and call the name of the target community. This will make the sky red and cause a serious, even deadly epidemic of diarrhoea.

Well to the south of Yirrkala is a *wokuti* place, a burial site. Most people are afraid to go there now. As with the Yingupungapu places, a man who enters such an area will contract leprosy or a similar disease.

The risks associated with entering dangerous Dreaming or burial places may be directly attributed to the spirit beings which dwell there. If a man who is a stranger to a certain area walks through it without permission and ritual protection, the spirit, described as *meldbudjumirri*, may steal his spirit or soul. The victim will become thinner and thinner and finally die. Although a *marrnggitj* can tell what has happened he is powerless to do anything about it. As described in Chapter 6, the leader of a clan which established a homeland centre south of Yirrkala said that he had suffered at the hands of the spirit people of this area. When he visited Yirrkala he suffered hallucinations and a 'darkness' of the mind. The doctor suggested that his symptoms might abate if he returned to his homeland centre. This man feared, however, that the spirit people living there might have resented the intrusion by human beings and therefore made him sick.

Sacred objects and *ceremonies* are also surrounded by an elaborate set of rules and restrictions. Sacred objects possess power which can be dangerous to those not authorised to handle them. For instance, a woman attributed a severe attack of coughing during the night to the proximity of her bed to a sacred object (*rangga*) which was wrapped and stored in a suitcase nearby.

Similarly the power activated during sacred ceremonies may be dangerous to the uninitiated or, if not correctly controlled, dangerous to all involved. After an epidemic of influenza struck Yirrkala, one man said that it had been caused by his dancing the dangerous (in his words, 'poison') octopus dance of his mother's clan during mortuary rites. He had, he said, unwittingly invoked the power and spirit of the totemic octopus while dancing and kicking up the dirt with great energy. This power is not inherently dangerous: this man has used it at times to heal others and protect himself. Rather it can cause sickness if it is released without adequate ritual restraint. A clan leader criticised the negligence of a younger leader in allowing men and women to dance together (instead of on separate grounds as the law dictates) at the opening of a pump at a homeland centre. He blamed this breach of the law for the leader's subsequent illness (pneumonia) and for the deaths of members of another clan who were 'bosses' for the ceremony.

On another occasion, many of the people at Elcho Island who had participated in mortuary rites there developed sores and boils at the conclusion of the ceremonies. Several children died. A woman who had been present recalled hearing spirits dancing as well. She was sent back to Elcho Island as an emissary by her father's brother who had led the ceremony to assure everyone that he had not done anything on purpose to make Elcho Island people ill. She explained to them that, since they had made a representation in the sand of the Yingapungapu area and put the dead man's clothes in it during the dancing, it must have been the mythical female spirit being associated with this particular *wangarr* area which had made them ill.

While the Dreamtime or *wangarr* beings may cause illness, the spirits of the dead are not often blamed for illnesses. Only once was I told of a physical illness caused by a spirit: a woman said that her brother's wife had become very sick because a *ngänuk* (or *mokuy*) stabbed her with its fingernail. Occasionally emotional disturbances or mental illness, particularly 'madness' (*bawa 'mirri*), are attributed to the actions of spirits. One man who was receiving intermittent psychiatric care explained that several *ngänuk* had come from the cemetery one night to visit him. One *ngänuk* now stays with him and talks with him, tempting him to do rash things, to make trouble. Even as he told me this, this man said he could hear a spirit in his head telling him to do things, but he refused to co-operate with it. Sometimes the spirit chases him with a knife or tells him that his wife is running after other men. She, however, just laughs at this, telling her husband it is not true.

All people are at risk if they ignore the laws relating to sacred matters. Many statements about the causes of illness (such as, 'I became sick because I hunted in a sacred area'), however, are ambiguous. It was not always clear to me whether the speakers thought retribution was direct or mediated by a sorcerer (indirect). It seems clear that, while most causal statements implicate a human agent, at least some illnesses are the immediate result of ritually unprotected or illegal associations with powerful places, objects or spirit beings.

In both ritual and secular contexts, various prohibitions dictate the types of *food* which may be eaten by initiates during sacred ceremonies, by participants in other rituals and by menstruating or pregnant women. Several people, for instance, suggested that some of the now middle-aged men at Yirrkala had contracted leprosy as the result of participating in the Gunapipi ceremony between 25 and 30 years ago. This ceremony had been imported from clans to the south and west, and many of the Yirrkala participants did not know the rules connected with it. Although they were told to eat only lean animals and fish, some ate fatty animals and, as a result, were stricken with leprosy. Similarly, during circumcision, young boys may not eat *madayin* (sacred) foods until they have participated in a final ceremony which frees them from this restriction.

During pregnancy, young women are forbidden to eat certain foods, particularly those with totemic associations. The cleft palate of a young child and the failure of his infant brother to thrive were attributed to their mother eating emu during her pregnancy. Ideally a pregnant woman should not eat sacred animals such as crocodile, emu, brolga, porcupine, bush turkey, a certain turtle (*malarrka*) and its eggs, and certain fish. If she eats certain species of fish, her baby will be blind or its skin soft. She can, however, eat kangaroo, wallaby, goose, duck, shellfish, yams, and the corms of the spike rush. One woman maintained that, if a pregnant woman eats animals which contain no fat, the child will grow with crooked legs or sicken and die after birth. The mother should also observe certain dietary restrictions in the early months of a baby's life and others throughout the growing-up years.

Whereas the food taboos connected with pregnancy are sometimes implicated in sickness, breaches of taboos which apply to a menstruating woman are not usually said to cause illness either to the woman or to others. However, a woman must not eat any food caught, gathered, or given to her by a male relative while she is menstruating. If she does so, it is said, an accident will befall this man the next time he goes out hunting.

Breaches of Social Norms

Breaches of social norms, if punished at all, are almost always punished by sorcery rather than rebounding directly on the offender. Again it is difficult to determine precisely what is meant when a person attributes an illness to, for instance, a 'wrong relationship'. Unless it is possible to elicit more information — and often, since direct questions about a person's private life are considered rude, it is not — it is difficult to know whether the speaker means that punishment has been meted out by a sorcerer or that the relationship itself has resulted directly in illness. The latter possibility is probably entertained. A senior woman of the community suggested that the girlfriend of a ritual leader of the community who was in the wrong relationship to him for marriage had become ill and died because of their irregular liaison.

Anger and recriminations almost always ensue if a young person rejects her (or his) betrothed in favour of a lover. Not only does this deprive her betrothed of his rightful wife but the 'promise' of her boyfriend is then unable to marry him. The parents of the woman are placed in the unenviable position of having received gifts and services over the years from the potential son-in-law and having to compensate him for the breach of contract. One young woman who had taken a boyfriend fell ill and was rushed to hospital one night. The attending doctor said that she had been drinking. Her relatives excused this as a reaction to the recent death of her deceased father's brother (her classificatory father). She remained sick, however, and spent several weeks in hospital in the following months. Although she had a low grade fever and was considered ill by hospital staff, they were unable to diagnose her condition. Throughout the illness her father's sister who was the mother of her betrothed, and had been very upset by her liaison with another man, maintained firmly and often that it was the result of their association.

Certain behavioural restrictions surround pregnancy and the spacing of births. It is often said that to ignore these is to court illness for a young child. For instance, widespread agreement exists that if a woman becomes pregnant before her last child is 'on its feet', both mother and child will become sick. In particular, the infant will become weak, thin, sickly and 'lose blood' (become anaemic). The mechanism thought to bring about this deterioration in the child's condition is not clear. Several women (and men) said that the child does not get enough breast milk when his mother becomes pregnant again. When the baby is born he is displaced from the breast completely. One maintained that it is 'like magic', that the young child senses the pregnancy and sickens. Others simply observed the connection and did not suggest a mechanism. Whatever the postulated cause of the sickliness of a child displaced by a new sibling, a long interval between births is strongly advocated by many people. The average birth interval preferred by 92 women interviewed about their knowledge, attitudes and practices with respect to child-bearing was four years (These results are discussed in Reid 1979a, and Reid and Gurruwiwi 1979.) The father of five children stated most vehemently that a girl who has her first child before the age of 16 or 17 will become weak and that, if a woman has a second child before her last baby is walking, the first child will also become weak.

In summary, serious illness and death may be attributed either to human agents (sorcerers) or to the effect, direct or mediated, of the breach of a religious law or social norm. By far the most commonly postulated cause of illness is sorcery. In either case, illness and death are not viewed as natural or chance events, but as the outcome of hostility between individuals or groups or as the outcome of a failure to observe the laws of behaviour governing the relationships between people, the land and the supernatural.

The causal beliefs outlined in this chapter can be regarded as a social paradigm or sociomedical theory.[3] Though Yolngu would not, of course, describe them in these terms, the proximate and ultimate causes of sickness constitute an explanatory framework, a framework embedded in the fabric of personal and political relationships as expressed in the social life of the community. By analogy with the theories of Western science, the sociomedical theory of illness and death in north-east Arnhem Land can be seen as consisting of the following elements: a set of independent variables, the social and political relationships and religious life of the community; the values of these variables, such as hostility, peace, amity, jealousy, harmony, anger; the dependent variable, the illness or death to be explained; and the intervening variable or mechanism of causation (if any), such as sorcery.

The primary function of the sociomedical theory is to provide understanding when the loss of a member of the society is a reality or a threat. The theory links perhaps the most uncertain, and therefore anxiety-ridden area of human existence, that of health and ill-health, to the most pervasive and culturally structured area, that of human relations. It explains variations in one by variations in the other: if personal or clan conflicts become more frequent, the incidence of sickness will rise. The immediate cause of the illness or death is usually sorcery. The ultimate causes, however, are disturbances in social relationships.

Yolngu consider that any explanation of a sickness or death which does not identify a proximate and ultimate cause is incomplete. As Evans-Pritchard observed, anthropomorphic and spiritual explanations of sickness and death are deeply satisfying, for they tell not only how a person has been afflicted, but why (1937:67-70). When termites eat through the supports of an Azande granary and it falls and kills a person underneath it is not enough to say that his luck ran out. The death requires answers. The victim's fellows are fully aware of how it collapsed (the termites) but want to know why it fell on him and not someone else. For a Zande, witchcraft provides the

---

3. Barnes (1969) defines a paradigm as 'a set of categories, theories and procedures learnt in connexion with concrete examples, accepted by the entire reference group and applied to deal with problems in concrete situations' (1969:97). A paradigm includes both theory and some exemplary applications to the results of experiment and observation. I am taking a somewhat narrower view of the aetiological beliefs described in this chapter and designating them a theory; that is, an explanation of certain phenomena which is based on principles or variables independent of the phenomena to be explained. The terms 'model', 'paradigm' and 'theory' tend to be used interchangeably by such authors as Barnes (1969), Horton (1964) and Marwick (1974).

answer. For a Yolngu, sorcery. The concept of accident, as one young Yolngu woman explicitly pointed out (p. 102), is not acceptable to the people of Yirrkala. Neither are notions of fate or chance. They want to know not only *how* someone has come to be afflicted, but *why*.

The conviction that there is a causal relationship between social and somatic phenomena requires only one assumption: that power exists in the universe which can be mobilised by human beings in certain known ways for their own ends, be they bad or good. All other relationships postulated by the theory flow logically from this assumption. It follows that diagnoses of the cause of illness which use this theory are not only statements about bodily symptoms and disease processes but are statements about social processes and their implications.

Clearly it is not sufficient simply to locate and explain an illness or death. A diagnosis or divination contains within it an indication of the most appropriate response. If diagnoses are statements about the malevolent uses of power, treatments will be attempts to mobilise power for healing and reverse the damage the sorcerer has done. The person who has access to the power necessary to heal is the traditional healer or *marrnggitj*. It is he (or she) who can extract and neutralise objects of sorcery, strengthen and cure a patient, divine the cause of death, and protect group members from further assaults. In the following chapter the making, powers, and each of the functions of the *marrnggitj* are discussed.

3 *Marrnggitj*: The Yolngu healer

The *marrnggitj* is the traditional healer of eastern Arnhem Land. He is, according to Warner (1958), 'the reverse of the coin on whose other surface appears the black sorcerer'. He possesses special powers which enable him to heal the sick and to divine the cause of an illness or death. It is the *marrnggitj* to whom community members look for reassurance, healing, explanation and protection when serious illness and death threaten[1].

The way in which a man (or woman) becomes a *marrnggitj*, the abilities and powers which he possesses and the types of cures and divinations he is able to effect have been described by Thomson (1961), Warner (1958) and Webb (1936, n.d.). Each recorded the life histories and activities of *marrnggitj* living in central and eastern Arnhem Land in the 1920s and 1930s. Webb wrote that,

> I[n] East Arnhem Land there are two classes of magicians or medicine-men. Members of the one, whose operations are wholly of an evil character, are known as *ragalk*, while members of the other, whose operations are always of a benign character are known as *marrngit* . . . (1936:336).

Of *galka* and *marrnggitj* Warner wrote:

> There is here a kind of warfare between the forces which do good and those which do harm to man. The latter are related to an organized set of concrete techniques embodied in the person of the black magician, while an entirely different set gives practical expression, in the personality of the white magician, to those forces which control the effects of black magic (1958:193).

Both Warner and Webb agree that, in his social personality and role as a member of his local group, the *marrnggitj* is different from his fellows only in the magical powers which he possesses. There are, writes Warner, 'no indications of the psychopathic personality,

---

1. The role of the *margidjbu* of western Arnhem Land as described by Catherine Berndt (1964) is similar to that of the *marrnggitj* in that he is the individual to whom community members turn in times of illness and death for healing, information and emotional support. In a most interesting paper on the concept of abnormality in western Arnhem Land Ronald and Catherine Berndt (1951) also analyse the role of the *margidjbu*, the concept of *bengwar* (silliness) and ideas of sorcery, and provide emic and etic perspectives on the distinctions between them. As these papers and Eastwell's (1973) article on healers in modern Arnhem Land show, the similarities between east and west are striking.

for psychologically and physically they were a very normal group' (1958:210). According to Webb, the office of healer is not inherited and the descending of powers on any particular man 'appears to be quite capricious and without any discoverable governing principle' (1936:337).

The descriptions of the *marrnggitj* given by Thomson,[2] Warner, and by Webb closely parallel the making, roles and personalities of *marrnggitj* living in, or affiliated with, Yirrkala today. In this chapter the way in which contemporary *marrnggitj* at Yirrkala became healers, the attitudes of community members towards their work and their social roles in the community are described.

Making and Powers

The process of becoming a *marrnggitj* has several identifiable stages. Typically the *marrnggitj* undergoes, at some time in his or her life, a frightening supernatural experience by means of which he becomes 'clever'. This may involve an encounter with spirits who adopt him and confer on him their powers, a confrontation by the spirits of the dead, an experience such as dying and coming to life again or living for some time in a death-like state.

Second, while few, if any people of Yirrkala dispute the existence of the types of powers and abilities which the healer claims to possess, the actual visitation of such powers on an individual must be demonstrated. He must show that he is, in fact, able to cure the sick. Third, the healer must attract a clientele and establish his practice. Once his claim to the role is validated by those who have seen and believed, the sick begin to seek him out for treatment and his practice gradually expands.

Several *marrnggitj* live at Yirrkala or in its affiliated homeland centres. Their professional careers have broadly followed this pattern. In the following pages the life histories of four such healers are given. The first and second, those of an adult male *marrnggitj* and a former child *marrnggitj*, were related by the *marrnggitj* themselves. The third, that of Nyurrulnga, a child *marrnggitj*, was given by his parents. The fourth, that of a female *marrnggitj* who lives at a homeland centre to the west, was given by distant relatives. The last

---

2. Thomson (1961) found that the spirit familiars of the healer were called *marrngit* among the tribes near Milingimbi and the healers, *marrngitmirri* ('having' or 'with' *marrngit*). At Yirrkala these spirits are called *manggata* or *djamarrkuli* (children), and the healer himself *marrnggitj*. As at Yirrkala, there were some differences of opinion among Thomson's informants about whether women could be *marrnggitj*; whether the office was inherited and what form familiars take. However, the healers' making and powers are essentially the same in both areas.

account reflects a lack of consensus about the source of her powers but an agreement that they followed a critical personal experience.

An Adult Male *Marrnggitj*

This man (Plate 5) was born to the west of Yirrkala but grew up in the community. His mother had six children, three of whom are still alive. They and his parents live at Elcho Island. He has a young son by a former wife but is now living at Yirrkala with his second wife. The way in which he acquired his powers and began to practice as a healer is described in his own words:

> When I was young I walked back to Yirrkala from Caledon Bay after visiting relatives there. One night, as I was sleeping, I heard voices like wind rustling in the leaves. I thought it might be *galka* and was very frightened. Then I felt something like an electric shock and some of this power that I have now, the little children [spirit familiars] or *manggata* entered me. I slept as though I was unconscious and in the morning woke up afraid that I had been attacked by *galka*. I thought I might die or be attacked by a crocodile as I was swimming across rivers on the way home.
> When I arrived at Yirrkala I went to join some

5 A *marrnggitj* (healer-diviner) of Yirrkala with his diagnostic and healing stones (*milirrk*)

relatives at Dambaliya [an island off the coast]. At sunset one day, as I was cooking a fish alone on a remote beach, I saw someone coming. I thought it was one of my brothers, but as the figure got closer it became huge and I could see it was carrying a *matjinydji* [special dillybag] across its chest and had fins running down its side and legs. 'He's a *mokuy* [spirit]', I thought. 'What's he going to do to me?' I was frightened and ran back and forth from the sea to the bush, but in each place he appeared next to me. I decided to dig a hole and bury myself in the sand, but the *mokuy* just shrank to the size of a beetle and ran up and down my back. Suddenly I realised I was deaf, that my heart had stopped beating and that I was no longer afraid.

'Why were you afraid'?, it asked. 'Don't you want my *gilapa* [magic things]? If you hadn't been afraid I'd have given you all of them. But now I've decided to give you half. I'll give you three *gilapa*.' These are the stones I now use to heal people. By this time I wanted to get back to camp but it was high tide and I could not cross the rivers. However, the *mokuy* told me to put my spear and spear-thrower into his pouch and to climb on his back. He then soared like a bird across each river until we were close to the camp. There he disappeared.

When I arrived at the camp I couldn't speak to anyone. My tongue was wrong. My ears, mouth and nose had all grown large until I looked like a *mokuy*. When the children saw me they screamed. Throughout the night I dreamed of spirits, snakes, *galka* and people fighting — all the bad and sinful things. The next day everything I saw was red and trees and animals looked like *mokuy*. I was sure I was going to die at the hands of these things.

We left later that day to go back to Yirrkala by dugout canoe. I could hear a voice telling me not to reveal that I was a *marrnggitj* for at least three years.

One day, three years later, a man became very ill at Yirrkala. He had been speared through the skull by the wire of a *galka*. The *galka* had meant to attack someone else and, when he saw he had stabbed the wrong man said to him, 'Go to [name of this *marrnggitj*]; he will cure you'. People heard him running around like a madman in his pain calling my name and so came and fetched me. By the time I arrived he was unconscious. I said, 'I'll try to make him well. If I can't it means I'm not really a *marrnggitj*'. I put the large stone the *mokuy* had given me on his head and saw that there was a large sore and *manggimanggi* inside his skull. I swept my hand over his head and, when I opened it, the *manggimanggi* was in my palm. When I realised what I had done, I thought to myself, 'I *am* a *marrnggitj*'. The next day this man was well and went back to work.

About eight years ago, 10 years after this happened, my stepbrother died. I was so sad after the funeral that I decided to go and sleep by his grave. That night the ground shook like an earthquake and several *mokuy* rose from the grave. The boss *mokuy* said to me, 'Why did you come to the cemetery'? 'I was grieving for my brother,' I replied. 'What do you want'?, he asked. 'I want to become clever'. He told me that he was the boss because the dead man had come to him and I said I would follow him. He then gave me another *gilapa*.

This *marrnggitj* now possesses a special *malaka* or small dillybag, and a total of ten healing stones (*gilapa* or *milirrk*) which he uses to treat people. He is also aided by an unspecified number of spirit familiars or *manggata* which possess magic of their own and are only visible to him. At dawn and sunset they come to him and affect his eyes so that he can see things others cannot. At night they protect him from harm.

The *marrnggitj* says that the various stones have different powers. One can be placed in water which, when drunk by anyone suffering from an illness of the stomach, liver or kidneys, will cure the damage to these organs. Another is used to heal internal sores by pulling the flesh and sinews together. A small stone erases all superficial signs of a sore by healing the flesh and skin completely. A stone which is striped with red bands of 'blood' will restore a patient's 'bad blood'. Another is an 'X-ray stone' which enables the *marrnggitj* to see inside the patient's body. One large stone helps him to divine the identity of the killer after a death in the community.

A Former Child *Marrnggitj*

At least three individuals at Yirrkala claim, or are claimed, to have had powers which they have either lost or now choose not to exercise. Few people seem to know of the early feats of curing of a man in his mid-twenties. A close classificatory father's sister said she had never heard about them although one distant relative recalled the young man's abilities and maintained that he had lost his powers after becoming partially deaf. Another older male relative said that this man had never actually been a *marrnggitj*; he was just a 'strong dreamer' (that is, he was clairvoyant). The man himself still possesses healing objects but remembers little of his early experiences and his healing activities as a boy of five. Many of them were later recounted to him by his mother. In his words:

> My brother and I were twins. I was born second. After my birth I was taken and left in the sacred sandhills of my mother's clan territory. However, my mother told the wife of one of the missionaries that I was there and she came with my relatives to get me. When they found me I was alive and well, having been protected by the sacred goannas which were covering me to shade me from the sun. The missionary brought me back to Yirrkala and gave me to my grandfather's wife who cared for me. After this I was given a name meaning 'king' because I was king of the sandhills. My two grandfathers told me this story when they were alive, but at first I couldn't believe it. I'm not a king.
>
> When I was five years old I ran away back to my mother's country and people. I was really happy there. I was full of joy. I really wanted to go back to those hills and used to dream about the [creator being] of that area. I had a little stone which used to belong to my mother's paternal grandfather who was a *marrnggitj* and which came from the hills. It is a sacred stone.
>
> While I was living there I used this stone and my three children [spirit familiars] to heal my grandfather who had been bitten by a shark and a woman who was attacked by someone using *manggimanggi*.
>
> By the time I went to school I was really a *marrnggitj* and had two stones (one of them from the kingfisher's eye) and two octopus' eyes. The two stones came from the sky. I found them twinkling on the ground. The octopus' eyes are sacred to two clans and are being kept by [the head of one of them].
>
> By the time I was seven I had forgotten most I learned about being a *marrnggitj*. However, I still use my stones occasionally. Recently my *djamarrkuli* [children or spirit familiars] came out of one of them and told me that a man on another settlement was very sick and about to die. When my brother's daughter arrived by plane from the settlement the next morning she confirmed this. I plan to take my sacred stone to the settlement and, with the help of my *djamarrkuli*, identify his murderer [sorcerer]. Once I know his name I'll tell the police in Nhulunbuy. They'll

put him in gaol. My mother has told me she does not like me taking any part in matters concerning death and dying and lies awake at night worrying about me.

I have been trained as a health worker. When the members of my family and clan move to our homeland centre I'll be a *marrnggitj* for them. We won't call the doctor. I've learned a lot from Dr Raven [a pseudonym] and I've worked in two ways. If someone gets sick I might use medicine from the doctor to make the job easier. Some *marrnggitj* work takes 15 minutes — a long time. It's good to work both ways.

A Practising Child *Marrnggitj*

A young boy of the community is reputed to be both a healer and clairvoyant. His mother, father and other relatives all attest to his unusual abilities. His school teacher, a young man of the community, has observed that he is very bright and can read people's minds. His mother and father described his development in the following terms:

Nyurrulnga [a pseudonym suggested by the boy's father] was born prematurely. At birth he was so small that he had to be placed in an incubator where he could not open his eyes or his mouth. He had to stay there for two and a half months. When he was three he began to behave in ways which made us suspect he was different from other children. When someone died he would act like an old person, dragging his feet along the ground. At night he would leave the house and play with a special dog which is an animal of his mother's clan's Dreaming. We think his mother's *märi* [mother's mother's brother; deceased] gave the dog to him. When [the female *marrnggitj*] visited Yirrkala, her *manggata* told her our son had special powers and she relayed this to us. It was shortly after this that he began healing.

When we were living at our homeland, Nyurrulnga's sister broke her leg. She was screaming in pain and her leg began to swell. Nyurrulnga told her she must go with him and swim in the sea, because it is the home of some of the spirit people of our clan. They are like sons and daughters to Nyurrulnga as well. They carried his sister as she swam. At night Nyurrulnga sat with her and continued to heal her. The next day we were so worried that we took her by car to Nhulunbuy Hospital even though Nyurrulnga said she was, as a result of his work, already recovering. This was so. When we got there the staff simply bandaged her leg and sent her home.

Nyurrulnga is not only a *marrnggitj*. He can tell us exactly who is coming by car to our homeland centre even though we do not have a radio. When we are there and someone dies at Yirrkala he tells us about it. In addition, he now has five magical stones which have been given to him by the spirit people of our clan. One has eyes. Another contains spirit familiars which enter a sick person's body and run around inside healing the patient. These stones are still being given to him. We don't really know where or how he gets them. They are given to him in a sacred way. The spirit people leave the stones for the boy to find. When a person is ill the stones and the spirit people help Nyurrulnga to heal him. For instance, when [a clan leader] was sick in hospital, Nyurrulnga treated him. That night [the leader] dreamt he saw two men dancing in the ward. Nyurrulnga said they were our spirit people who had stayed to heal him. [The leader told me they were the spirits of his own ancestors]. That day, when we told him to go to school, Nyurrulnga refused, saying that he wanted to stay home and wait for his spirit people whom he suspected had slept at Nhulunbuy Hospital.

Initially I [his father] didn't believe in him. However, one day he threw something into the air and told me to fly up and catch it. I said I couldn't, so he flew around himself, up to the ceiling. The next day I told him I believed him. Now I protect him. He must not drink hot tea because this will kill his power. We have to be careful of people who may be jealous of his powers and try to kill him. I am a Christian and believe that his power and acts are like miracles. Perhaps Christ has chosen him as a little boy through whom He can perform miracles of healing.

A Female *Marrnggitj*

A female *marrnggitj* of wide repute who has a flourishing practice lives at Gurrumurru, west of Yirrkala. Her skills are such that she is visited by patients from Milingimbi, Elcho Island and Yirrkala and by residents of her own and neighbouring communities, an unusually large practice for a Yolngu practitioner, most of whom are consulted only by people who have known them well for many years. When she visits the main settlements she is normally consulted by several patients and is often reimbursed, sometimes handsomely, for her ministrations. (Her immediate family members, though, do not pay.) Her services are so highly valued that one man expressed great concern at the rumours that the medical authorities were attempting to persuade her to go and work at Darwin or Nhulunbuy Hospitals. Not only, he said, would she then be unavailable to her usual clients, but doctors there might be jealous of her powers and try to kill her.

I was not able to talk with this woman personally because she rarely visits Yirrkala. A ritual leader and active church member explained that this is because she was once severely punished by missionaries for her professional activities and therefore prefers to stay at Gurrumurru. Nevertheless, distant relatives gave me three independent accounts of the way in which she acquired her powers. I do not know whether these accounts would coincide with her own, but they indicate the types of experiences individuals are expected to undergo to become *marrnggitj*. Each also reflects the view and personal convictions of the speaker.

A young ritual leader, who is not related to the *marrnggitj*, maintains that 'all her family were *galka*' and that her sister's husband 'taught her *marrnggitj*'. A young married woman said that she had heard that this woman was gored and killed by a buffalo while out hunting one day and that her husband was so afraid that he ran away and left her. When he returned with several people to collect her body, she was sitting up unharmed. This is how she became powerful. A community leader from Elcho Island, who is an avowed Christian and staunch member of the church, said that this woman once died and, as was customary, was left in a high tree after the mortuary rites had ended. While she was dead, angels came down from heaven and gave her the twelve *manggata* she has today. Of these, the three most important are James, Peter and John. After three days and three nights in the tree she woke from the dead and God told her where to go to find the camp of her relatives.

In general, the *marrnggitj* of Yirrkala fit closely Cawte's (1974) characterisation of Aboriginal healers as altruistic rather than psychopathic or mystic personalities. Of the *marrnggitj* whom he knew and interviewed, Warner writes:

> The individuality of the white magician is not different from that of the ordinary man. The only noticeable tendency in all the observed healers was their joviality and pleasantness in their ordinary social relations . . .
> (1958:210).

Similarly, Webb (1936):

> The *marnggitj* occupies no special place, exercises no special functions outside his profession, and possesses no

special influence in the life of his horde or tribe (1936:337).

Thomson (1961) takes some exception to Webb's statement, pointing out that, in times of serious illness or death, the influence of the *marrnggitj* may be one of life or death. However, he agrees that *marrnggitj* are differentiated from their fellows only by the possession of special powers and the patronage of spirit familiars.

While it is true that the *marrnggitj* at Yirrkala are ordinary members of the community with their own families and fairly typical lives, it is possible to identify personal or familial factors which may have contributed to their assuming the role. The adult male *marrnggitj* belongs to a family which has a history of psychiatric illness and has himself married into such a family. In conversation and day-to-day activities, however, he is much like any other person. He is, at present, a heavy drinker and several people have expressed concern about the viability of his powers if he continues drinking. The young man who was a child *marrnggitj* traces his powers to the time when he, as the second of a pair of twins, was left to die. The child *marrnggitj*, Nyurrulnga, was born prematurely and seemed to his mother to be barely alive for several months. He is, in addition, the loved and admired youngest son in a marriage which was, at the time of the study, very stormy.

Whatever the predisposing personal attributes of those who become *marrnggitj*, there is evidence that becoming a *marrnggitj* is as much a matter of the collective wishes of the group as it is of a person's inclinations. Rather than individuals being born *marrnggitj* or achieving this status, the office appears largely to be thrust upon them. Since the healer is such a powerful source of reassurance and understanding at times of illness there is probably ongoing pressure on individuals who show signs of healing ability to develop and exercise their powers. Nyurrulnga's career, for instance, is being fostered and promoted by the attention of his admiring parents and by the expressed needs of the sick. This fostering may even take the form of overt teaching of the skills which a *marrnggitj* should master. For instance, when a clan leader was hospitalised with pneumonia, he specifically asked the boy to come and treat him. As Nyurrulnga began his work, this man told him not to use too much water and showed the boy how to massage a patient by spreading his hands wide and drawing them from the middle to the side of his chest and abdomen.

Just as it is expected that a *marrnggitj* will work (and be made) in a certain way, so people are always alert to the possibility that a new *marrnggitj* may emerge. One middle-aged woman told how *guwak*, the totemic night bird of her clan, often follows her around, protecting her from wild buffalo and other dangers. One night, as she was walking towards her brother's house, her brother heard the bird coming as well. When she arrived he asked her 'Why is *guwak* following you around? Are you clever?' She said she did not know.

Some individuals may aspire to the position of *marrnggitj*. An adolescent girl related an occasion on which she was very ill and her mother's brother, who was drunk at the time, came and massaged her with water as he had seen a *marrnggitj* do. The next morning she felt considerably better and her uncle went home saying to the girl's mother and sister before he left, 'You two couldn't have done this to her. You were trying to help her and couldn't.' He walked off, she reported, very proud of himself, saying drunkenly, 'I just healed my *waku*! [sister's child]'.

Other people who are not actually *marrnggitj* possess objects which are powerful and which they occasionally use to treat themselves or members of their immediate families. I was told of two older men who had, as pearl divers in their youth, obtained octopus *gilapa* (eyes or other magical objects associated with the octopus) which they occasionally use to treat relatives. One of these men says he is also able to heal simply by stretching his hand over the afflicted person and letting his personal power (derived from the totemic creator beings of his clan) heal the patient. At least one of the women health workers possesses an object which has healing powers. The conviction that certain objects are powerful prompts individuals to be alert for them. One man was impressed by a 'worry stone' which belonged to a European friend. He borrowed it both to heal and to calm himself.

In summary, the role of the *marrnggitj* is well established and widely recognised in eastern Arnhem Land and may be perpetuated by the expectations of community members. While the presence of relatives at the sick bed and their efforts to treat the patient are crucial to the care of the sick, the absence of a *marrnggitj* when his skills are required would constitute a real deprivation for those in need.

Community Attitudes

The claim of a person that he has healing powers is not sufficient to establish him as a *marrnggitj* in the eyes of community members. For most people at Yirrkala, as in other societies (see Geertz, 1960:90; Gluckman 1968), seeing is believing. Until an individual has convincingly demonstrated his abilities, attitudes towards him range from admiration to disbelief. The claims of aspirants are assessed by community members with a critical eye. Some people openly voice their doubts. Nyurrulnga's father said he would not believe a *marrnggitj* unless, like his son, he could prove that he was not just a 'copy *marrnggitj*'. Another man, whose sister had been convincingly healed by the adult male *marrnggitj*, said:

> I was never treated by a *marrnggitj*. It's not that I don't believe it. It's a matter of whether the *marrnggitj* is true or not and can prove it.

An older woman who had just lost her mother was more sceptical:

> I don't really believe in *marrnggitj* or really believe what he does, because when [the female *marrnggitj*] tried to help my mother who was very sick, she got worse and worse. That was just before my mother died.

A reputed *marrnggitj* from Elcho Island, who said he himself is only clairvoyant, expressed doubts about the adult male *marrnggitj*:

> I don't believe in him. He heals people for a half a day and then goes to the hotel. He is just fooling people. If a man eats sand and mud [alluding to drinking alcohol] is he a doctor? Alcohol is why people are losing themselves and their *marrnggitj*. They are becoming like leaves floating on the sea.

Scepticism may be reinforced by evidence of fraud. A woman who suffered from a serious heart complaint and had had considerable experience of Western medicine said she would not believe in a *marrnggitj* until she saw evidence of his (or her) powers herself. She preferred to consult the doctor. To justify her doubts she recalled an occasion on which a *marrnggitj* treated her brother's wife and drew from the patient's body a small black lump which the *marrnggitj* claimed was the cause of her discomfort. The next morning this woman returned to the spot and found lumps of charcoal lying on the floor near her sister-in-law's bed. She showed these to her brothers and they all 'had a good laugh'.

Sceptics may be won over by a convincing display of power and skill. A community leader at Elcho Island explained that he had not believed in *marrnggitj* at all until he saw the female *marrnggitj* working. Although he scrutinised her hands carefully and could see that she was not concealing anything, when she rubbed her hands over the patient's body she pulled out an object. A young woman at Yirrkala related a similar experience:

> I used to doubt [the adult male *marrnggitj*]. 'He's not a *marrnggitj*', I'd say. But my brother's wife was attacked by a spirit which stabbed her in the back with a long fingernail . . . [The *marrnggitj* extracted the fingernail] . . . When he opened his hand, there it was. It had blood on it. I just looked at it. I believed him then.

While sound evidence of the abilities of a *marrnggitj* is a prerequisite for a favourable reputation, failure to cure is not necessarily taken as evidence of fraud. As a senior clan leader explained:

> *Galka* can sometimes be cured. If the wound is only small and has been covered by the *galka*, the *marrnggitj* can see the injury to the muscle or other wounds inside even though the *galka* has covered the cut because the *marrnggitj* has special *wulä* [dried blood of a sorcery victim] in his dillybag. If the wound is inside and very bad and filled with grass, the *marrnggitj* can't cure him. He can say [divine] that the sick person has been attacked by a *galka* but he can't do anything.

The doubts which people express about certain *marrnggitj* and the acknowledged inability of *marrnggitj* to cure some illnesses enable clients to accept failed treatments and even charlatans without having to abandon their belief in spiritual healing. When John, a young man of the community, died, for instance, no-one blamed the *marrnggitj*. John's relatives (who were also related to the *marrnggitj*) said the *galka* had fooled him. He had pierced the underside of John's heart to drain out his blood, an injury which the *marrnggitj* could not 'see'. In any case, Yolngu wisdom holds that *galka* injuries are notoriously difficult to treat. No *marrnggitj* could be expected to make much therapeutic headway with a patient whose vital organs had been removed. That John died was taken as proof that the organs were missing. If his attacker had used a lesser form of sorcery he might have lived. His recovery would both have confirmed a lesser cause (or perhaps suggested an inept sorcerer) and reflected creditably on the *marrnggitj* (pp. 99-101).

Cases such as these and the recovery of patients after treatment by a *marrnggitj* form the basis of his reputation. The faith and gratitude of patients and relatives are powerful forces in perpetuating and enhancing the reputation of the able *marrnggitj* and ensuring the likelihood of further success.

Social Role

The most crucial task of traditional healers, as seen by their clients, is to combat the effects of sorcery worked on members of the community. Because most people of Yirrkala believe that *marrnggitj* are able to counteract the effects of all but the most destructive forms of sorcery, *marrnggitj* are most often called when someone is seriously ill and those close to the patient fear for his life. These days this is often when Western medicine has proved ineffective and patient and family are frightened and upset.

On one such occasion the adult male *marrnggitj* was called to treat a woman, Mandjinga (pseudonym), who claimed to have been attacked by a *galka* and had not spoken or taken food for several days. The events which ensued illustrate the way people respond to serious illness at Yirrkala and are referred to again later. But the case is presented in full here as an example of the role which the *marrnggitj* plays in a crisis.

At the time of this incident, Mandjinga was in her late twenties and had one infant daughter. The child was ill and underweight and had been in hospital for several weeks. Her husband, whom she had married against her family's wishes as she was promised to another man, had been drinking heavily. When he was not drinking he was employed in a local industry. During several of his drinking bouts he had beaten Mandjinga and, more recently, had threatened to hit their baby daughter (a very frightening threat in a community which indulges children and condemns physical punishment of the young). Mandjinga had been admitted to the hospital in Nhulunbuy at least once with severe bruising. It was, in addition, rumoured that her husband was involved with (or pursuing) another woman.

The day before the onset of the illness episode Mandjinga was drawn and stooped – she appeared to be in pain and looked very unhappy. She said she had pain in her side and lower back and as well described to me the symptoms of chronic cystitis. One of the Aboriginal health workers who was also a member of Mandjinga's immediate family said that Mandjinga's husband had recently beaten her but this story was not subsequently confirmed by any other family members or health centre staff. Mandjinga herself said she had been to the health centre repeatedly over a period of months complaining of abdominal pain and pain when she urinated but (in her opinion) the nursing sister and Aboriginal health workers did not believe her and did not give her the treatment she needed.

> *Saturday:* By midday most people at Yirrkala had heard that Mandjinga had been taken to hospital at dawn. She managed to tell those who found her that she had gone outside during the night to investigate a noise and been assaulted by a *galka*. Before collapsing she called out to her husband and neighbours, all of whom except her husband came running to help her. He ran away. Mandjinga later told me that, when the *galka* struck, she felt great pain as though something had hit her in the chest. She then felt as though she was in a whirlwind and had to hold on to the house to stay upright. The *galka* struck her again on her head and the nape of her neck with an old stone axehead

and she lost consciousness. (Some men of her family later searched for the axehead, said to be the *galka's* weapon, found it and threw it into the cold water of the creek.) She said she did not remember anything until she woke up in the hospital twenty-four hours later.

The health worker who was called to Mandjinga's aid later told me that when she arrived at the house, Mandjinga stared at her with a fixed, unseeing gaze. This blank stare terrified her. She was convinced that the woman must have been attacked by *galka*. This was not the first time she had seen her in this state: Mandjinga, she said, had been attacked by *galka* before. The health worker put her in a car and drove her to Nhulunbuy Hospital. She was found by staff to have a cut to one hand and severe bruises below the right armpit and in the centre of her chest.

Sunday: At the request of Mandjinga's family I rang the hospital to inquire after her. The nursing sister said that the patient was still in pain but that, otherwise, she was at a loss to explain her state. The sister felt her condition might have a psychiatric as well as physical basis. She had known Mandjinga some years before and recalled that she had had previous psychiatric problems but 'usually came good after a while'. The sister later told me she had asked that Mandjinga be placed in the surgical, rather than the medical ward, so she could personally take care of her.

Later that day I went into town and joined a group of about 40 adults and an equal number of children who had camped outside the hospital. Most were of the patient's clan; some were members of closely related clans. All talk was of the *galka* attack. Fears were expressed that he might return to finish his work. Mandjinga's paternal uncle (her father is dead) was extremely concerned because her symptoms were clearly those of a victim of a *galka* attack. He noted in particular that her injury had not bled. He feared that the bad blood and tissues would damage her heart, lungs or other organs as well.

When I visited Mandjinga in the ward she was in what seemed to be a stupor. She whispered that her head was not good and that her body was sore. Later in the day, however, she told me she was able to think more clearly and felt a little hungry. The nursing sister brought some biscuits and tea which, with gentle urging, she consumed. When I relayed this hopeful sign to a senior man of another clan he maintained that it is of no benefit to a patient to force him or her to eat. He also pointed out that in any case, victims of *galka* always rally during the day and go downhill at night.

Monday: By Monday Mandjinga was propped up in bed but still refused to look at visitors who walked into the ward. She had, however, eaten porridge for breakfast. She managed a barely perceptible smile when I made a joke. Her family remained extremely concerned, pointing out that, although hospital staff had assured them that she would be much better within twenty-four hours of admission, she was still seriously ill. During the day the adult male *marrnggitj* came to visit and treat her but was 'caught' and sent away by the nursing sister who saw that her nightdress was open and her breasts exposed and thought he was (in her words) 'molesting' her. The nursing sister told me later how glad she was that she had found him in time for she 'knows about such people' and is frightened of the harm they can do.

Tuesday: Early on Tuesday morning a truck left Yirrkala for Nhulunbuy to bring Mandjinga home. The ward sister said that the doctor was sending Mandjinga home because she seemed more responsive than when she was first admitted. The sister said she herself felt that Mandjinga was depressed and would benefit if cared for by her relatives, particularly as the regional psychiatrist only visits north-east Arnhem Land twice a year.

When the truck arrived at Yirrkala, Mandjinga was helped to a mattress under a shelter in the open. Immediately she was settled her mother and other female relatives began to wail and continued weeping intermittently for the rest of the day. Throughout the day other relatives arrived and gathered around the patient's bed. A classificatory daughter sat next to her massaging her arms from shoulder to wrist while an older woman searched for her pulse. (The pulse is called *wangi* [wind]. When it is faint and slow or very fast it is moving up the arm towards the torso and the patient is dying. It is necessary to massage it back down the arm to the wrist to make it strong.) One of the women asked me rather tentatively what I thought of the hospital sister's opinion that Mandjinga had improved. I said, guardedly that I had my doubts. She vehemently agreed and insisted that the sister was wrong.

Later in the day the patient whispered that she wanted the senior men of her moiety to be summoned to sing the sacred songs of her clan. These are always sung for people who are very sick or are dying. The men arrived later in the afternoon and began to sing. I was asked to send a telegram to her brother who was in Sydney telling him to come home. The *marrnggitj*, who was drinking at Nhulunbuy hotel, was summoned to treat Mandjinga. He arrived just before sunset.

By dusk a large crowd had gathered around the shelter under which Mandjinga was lying. The *marrnggitj* was sitting on one side of her mattress. Family members crowded around her. Opposite sat the wife of one of the mission staff (Judith). She offered to pray for Mandjinga and one of the women immediately quelled the noise with a look and wave of her hand. Judith prayed that Mandjinga would look to Christ and listen to His voice, rather than the voices of evil, for healing power. She prayed that Mandjinga would be guided back to the Lord from whom she had lately strayed and renounce the forces of darkness. The prayer was translated. Mandjinga attempted to whisper something to Judith who, overcome, began to weep. She was accompanied home by one of the women but left behind two cassette tapes of hymns and Bible readings in the local language asking that they be played to Mandjinga. Those left behind commented with warm approval on Judith's obvious concern and kindness in coming to see Mandjinga.

The *marrnggitj* then took two of his magical stones or *milirrk* out of a cup of cold water and placed one between Mandjinga's breasts. The other was placed against her side. He indicated to those in direct line with the stones that they should move aside. He then leant down, peering intently so that he appeared to be looking through her body in the line of the two stones. Then he used another stone to treat her internal wounds and continued to examine and treat her in this way during the following three hours.

At one stage the *marrnggitj* appeared to be having a conversation with an invisible presence. I assumed he was consulting his *manggata* (spirit familiars). Suddenly he looked up and announced that a ligament or muscle which ran from Mandijnga's chest to her neck was broken and that she had a large internal sore. Furthermore, the person who attacked her belonged to the Ngarritj subsection (one of eight subsections). He said he was unable to ascertain her attacker's personal name.

After several hours the *marrnggitj* announced to all that he was not sure whether Mandjinga would live or die. A wail went up from the women. The poor prognosis of the *marrnggitj* was repeated to me, whereupon, overcome by fatigue, everyone else's expressions of grief and a genuine fear for Mandjinga's life, I began to cry. One of the women told Mandjinga that I was very distressed and she weakly beckoned me and whispered that as a result of the treatment by the *marrnggitj* she could now breathe more easily and that I should not worry.

By about 11 p.m. Mandjinga's husband had returned from shift work. Her baby daughter had also been brought from Nhulunbuy hospital and joyfully thrust her milk bottle into her mother's hand. Mandjinga did not respond to her daughter's advances and so the child, protesting and crying, was taken away by her mother's sister. At this moment Mandjinga appeared to faint. The *marrnggitj* was summoned and placed his *milirrk* on her chest shaking his head negatively. After some time, however, she was revived. She then turned over and went to sleep.

Wednesday: The *marrnggitj* stayed with Mandjinga in order to continue her treatment and protect her from the *galka* whom it was feared would attack her again. I was told that the *galka* had, in fact, been seen that night in the bushes near the house but been chased away. Many of Mandjinga's relatives went home or back to work. Only immediate family members stayed with her. The crisis was over.

Thursday: Mandjinga ate the breakfast prepared for her and appeared much improved. She spoke at length about her ordeal and said that Judith had visited her again and told her not to listen to the 'witchdoctor' because the 'witchdoctor' listens to evil spirits. She continued: 'But I told her that in the afternoon before [the *marrnggitj*] arrived I had almost died. After [the *marrnggitj*] worked, my breath came more easily. I can only believe [the *marrnggitj*] because nobody else, not even Jesus could help me. She said I can't believe in Christ and the witchdoctor at the same time. I was upset by what she said.' Mandjinga seemed very disturbed by Judith's exhortations. She paused after saying this, looked at me and said, 'What do you believe?'

I later talked with Judith who said that when she had visited Mandjinga that morning she found the 'witchdoctor' sitting there. He had her nightdress open so that her breasts were visible and was rubbing one of his stones over Mandjinga's chest. The 'witchdoctor' must, Judith said, have been quite brazen to do such unspeakable things in front of so many people. She was pleased to hear from me that the singers and *marrnggitj* had not been in evidence when I arrived some time later. Judith also described how, when Mandjinga had taken the religious cassettes and put them under the pillow, she had seen there the stones belonging to the *marrnggitj*. She immediately 'faced Mandjinga up with it' and told her she would have to make a choice between the 'witchdoctor' (the ways of Satan) and Jesus. At this Mandjinga removed the stones and replaced them with pictures of Jesus. Judith remarked that Yolngu often pray to God and then consult the 'witchdoctor'. When they recover they have no idea who cured them.

Judith was also puzzled by the fact that Mandjinga had been sent home by hospital staff when clearly so ill. She wondered if they found out that she had been admitted for sorcery and wanted nothing more to do with it. Judith herself had gone to see the nursing sister at Yirrkala health centre about Mandjinga. The sister agreed with her that the patient's illness was being attributed to sorcery but said that this was their (her family and the community's) business, that she did not wish to talk about it and would have nothing more to do with it unless specifically asked. Later, one of the health workers told me that the sister had expressed an opinion that Mandjinga should return to hospital. The health worker told the sister that the family would not allow this and undertook to explain to her that this was not a 'common illness' but one caused by *galka* which only *marrnggitj* can help.

Mandjinga herself affirmed that her illness was of a class not amenable to treatment by nurses and doctors. She said she had only had ordinary illnesses before. Doctors, she maintained, know how to diagnose and treat external sores, common illnesses like tuberculosis and hookworm and illnesses which cause a temperature or high blood pressure (her own words). But many people die 'just like that', (she snapped her fingers) without any of these symptoms. This is caused by a *galka* sickness which doctors and nurses know nothing about.

Friday: In the morning Mandjinga told me of her intention to go and live at a homeland centre. She hoped that her husband would join her and that this would stop him drinking.

While we were talking, Judith arrived. She said that, since she had seen how frightened Mandjinga was, she had recorded some verses from the Bible which concerned the absence of fear within those who have the power and peace

of God. These she left with Mandjinga. At lunchtime
several family members arrived home from work and sat
around talking about the powers of the *marrnggitj*. There
was considerable discussion about the missionary's wife's
comment that only Christ has healing power and that the
marrnggitj gets his from Satan. The *marrnggitj* joined the
group and said that, although missionaries and others do
not believe in him, he is in fact the best doctor. The
patient's brother agreed that very few Europeans know or
understand the work of the *marrnggitj*.

Saturday: I saw Mandjinga late in the afternoon carrying
some of her belongings back to her own home. She walked
very slowly and weakly and sat down after she had walked
a short distance. She went to stay at her brother's house
where she felt she would be safe until she left for the
homeland centre. When I saw her at his house later she told
me she was eating better and had had some soup and mud-
crabs. However, she looked unhappy and clearly did not
want to talk. She still put her hand to her head in a
distracted way, as though bothered or preoccupied, a
gesture I had first noticed during her illness. Shortly
thereafter she left for the homeland centre and stayed there
for some months.

In 1977, two years after this incident, Mandjinga's marriage was
still unstable. Her older sister had helped her contact the Aboriginal
Legal Aid Service in Darwin and a restraining order had been issued
to keep her husband away from her. Mandjinga, however, was
ambivalent about a separation and in 1978 when I returned to
Yirrkala, was well and living with her husband. The following year,
during another visit, she was back in hospital and showed me how
her abdomen was 'hot and hard' and distended. None of her family,
she said, had visited her in hospital or cared about her. (The doctor
found she had chronic pelvic inflammatory disease, probably of
several years standing.) Three years later, in 1981, she was living
with her sister at a homeland centre. When I asked her how she was,
she replied with feeling, 'Good, I left my husband a year ago and
now I'm fine and healthy',
 Clearly this case lends itself to comment on numerous counts,
especially the factors which precipitated Mandjinga's sudden
collapse and decline, her interpretation of her collapse and the
influence of Christian views on Yolngu medical belief and practice.
But the case is presented here primarily to illuminate the role of the
marrnggitj. As it shows, he (or she) is a person who in a crisis is able to
bring reassurance to patient and family, to create a setting in which

love and concern are evident, and to instil in the sufferer the confidence which promotes healing.

Not all healing sessions are conducted for the seriously ill. The adult male *marrnggitj* is sometimes asked, for instance, to treat infants who are unwell and may simply massage the child briefly and hand him back to his mother. I was also present one evening when the child *marrnggitj*, Nyurrulnga, was asked to treat a young child who was somewhat ill:

> When I entered the house with Nyurrulnga's father, Nyurrulnga was sitting on his mother's lap. Three curious children were sitting next to her, and a woman and her struggling and screaming grandchild (the patient) were seated opposite. Nyurrulnga took his magical stone and placed it against the child's back while the grandmother restrained the child. He said he was healing a cracked bone in the child's back. He then dipped the stone in a can of water and rubbed water and stone over the child's stomach. There was anything but an aura of concentration about Nyurrulnga. He scarcely looked at what he was doing. He frequently stopped to pull his mother's head downwards and whisper in her ear. If it was about his work she conveyed his comments to us.
>
> After some time Nyurrulnga handed the stone to his father who affirmed that it was hot. It had, the father said, taken the heat from the little boy's body. Nyurrulnga then took the stone and, while holding it, contorted and cracked his fingers. His father told me that he was straightening the displaced bones and veins in the child's body. By this time the child had quietened remarkably and had nestled against his grandmother. She commented that he felt cooler and he nodded affirmatively when she asked him if he felt better. Throughout this session Nyurrulnga did not keep still. His incessant activity was also noticeable at other times. He stood on his father's shoulders, turned somersaults and moved around constantly. When we returned to another house to eat, Nyurrulnga continued to be very active. With no warning he suddenly slumped in a chair, unable to stay awake. His father said he was always like that after he had healed someone. The sickness went into him and the healing process went on in this way. After a night's sleep, however, he was always all right again.

In addition to their role as healers, *marrnggitj* may be called upon, as described in Mandjinga's case, to divine the identity of the sorcerer. When a man died at Elcho Island, his father asked this *marrnggitj* to fly over by plane, telling the people, as he related it, 'I have a good witchdoctor — not a witchdoctor but a clever doctor from Yirrkala'. When he arrived, the *marrnggitj* surveyed the area closely and found a paperbark receptacle containing the dead man's blood. When he walked into the bush to collect the rest of the blood he found that the *galka* had taken it away and that only footprints were left. He told the father of the deceased to whom they belonged. At the time at which he related these events to me the father was giving some thought to handing this information over to the police.

In summary, the *marrnggitj*, like traditional Aboriginal healers described from other parts of Australia (Elkin 1977) performs several of the functions associated in Western society with the doctor (healing the body), the therapist (healing the mind), the priest (comforting and instilling faith) and the coroner (determining the cause of death). His work as a healer and diviner reinforces community convictions about the reality and danger of sorcery. His presence and activities in times of serious illness and death are visible reminders to individuals of the threats posed to their health and safety by strangers and of the need for care both in their dealings with others and in the observations of religious strictures.

4 Sorcerer and Healer: A Matter of Boundaries

The early ethnographic accounts of Yolngu sorcery and healing are unequivocal. The *galka* is bad. The *marrnggitj* is good. One kills. The other cures. The concept of the witchdoctor – one who can be either benign or dangerous – is not part of the Yolngu cosmology. Most Yolngu at Yirrkala when asked, are also quite vehement about this dichotomy. The *marrnggitj* they know do not work sorcery, and there are no *galka*, they commonly say, in the community. The ideal separation of the two is reflected in Yolngu beliefs about the body and the ways it is affected by the work of the sorcerer or the healer.

During life the body is a repository of the soul and container of those substances which give a person life, vitality and strength. The integrity of the boundaries of the body is a pervasive theme in statements about sorcery and healing. Any attack on the body is dangerous not only to the victim but to his kin. Much anxiety about ill health and most descriptions of the work of *marrnggitj* and *galka* focus on the vulnerability of the body and especially on the properties of blood and its importance.

Blood is essential for life. It is also a source of power and, if improperly shed or used, danger. Whereas blood contained and controlled gives life and strength, blood uncontained, uncontrolled or violently shed is a source of danger, illness, and death. The power inherent in blood is not, in itself, either beneficial or dangerous. As with spiritual power, its effects depend on the context and way in which it is shed.

It is dangerous, as described in Chapter 2, for a menstruating woman to accept food which he has hunted from a male relative. If she does so, an accident will befall him the next time he is out hunting. Until about 15 or 20 years ago, when a girl menstruated for the first time she was isolated for several days and a small ceremony was performed by her close male relatives. Sacred songs were sung, and, when the bleeding had finished, she was painted with red ochre. After this, a purification or 'smoking' ritual was carried out (similar to that performed after a woman has given birth or after a young boy has been circumcised). A fire was made and *girrigirri* (the inner bark of the stringy-bark tree [*Eucalyptus tetradonta*]) was boiled in a container on the fire. The girl drank some of the liquid or sucked the bark. A large stone was then placed on the fire and covered with leaves and *girrigirri*. The girl then sat on the warm stone ('to stop the period pain') for a few minutes and then bent over the fire to inhale the steam and smoke. She was then free to interact normally with those around her and to eat those foods which are prohibited during menstruation.

The absence of blood is invoked to explain a variety of afflictions. When speaking of a sickly child, mothers frequently say the child 'hasn't got enough blood' and refer to iron tablets dispensed at the health centre as giving the child 'more blood'. (Transfusions are also regarded favourably since they give the patient 'new blood'). When an older man was admitted to hospital after prolonged bouts of drinking, one woman explained that there was only alcohol in his veins where there should have been blood. After a chronic drinker died, one of the health workers said that she had heard that, when he was opened up by the doctors, they found that the skull cavity and blood vessels were filled with alcohol. He had no blood left at all.

Blood and its symbolism are also important in the context of religious ceremonies and myths. Some people believe that a few of those men who have (or have had) leprosy, originally contracted it as a result of participating in Gunapipi rites, which involve the ritual letting of blood. But the power of blood can also be beneficial. A brackish lagoon on one clan territory which is said to have curative properties was formed when the menstrual blood of a female ancestral spirit flowed into the hollow.

Whenever blood (or, less importantly, pus, urine or faeces) is shed by someone with a serious injury or illness he or she becomes subject to the restrictions contingent on contact with a dangerous or polluting substance. This rule includes contact with dead bodies

6 A *bukulup* (*liyalupthun*) or washing ceremony held at the end of a funeral

during funerals. A person so restricted may not give cigarettes or food to his father (*bapa*), mother (*ngändi*), brother (*wawa*), sister (*yapa*), mother's brother (*ngäpipi*) or father's sister (*mukul bapa*). Other close kin, especially those who have cared for the person or dressed his (or her) wounds, are also subject to these restrictions. They are lifted by a purification ceremony called *bukulup* or *liyalupthun* (lit. 'facewash' or 'forehead wash') (Plate 6). This washing ceremony is said to 'free' patient and relatives. It reincorporates the individual who has been alienated by sickness and diverts the debilitating effects of his condition from others. In some cases, the ceremony may be concluded by painting the patient with red ochre. The ochre symbolises the blood which was lost and restores his strength.[1]

The notion of blood as the primary source of strength pervades Yolngu thought about health and sickness. It also reinforces the differences between the *galka* and the *marrnggitj*, for each deals with the body and its blood in distinctive and opposite ways.

Typically, as described in Chapter 2, the *galka* breaches the boundaries of the body, damaging, disorganising and destroying internal organs and extracting blood. If the victim survives a *galka* attack, it is only because the *galka* did not finish his work. If the *galka* manages to complete the operation no one, not even a *marrnggitj*, can save the victim. The middle-aged woman who survived a *galka* attack (pp. 39-40) attributes her survival to the fact that she was recognised by one of the *galka* as a kinswoman. He suspended the operation and threw her blood into a lagoon rather than burying it

---

1. Warner (1958:228) described the *bukulup* performed at Milingimbi in the period 1926-9 as a corporate healing ceremony which mobilised the power of the totemic well, rituals and objects to restore the patient to health and avert illness from the group generally. White (in Scarlett *et al.* 1982) found in the 1970s that at Donydji, a homeland centre to the south-west of Yirrkala, the *bukulup* was seen by some younger men as a healing rite, as well as a means of countering destructive and worrying influences such as suspected sorcery. Berndt (1965b:198-201) interprets a *bukulup* held at Elcho Island in 1961 following the return of a man who had been in Darwin hospital for treatment of an injury as washing away any lingering unpleasantness, blame, grief or other discordant influences. This interpretation, if rather broader, is closer to my own. At Yirrkala the *bukulup* is always held after a sick or injured person has recovered.

Because my findings were at variance with Warner's I questioned participants closely about the stated function of the *bukulup*. All said it was not to cure the person but to 'free' him and his family. Keen (1977b:168) similarly found in the 1970s at Milingimbi that washing ceremonies are used to release people from the prohibitions incurred through having an open wound or sore. (The *bukulup* is also held at the end of a funeral for the same reason: to purify participants and release them from the state of ritual pollution caused by contact with the dead bodies. Whether intended or not it also brings some closure to the ceremony and the tension and grief surrounding the death.)

for later retrieval and use. When Mandjinga was recovering (p. 74), the *marrnggitj* stayed with her to protect her from another attempt on her life. One man at Yirrkala lives with the chronic effects of a *galka* attack. It is said that, although a European doctor managed to reverse some of the effects of the attack by performing surgery and removing the leaves and grass left by the *galka* in the man's thoracic cavity, he could not replace the lost organs. (This operation is described by Philip Roberts in *I, the Aboriginal* [Lockwood 1962:23].) His present weakness and the partial paralysis of his legs are said to be legacies of this attack.

Yolngu remember the doctor who performed this operation with great fondness and admiration. In their opinion he had exceptional, *marrnggitj*-like, powers. When he died of a heart attack in the late 1950s in Darwin it was widely rumoured by Yolngu that the other doctors had put poison in his tea because they were jealous of him – behaviour which is expected between *marrnggitj*. In medical crises relatives still ask if there are any other doctors in cities in the south like him who would be willing to fly up, at the clan's expense, to see the patient. But this is the only favourable account of surgery which I recorded during the study. Most people at Yirrkala express a deep fear of surgery and are very reluctant to give permission for an operation. 'The person who has been operated on', one man said, 'will not live long with his family'. In describing its dangers people claim that surgery will 'waste the blood' and 'spoil the body'. One man who underwent abdominal surgery in Darwin asked me to write to his doctors or to the Department of Health requesting monetary compensation for the blood and strength he had lost. 'My body is weak', he said. 'There's no blood in it'.

It seems likely that the fear of surgery derives at least in part from the fact that it involves cutting the body and may mean the loss of blood and organs. While it is the absolute loss of both which frightens people, surgical procedures also bear a striking resemblance to the operations carried out by the *galka*. Although the parallel between the two is not made explicitly, some people deeply mistrust strange surgeons and fear they will (presumably like *galka*) use the opportunity to kill their Aboriginal patients. The greater the personal distance between patient and doctor (that is, the less well the doctor is known), the stronger the suspicion.

Other techniques of sorcery also have the effect of striking at the victim's life essence by utilising his urine, faeces, sweat, or other bodily excretions (usually impregnated in his clothes). Each person needs to be watchful and ensure that no strangers have access to his personal possessions. Suggestions of sorcery worked on an individual by a jealous spouse, brother or sister are lent plausibility by their ease of access to each other's clothes, urine and faeces.

The body is vulnerable not only to the loss of blood, but to heat and dryness (cf. Wiminydji and Peile [1978] for the Gugadja). There is in this also a distinction between sorcerer and healer. The sorcerer aggravates his assault by utilising heat, fire or the sun to strengthen his weapons or to enhance the effect of his attack on the victim's body. The *galka* leaves his victim's blood to dry buried in the ground. This not only gives him power, but ensures that his victim will die. Some *galka* may heat a wire and insert it into the victim's skull. Other techniques of sorcery also employ heat: 'spoiling' the body by burning a man's sweaty clothes and leaving the *manggimanggi* in the sun to increase its efficacy and strength. Serious urogenital or abdominal illness results from heating or drying the urine or faeces. Systemic illness results from stabbing a person's footprint or impression with a hot wire. By the same token a *galka* can be made to fall prey to his own methods. Some say that a hot wire inserted into the body of a dead man will evoke a scream of pain from his killer, wherever he is, and lead to a long, agonising and fatal illness.

Whereas sorcerers attack the body, the work of the *marrnggitj* is directed towards restoring bodily tissues, blood and health. This he does without cutting the body. The adult male *marrnggitj* explained that his stones enable him to see inside the body, to restore old black blood, to give new blood, and to mend internal and external tissues. His spirit familiars, which he said can enter and travel around inside the sick person, aid him in his work. The female *marrnggitj* is particularly renowned for her ability to extract objects inserted by a sorcerer without actually breaking the skin. Whereas the sorcerer uses heat and fire to enhance the effectiveness of his techniques, the healer utilises the healing qualities of cool water in his work. If the healer extracts an object he will always throw it in a lagoon or stream to annul its harmful power. (The men who found the axe head used in the attack on Mandjinga threw it in the creek for the same reason.) If he does not do this, the patient will continue to sicken. The adult male *marrnggitj* keeps his *milirrk* or special stones in a container of cold water to, as he describes it, 'refresh' them. Excessive heat is dangerous to the *marrnggitj*. He should drink only lukewarm or cold beverages and work at twilight or at night. Some people are concerned about the heavy drinking of one of the *marrnggitj* of Yirrkala because alcohol is deemed to be hot and therefore a threat to his powers. When the child *marrnggitj* began to lose interest in healing, three years after his parents first told me of his powers, his father said it was because he had drunk too much hot tea. 'Children', he said, 'don't know what to eat and drink'.

It is clear from their treatment of the body and its blood, their techniques and their intentions, that *galka* and healer are figures starkly opposed in Yolngu thought, symbolising much that is feared or valued in life. But in reality the boundary between the two is not always as sharp in people's minds as they claim and *galka* and *marrnggitj* do not always conform to the ideal characterisations. *Galka* for instance are sometimes said to be at work uncomfortably close to home. In 1979 a young man was found dead on a bench near the Nhulunbuy hotel where he had been drinking. There was evidence that he had been hit over the head with a weapon, possibly a piece of wood, during a fight. But his family, according to one of the women health workers, indiscriminately accused everyone of using sorcery. They particularly suspected her own clan which owns the land on which Yirrkala is built. A public accusation of this sort within Yirrkala is rare and very serious. The head of the accused clan, exercising his right as a landowner, responded by closing the community store, health centre, offices and bank for a week. He also called a large public meeting at which the health workers explained the cause of death as described to them by the doctor (p. 152). I asked the health worker who described the meeting to me whether there were any *galka* at all at Yirrkala. 'No', she replied firmly, but then paused and added, 'not unless people here go and learn *galka* from other places, like Numbulwar, Elcho Island, Groote Eylandt, Katherine and Milingimbi'.

Galka are a special type of sorcerer. They are specialists who have learned their trade and have privileged access to the realm of the dead and its powers. By contrast, everyone is potentially capable of working *manggimanggi, biyi', burrpuy, barrakbarrak* and *nyira*. But, as with *galka*, accusations are almost never overt. People keep their suspicions to themselves and discuss them only with close and trusted kin. When asked directly about its use, they will say, sometimes indignantly, that no one at Yirrkala performs sorcery. There is, consequently, a problem in documenting accusations of sorcery among the Yolngu. Unlike some African societies where witch-finding and witch trials are in the public domain, the Yolngu worry that accusations may reach the ears of the suspect and escalate hostilities. A sorcery accusation is slanderous and slander invites trouble: be it anger, violence or further retaliation by sorcery.

During eight years of contact with the community, rumours of sorcery to which I am privy have become more numerous and much closer to home ('home' being the family and clan of the speaker and his or her affines). 'They', the sorcerers, had become much closer to 'us' by 1981 than in 1974. One could hypothesise that the social strains at Yirrkala have increased over this period and that this is demonstrated by the increase in the number of suspicions of sorcery. Apart from the fact that this is a circular and untestable proposition, it seems more probable that the apparent increase is an artefact of the fieldwork process. (Kluckhohn [in Colson 1974:58] for the Navaho and Colson [1971:245] for the Tonga of Africa reached similar conclusions.)

After eight years I could be trusted. People had learned I did not gossip to the wrong people and was scrupulous in observing confidences. This conclusion is supported by the fact that only in later years was I apprised of conflicts going back several decades. I learned, for instance, that some people of the landowning clan accused after the death of the young man at the hotel believe that their former clan head, who died in 1967, was killed by *manggimanggi* worked by the young man's family. The accusation in 1979 was, as in most cases, one of a long series of conflicts between the two clans. In 1965 there was a killing at Yirrkala when a prominent leader was fatally stabbed and his assailants wounded. The antagonists were tried and one was convicted and gaoled for some time. A revenge spearing several years later ostensibly ended the matter and I was assured by the dead man's family when I first asked that all was forgiven. But when, in 1979, one of the attackers had a minor heart attack, a man closely related by marriage to the murder victim said the patient was still, and justifiably, 'worrying' about retaliation. In short, sorcerers, who ideally are 'out there', in crises may be found dangerously close at hand.

Similarly *marrnggitj* may not always conform to the Yolngu ideal; they can be ambiguous figures. One man suggested that the adult *marrnggitj* at Yirrkala is afraid someone will accuse him of being a *galka*. He therefore treats only his own kin. Another person associated the healing powers of the female *marrnggitj* with her familial relationships to *galka* – people who, like her, come from clans to the west. The hypothetical account of the making of 'clever' men given by one man shows how similar he considers the powers and making of *galka* and *marrnggitj* to be (p. 41).

When a clan leader died at Yirrkala, a small delegation of men visited a neighbouring community to ask a man of a closely allied clan, who had rubbed the deceased with sand (ostensibly in an attempt to cure him) whether he had done it in the 'bad way' or 'good way'. The accused was most upset and subsequently wrote a letter to the dead man's family proclaiming his good intentions. These accusations clearly worried this man for, when he was in Sydney a few years later and was re-introduced to me he said, 'Ah, yes. I remember. You were the person who once asked me if I was a *galka*'. I would not have dreamed of doing so – I had in fact once asked him if he was a *marrnggitj*. I protested, but he went on, 'People call me *galka* or *marrnggitj*, but I'm not. I'm just a strong dreamer [clairvoyant]. When something happens elsewhere I know about it'.

A nursing sister stationed at Milingimbi who has spent many years in this region told me that, when a senior officer of the Department of Health visited the settlement and proposed to Aboriginal leaders that the 'bush doctors' be given some medical training and supplies, the response was cool. Puzzled, she later asked one of those involved the reason for the lack of enthusiasm. He explained that bush doctors are already powerful and that giving them medical training and supplies would give them access to additional means of both helping and harming people.

At least one well known *marrnggitj* who lives to the west (on a homeland centre not associated with Yirrkala) both claims and is claimed to heal and perform sorcery. After a man at Yirrkala was killed in a fight, a lock of the victim's hair was sent by relatives of the deceased to this *marrnggitj* with a request that he avenge the murder. According to a relative of the dead man, the *marrnggitj* did as requested. As a result, it was said, the murderer's sister was injured in a buffalo attack and the man primarily responsible for the killing became ill and was hospitalised for some time. On a different occasion this *marrnggitj* told the leader of a visiting research team (John Cawte) that he has powerful objects which enable him to kill those whom he hates or who have angered him — especially those who have killed his relatives. Nowadays, however, he added, he is getting old and has a kind heart. He only uses his powerful objects to heal the sick.

It is apparent, then, that although people say that sorcerers are wholly evil and healers benign, in real life the distinction is not as clear as this. Their perceptions of particular *marrnggitj* and their opinions about the culpability of someone accused of sorcery are, in fact, affected by the social distance between themselves and the person in question.

People at Yirrkala perceive themselves as standing at varying distances from one another in social and geographical space. For any one person, it is rather like being at the centre of a series of concentric circles: in the first circle are one's closest and most trustworthy relatives (mother, father, spouse, children, grandchildren and others). In the second are other members of one's own clan and closely related affinal clans. They often own contiguous territories, have well-defined rights in each other's land and ceremonies, and can be trusted. In the third are people of clans which may intermarry and co-operate in ceremonies but have less informal social contact. In the fourth are members of territorially and socially distant clans which do not intermarry. They may join in large ceremonies but have little or no other contact. In the fifth are Yolngu whose clan territories are far away and who mainly live at Milingimbi, Elcho Island, Ramingining and Gapuwiyak. And last, beyond the Yolngu cultural bloc, are tribes from other parts of the region or of Australia who share neither the language, religion nor law of the Yolngu.

These conceptualisations of social distance are paralleled at Yirrkala in the configuration of the housing areas. The location and separation of the camps reflect clan alliances and territorial proximity of the estates of clans of the community. Although there are four camps, two (Balnguma Road and Beach Camp) have close links and can be effectively regarded as one. Balnguma Road and Galpu Road also have some cross-cutting ties, as do Top Camp and Balnguma Road. Broadly speaking, residential clusters reflect the disposition of clans in north-east Arnhem Land when the mission was established (cf. Bell [1980], Hiatt [1965] and Young [1981] who describe similar residential patterns for other Aboriginal communities in the Northern Territory). The Top Camp bloc were living around Caledon Bay and Trial Bay to the south. The Balnguma Road bloc were living in the immediate vicinity of Yirrkala and own the land on which the mission and the mining operations are situated today. Other clans were living to the west and further south and live at the settlement near groups with whom they have close ties. In every day life people rarely visit other camps. There are few causes for such visits and sustained contact between people of different camps usually occurs only during large funeral ceremonies.

Accusations of sorcery are most frequent between the major alliances, or directed at little known and, by definition, unfriendly Yolngu from other communities, or 'stranger Aborigines' from elsewhere in the Northern Territory. From the vantage point of a person at the centre of his (or her) kindred, danger and hostility increase with distance from the centre. Those people in his immediate social universe are ideally safe, peaceable, moral, known and predictable. The further one gets toward the periphery the more likely are people to be dangerous, belligerent, immoral, unknown and capricious. (Biernoff (1978) makes a similar observation about man-land relationships.) At the very edge of the traditionally known world are Aborigines who are substantially unsocialised according to Yolngu tenets of humanity.

As Lindenbaum has so aptly written for the Fore of New Guinea (1971:286):

> Statements about the cause of an illness, besides being attempts to explain misfortune, are also statements about the structure of the society, the dangers to which its composite units are exposed, and the measures that can be taken to protect those units. Little dangers come from within: big dangers from without.

These elements of the Yolngu world view — safety and danger, trust and suspicion — revolve around the issue of control. The values regulating personal relationships, the bonds of caring and mutual dependence, and the sanctions on antisocial behaviour minimise the chance of serious conflict between a person and his immediate kin. When conflict does occur every attempt is made to resolve it through reason and moral persuasion. If a fight does take place and someone is killed by a close relative everyone is anxious to resolve the matter and to restore harmony.

The *galka* can provide a convenient scapegoat when an internal killing threatens group solidarity: he is sometimes said to arrange his victim's death by suggesting, while the victim is in his thrall, that he go home and provoke a fight with a kinsman. In this fight the victim is killed. Although blaming a *galka* does not excuse the killing, it does provide a focus for anger outside the kin group. Even when the guilt of an offender is clear the processes of negotiation and reparation, spurred by the strong desire to keep peace among relatives, provide strong support for the resolution of a conflict. Social control is as much a matter of shared views and interests as it is of the ability to impose sanctions. The rarity with which people accuse close kin of sorcery reflects their affection for each other and their confidence in the mechanisms for maintaining or restoring peace in the clan. Whether as a result of internal constraint or external restraint, behaviour can usually be controlled.

This does not mean that safety within the kin group is absolute, that fights and conflicts of interest do not arise, or that kin do not use sorcery. But away from the centre the control which a person and his kin can exert over the behaviour of others is much attenuated. At the periphery the real ability which they have to control others is negligible and their anxiety about them accordingly high. Even if an individual makes an exceptional effort to maintain good relations with others he is not necessarily safe. The clan is corporate in its liability for the actions of its members. A sorcerer does not have to kill the person who has wronged him. A child, spouse, parent or other relative is an equally acceptable victim. Nor does vengeance have to be exacted on the heels of a fight. The clan of the aggrieved may wait years for satisfaction and even attack the descendants of the offender. A person's life can thus be jeopardised by the misdeeds of his relatives — living and dead. His own behaviour, conversely, has implications for his kin and descendants. Clan solidarity is therefore not just a matter of trust and commitment, it is also a product of mutual self-interest. Each person has a responsibility to his kin to be fair, moral and circumspect in his dealings with others. Even if he has no personal cause to fear people of other clans, it behoves him to be cautious, for he cannot know when or if he will be the unwitting victim of another's troubles.

There are many social implications of the outsider-insider dichotomy. One of the reasons why ongoing marriages between two clans are favoured is the control the families can exert over the behaviour of those who marry in. For instance, long before a young man, John, died, reportedly as a result of sorcery worked by his wife's lover, I had heard his brother's wives deplore the marriage.

He should, they maintained, have married his two 'promises', girls from their own clan who were their classificatory sisters. Such marriages would have kept the girls in the family under the watchful eye, and in the familiar company of their older sisters. As it was, John had chosen to marry a woman from a distant clan who had no relatives in John's clan's camp. Even if his sisters-in-law had felt free to broach with his wife the subject of her rumoured affair, she would not have heeded their admonitions. When he died their worst fears about having an outsider in the family were realised.

Though in principle the people in each individual's world can be arranged along an axis from trustworthy to dangerous and their places on the axis determined by their clan affiliations, in real life the complexities of shifting alliances, irregular marriages, friendship, divided loyalties, vested interests, and personal idiosyncracies intervene. No one person has exactly the same social universe as any other. Even sisters or brothers, who have almost identical kindreds, tread different paths through life and view events around them from different perspectives. Loyalties of birth and marriage, in particular, may be cross-cutting influences on a person's perception of the guilt or innocence of a suspected sorcerer. For instance, when John died suddenly (p. 100), his family blamed a young man from Milingimbi who was having an affair with John's wife. However, another man, who was closely related to John by marriage (his sisters had married into John's clan), nearly started a fight when he openly disputed this explanation. His own wife comes from the suspect's clan and he declared publicly that no one from her clan would have worked sorcery on John.

In another, unrelated, incident, in 1981, a middle-aged man, the brother of the head of clan A, who had been drinking with relatives in town, was found beaten and unconscious at Beach Camp where his drunken companions had left him. He was taken to hospital and died four days later. The death was explained to me on separate occasions by two women, Lipami and Bingyurra, who are step-sisters. They have the same father but Lipami's mother was from clan A and Bingyurra's mother from clan B. The mothers and their daughters have always been close, but it is actually Lipami who has the strongest ties to clan B. Her husband had a close relationship with the men of clan B when he was alive; others of her sisters married into clan B, and people from clan B, most of whom live elsewhere, always stay with her when they come to Yirrkala. Bingyurra, on the other hand, though the daughter of a clan B woman, married the head of clan A, so the man who died was her brother-in-law. Clan A and clan B historically have strained relations because of conflicts over rights in land, religious ceremonies, and sacred objects. So, although Bingyurra and Lipami are step-sisters, and although both have very close links by birth and marriage to clans A and B, their kindreds and loyalties, as reflected in their explanations, are quite different:

> Bingyurra related in enthusiastic detail that Ngukuku, a senior man of clan B, had killed her husband's brother. He and his two sons beat him up at the hotel, worked sorcery on him and left him for dead. He was taken to hospital and died four days later.' (An autopsy revealed that he had died of a massive pulmonary embolism. The hospital superintendent explained this to the dead man's brother, Bingyurra's husband.) Ngukuku, she said, had tried to kill at least five men, including her own sons. He keeps the old law, she said, and is called a devil by the children.
> Ngukuku had killed her brother-in-law because he wanted to marry a young girl and was refused permission by her husband, the head of clan A. Though the head of clan A paid him off with the gift of a car he was not satisfied and took his revenge. (I later heard that it was another clan which gave clan B the car.)
>
> Lipami was furious though not surprised when she heard this: 'He's one of our family; it makes us feel terrible when we hear him blamed'. In fact, she said, Ngukuku was not even on the truck when the dead man was beaten up. Ngukuku's son, who was driving, was taken into custody by the police, and had to 'explain Yolngu culture to them'. 'He's my *märi* (mother's mother's brother)' he told them 'I wouldn't do such a thing!' In fact, Lipami said, two men from clan C did it (the clan responsible for the death of one of Lipami's brothers 15 years before). The others only blame Ngukuku because he has travelled widely, has friends all over Arnhem Land, and because he does not gossip like some people. He talks straight to their face. That is why they are afraid of him. Moreover, she insisted, the head of clan A (Bingyurra's husband) had publicly said that no blame attached to Ngukuku's clan because the doctor told him his brother died when his heart became blocked and his blood pressure went up.

In summary, the sorcerer and healer personify the polarities in Yolngu concepts of social order and security: conflict and harmony, sickness and health, danger and safety, outsider and insider. Ideally the healer mobilises power to protect and restore health and to counter threats to life and peace in the community. The sorcerer brings harm and sickness. He represents the disruption which can ensue if people argue, clans fight and hostility is allowed to go unchecked. But a statement about suspected sorcery is not only an ideological or explanatory statement; it is a statement about the nature of people and relations between them. Sorcery accusations are marked by the same ambivalence and ambiguity which characterise life in any small community laced with shifting alliances, loyalties and grievances. Sorcerers are not always from a long way away and *marrnggitj* cannot always be trusted. Ultimately sorcerer and healer represent deviations from the norm and remind people of the need to be vigilant, law abiding, yet generous and open in their dealings with others.

5 The Search for Meaning

For the Yolngu the sociomedical theory provides a framework for understanding suffering and loss. It renders intelligible the most profound threats to social order and continuity and gives its adherents a sense of control over critical events in their lives. To understand how the changes to Yolngu society of the past fifty years have touched the theory one needs to appreciate when and how it is invoked. Specifically: when do people at Yirrkala seek an explanation of the cause of an illness or death; what form do their inquiries take, and what factors influence the decisions they reach? The first of these questions revolves around the issue of how people manage illness and how patient and family react to an illness. The second relates to the way in which people draw on the sociomedical theory to provide explanations for death and illness and decide between them. The third question, concerning factors that influence their deliberations and, eventually, their decisions, has to do with the relationship of the inquirer to the patient or dead person, his interests in a given situation and the means he may employ to advance his or his group's interests.

At the outset one important qualification must be made. People at Yirrkala speculate about sorcery when someone is seriously or chronically ill or has died. Such events are far less common in the community than the host of ailments and minor injuries which often trouble people. As in Western society, most people at Yirrkala who become ill are treated at home or at the health centre with little fuss or thought about the cause (cf. Lewis 1975:229). This study is about the explanations and strategies for dealing with serious, but relatively rare, events.

It has been suggested elsewhere (Scarlett *et al.* 1982) that the domain of 'natural' explanations and treatments for illness has been underrated or ignored in Aboriginal studies (cf. Gillies 1976; Janzen 1981; Wiminydji and Peile 1978). The older people of north-east Arnhem Land, for instance, know how to find and prepare at least 100 herbal medicines (Plate 7) and have several procedures for the care of the sick, such as massage, rest or a restricted diet, which do not require 'magical' intervention or inquiry. Yolngu do not live in a state of chronic anxiety about sorcery. Sorcery for them (as most probably for other Aboriginal groups: Biernoff 1982) is like cancer for Westerners. When individuals become so sick that there is good reason to believe they have been attacked they will be very anxious. Everyone else goes about daily life without giving it much thought.

7 Collecting the edible fruit and medicinal leaves of the tree *dhurrpinda* or *monydjutj* (*Buchanania obovata/arborescens*)

Illness Management and the Place of Explanation

The experience of being sick is familiar to many people of Yirrkala. Infectious diseases such as influenza or viral gastroenteritis spread quickly, particularly in the wet season when families crowd into houses to sleep sheltered from the rain. People also complain of a variety of chronic ailments such as backache, headaches, chest conditions, skin disorders and urinary tract infections. Many suffer from anaemia, parasite infestations such as hookworm (often implicated in anaemia) and recurrent eye and ear infections.

If every illness precipitated a search for its cause most people would be preoccupied with sickness and sorcery most of the time. They would be consuming topics of conversation. In fact searches for cause are not daily events and are certainly not prompted by every illness. Only critical illnesses are likely to prompt people to think about their aetiology. Even then, caring for a sick relative may so preoccupy them that they give little thought to the origin of his (or her) illness. Only death generates a collective intent among the bereaved to find out what caused the illness, or rather, since relatives almost invariably think of sorcery, who.

Through the first days, or even weeks, of most illnesses, people are less interested in cause than cure. Their management of most conditions proceeds step-wise as the illness slowly becomes more serious. As it gets worse, the patient requires more time-consuming and concerted care from his family. If one form of treatment fails, another is tried, and so on until the patient recovers or dies. Very few illnesses, of course, progress in exactly this way. Some wax and wane. Some never pass beyond the trivial stage. Some are self-terminating. Some are sudden and fatal. Some are chronic and linger for years. This sequence of events, though, is typical of at least most serious conditions at Yirrkala, and is well illustrated in the case of Mandjinga (pp. 70-6).

In its initial stages illness, as anywhere, is a personal matter. The patient decides that he is sick and what to do about it. Being sick means different things to different people. Many people at Yirrkala suffer some chronic pain or discomfort. The point at which a person defines himself as ill depends partly on his normal state of health. It also depends on whether he has symptoms which community members recognise as signifying illness. At Yirrkala, recurrent upper respiratory tract infections and the habitual smoking of pipes and cigarettes commonly cause a loose, productive cough. Such coughs alarm non-Aborigines, but do not unduly worry Yolngu.

The attitudes of family and sick person depend on how serious they consider the illness to be, and range from sympathetic inactivity to alarm. If a person has a cold, headache, sore, mild injury, stomach upset or other minor condition, he may simply retire temporarily from social life and rest. Everyone recognises that many illnesses are self-terminating and do not need any treatment at all. If treatment is called for, a member of the family, usually a female relative, may massage the afflicted areas of his body with water, prepare food which he can easily eat and digest, and borrow, buy or prepare medicine. Medicines can be bought at the store (aspirin, Vicks vapour rub, cough mixture), obtained at the health centre, or prepared from local plants. (A discussion of bush medicines is given in Scarlett et al., 1982). A Yolngu steam treatment, in which a patient lies on a bed of hot coals which has been covered by leaves and wet rushes and is then covered by sheets or sand, may be prepared by women. However, the steam bed takes a long time to make and is used infrequently today. Often a patient will go directly to the health centre for treatment, or, when it is closed, the health worker on duty. The general tenor of the situation is one of watchful concern. Those close to the sick person want him to recover, but, unless he is very old, very young or otherwise felt to be at risk, they are not seriously worried.

When a consensus exists that a person is ill, certain expectations come into effect. Willingness to help a patient, to procure medicines, to allow him to retire from his normal social obligations and lean on others depends on his fulfilling these expectations. He is required, for instance, not to malinger and place undue demands on the time and energy of others after it is fairly clear that he has recovered. He is also expected to make a reasonable and responsible effort to get better.

Responsible behaviour is situationally defined. A person who over-extends himself while ill to uphold certain crucial obligations is likely to receive sympathy and support from those around him even if it is clear that the exertion is exacerbating his condition. For instance, a clan leader who was hospitalised with pneumonia insisted on leading the mortuary ceremonies for his deceased aunt. Though his relatives were very worried about him, no one seriously attempted to dissuade him. Everyone recognised that this was his cherished wish and his duty.

By contrast, a person who wilfully disregards the Yolngu norms of patient behaviour without a good reason is simply a source of annoyance and worry. He may well find that the sympathy of those around him is withdrawn and he is no longer accorded the privileges of the sick role. A seven-year-old boy who had been treated at the health centre for a severely swollen and infected foot insisted on accompanying some relatives on a bumpy four hour drive to a homeland centre despite their protests that he was not well enough. Although he tolerated the pain with relatively little fuss, he was unable to sleep at the homeland centre and was obviously in great pain coming home. When he arrived at Yirrkala and his aunt was told how sick he had been, she brusquely rejected any suggestion of neglect and said impatiently and unsympathetically that it was his own fault. He had insisted on going to the homeland centre even though he felt ill and now he was suffering the consequences.

The approach to an illness in its early stages is pragmatic. The severity of the illness is weighed against the inconvenience and cost – in terms of time, effort and money – of obtaining treatment. If one medicine does not seem to work another may be tried. Alternatively several may be tried at the same time. The medicines of preference these days are mostly Western, not necessarily because they are considered to be more effective than herbal medicines or the steam treatment but because they are easier to obtain.

In the early stages of an illness its cause is irrelevant. As long as there is a consensus that the patient will recover, aetiology is of little interest. If pressed for an explanation of the cause of the illness, the patient or his kin will usually say that it is 'just a sickness [*rerri*]', or attribute it to neglect (by self or others), bad food, heavy smoking or other causes which do not implicate sorcerers or malevolent spirits.

If the patient does not respond to treatment, he and his family become anxious. Certain symptoms and behaviours are acknowledged by most people as cause for alarm and for treatments of a higher order than those already tried. Those which trigger a consensus that the patient is critically ill include:

(1) signs of internal bleeding – blood in stool, blood in phlegm, blood in vomit, blood in urine;
(2) one or a number of severe symptoms which persist for several days, such as uncontrollable vomiting, diarrhoea or high fever;
(3) the patient is unresponsive to his physical and social environment – he stares blankly or is unconscious;
(4) the patient refuses or is unable to speak;
(5) the patient refuses or is unable to eat or drink;
(6) the patient says that he is very ill, in particular that he is experiencing severe internal pain;
(7) the patient says he is going to die and calls for his sacred clan songs to be sung;
(8) the patient attempts to sing his clan songs himself or to imitate the dances of the totemic animals;
(9) the illness is both severe and chronic – it lingers unchanged or slowly becomes worse over an extended period of time;
(10) the illness is perceived to be 'spoiling' the body, as in a severe attack of boils or infected sores, leprosy or a severe urogenital condition.

These signs and symptoms, either alone or in combination, are all causes for apprehension. They are almost always indicators to patient and kin that the illness is critical and that more intensive treatment should be sought.

The Western medical options available when a patient is critically ill include consulting the visiting doctor, referral and admission to Nhulunbuy Hospital and, occasionally, evacuation to Darwin or a hospital in a capital city in southern Australia. If the patient is considered seriously ill, close and distant relatives will always gather nearby, at home or at hospital, to show their concern, to cry, to comfort or simply to sit. Relatives have an obligation to stay as close as possible to a sick person and will camp outside Nhulunbuy Hospital after a relative has been admitted even though no facilities exist for campers and it is obvious to all that some hospital staff and townspeople do not approve.

When a person is seriously ill, Western medicines and treatments are usually sought first. However, if the patient does not seem to be recovering the *marrnggitj* may be consulted. The *marrnggitj* is thought to be able to cure certain illnesses, particularly those caused by sorcery, which fall outside the Western doctor's field of expertise. Doctors, on the other hand, as the adult male *marrnggitj* pointed out, have the means to cure some illnesses which *marrnggitj* cannot. Illnesses caused by *galka* may defy the attempts of both doctor and *marrnggitj* to effect a cure. On the whole, community members see doctors and *marrnggitj* as having different but complementary abilities. People acknowledge that *marrnggitj* are not allowed to work in hospitals because, unlike doctors, they have not studied at university for many years, but recognise their special skills in diagnosing and healing illnesses caused by sorcery. Some say the *marrnggitj* are best able to divine the cause of an illness and the doctor to treat the symptoms. Thus one young woman said when I asked her what the best treatment for the symptoms of nephritis (or cystitis) would be: 'Go to a *marrnggitj* to see what caused it and then go to a doctor for medicine'.

Although the various courses of action available can be characterised as a 'hierarchy of resort' (Schwartz 1969), they are not always used serially. If several are available or if the patient suddenly becomes seriously ill the shotgun approach is taken and several are used at once, the rationale being that at least one may work.

If a series of options has been tried and the patient's condition is still deteriorating, the senior men of his clan and other clans of the same moiety are called in to sing the sacred songs, the songs which celebrate the land and the Dreaming. These songs are said to remind the patient that all care about him, to 'make him happy' and to orient him towards his ancestors, land and sacred heritage. Should he die, the singing will 'bring his spirit back to the spirit land community'. It will ensure that his spirit does not linger and haunt his relatives but returns to the land of his clan or a place of the dead.[1]

---

1. When the men are singing they are not, as some non-Aborigines suppose, 'singing a man to death'. People may and do recover after the senior men have gathered to sing. The singing or *manikay* prepares a person for death and offers tranquility in the face of suffering. As one leader said, 'this *manikay* is only for guessing about the death'. That many people *do* die after singing

When patient and family decide an illness is critical, they not only seek more serious treatment but begin speculating about its cause. They analyse the patient's personal troubles, recall feuds between his clan and others and talk about any recent occurrences which indicate the activities of a sorcerer. A frequent topic of conversation is the unusual appearance in the camp of buffalo, owls or snakes – in fact, of any animals which might be *galka* in animal form. People seek the cause of an illness partly because they value an explanation in and of itself. The cause of an illness also helps relatives to decide what should be done to protect the patient and themselves from further attacks. Explanations are not primarily sought as a guide to treatment.

Since cause is rarely a major consideration in illness management, people may speculate, but a reasonably firm Yolngu diagnosis is usually retrospective, made when the outcome of the illness is known. The cause is indicated by the outcome of treatment rather than dictating treatment. Though several hypotheses may be entertained, it is usually impossible to know for sure what is causing an illness and so aetiology is not a reliable basis for action. (A rare exception to this sequence of events is the case of John, below, who gave a definitive explanation of his own illness before he died and, on the basis of his own conclusions and the opinion of the *marrnggitj*, refused to go to hospital.) The most appropriate course of treatment is generally decided by such factors as severity, the medical help available and the time, energy and resources needed to obtain any given treatment. If a patient recovers, however ill he may have been, the family and patient often lose interest in what caused the illness, or decide that it was not caused by sorcery at all. The only indisputable proof that a person has been attacked by a sorcerer is his death. And only then are urgent efforts made to find out exactly how and why the death occurred.

Sorcery and Problem Solving

When someone dies at Yirrkala, the first reactions of all affected are shock and grief. In such a small community a death touches not only the immediate family but a large number of relatives, most of whom have known the dead person all of his life. If the person was young or

---

begins is a function of the fact that it is only initiated for the seriously ill. A medical officer who treated dying patients at Yirrkala described the singing as easing the patient's path to heaven. It is possible that this practice may have been confused by some non-Aborigines with the 'singing' of a man by a sorcerer in order to kill him (called *nyira* at Yirrkala but known by other names elsewhere in Australia). The singing of the *manikay* has nothing to do with *nyira* at all.

middle-aged, the death is particularly distressing, for it also means the loss of one who has many responsibilities — as a mother, father, or leader and holder of sacred knowledge. A death sets in motion an elaborate sequence of rituals which continue for days or weeks and provide a vehicle for the expression of anger and grief and a means of dealing with the loss (Reid 1979b). When the first shock of the death has passed, it becomes a central topic of conversation. Attempts to find out why a person has died are both limited and guided by the sociomedical theory. The relatives of the dead person explore his relationships and personal history, the clan's history and its conflicts, the circumstances leading up to the death and any other factors which might help them to decide why he died (the ultimate cause) and how (the proximate cause). Evidence is culled from both the social and medical arenas. His symptoms before death, marks on his body and the nature of the death are all grist to the mill of inquiry. The death of a prominent young man in 1980 starkly illustrates the interplay of all these factors.

> John, a 30-year-old man who had been staying in Darwin, came home to Yirrkala for his uncle's funeral. He had been sick in Darwin and seen the doctor who gave him analgesics for a painful shoulder. He took about a dozen of these a day for a week or so. John was the father of three children, a fine exhibition dancer who had travelled with Aboriginal dance groups abroad and the eldest son of one lineage of a clan and thus a future leader. When he was at Yirrkala he was an intermittent but heavy drinker.
> At Yirrkala he began to feel worse and saw the visiting doctor complaining of lethargy, loss of appetite and the discomfort of what, on examination, appeared to be an enlarged liver. The examination and blood tests indicated hepatitis — either infectious, drug-induced or alcoholic. The doctor arranged for him to be evacuated to Darwin Hospital for further tests and care.
> On the day John was to leave, his family came to the doctor's house in Nhulunbuy early in the morning and said he would not be going. His illness, they told her, was due to *galka*. John had told them the story and the *marrnggitj* had confirmed that a *galka* had cut him open and taken two organs from his groin, leaving only one. John had said to them, 'I will not go to Darwin or to Nhulunbuy Hospital. If I do I will come back in a coffin'. The family asked, though, if the doctor would take an X-ray of John to see what was wrong inside. She refused, explaining that this would not reveal anything they did not already know but visited him and took blood for further tests. The results

indicated a deterioration in his condition and evidence of renal failure.

I arrived from Sydney that day to find the family distracted by anxiety and grief. They told me John was dying and that I was to come and see him immediately to say goodbye. He was lying on a mattress under a tree surrounded by his sisters and other relatives who were attending to his needs. Some were wailing. Most sat quietly, their faces vacant with shock. Men sitting nearby were singing the sacred clan songs. When I looked at John I did not know him. His hair was cropped short, his cheeks and eyes sunken, his body thin, and his abdomen which, despite my protestations, he struggled to show me, taut and swollen. Grimacing with pain he told me I would not see him again. When I moved away to sit with the family the *marrnggitj* came to massage and treat him. The next day, at dawn, he woke one of his aunts (*mukul*), said, 'I'm going now', and died. The health workers were on hand and tried artificial resuscitation, but to no avail.

The doctor said that, when she came the next day to see the clan head and family they were almost incoherent with grief and anger. She was permitted to view the body but was told the family would not consent to an autopsy: 'Definitely not; it's fine to cut animals' bodies, but not people'. But the clan head insisted she take part in the ritual washing of the body, a clear signal to her that she was in no way being blamed and that her help and concern had been appreciated. She, nevertheless, said she was shattered by the death, by her inability to avert the tragedy, and by the obvious concurrence of the health workers with the diagnosis of *galka*. She had been wondering if the whole incident would diminish the status of Western medicine in the eyes of the community, but was reassured to find that people were still coming to the health centre in the same numbers.

The body was not taken, as is usual, to the morgue at Nhulunbuy Hospital, nor was it kept in the mobile refrigerated coffin which the electrician at Yirrkala had helped the people make for use in prolonged funeral ceremonies. The mortuary rituals started immediately and, after four days, the body was buried. All the while macabre stories about the decomposition of the body and related signs of *galka* circulated throughout the community.

After the funeral, members of John's family talked about the circumstances surrounding his death as he had related them before he died. His wife had formed a relationship with a man from Milingimbi who was living at Yirrkala and had had a child by him. John had accepted the child as his own, but the child's father had been in Darwin at the same time as John, and one day at the hotel there claimed to be a *galka* and threatened to kill him if he did not give up the child. He and three other Milingimbi men then attacked John. Shortly before he died the wife's lover had left Yirrkala and gone to a homeland centre a long way away, clear evidence of his guilt.

The *marrnggitj* had done his best to cure John but the *galka* had fooled him by removing the fat from John's abdomen and piercing his heart on the underside (where the *marrnggitj* could not 'see' the damage) to drain away the blood. And besides this, the wife of the *marrnggitj* had taken his *milirrk* (healing stones) with her to a homeland centre. But, said John's aunt, the grandmother of one of his 'promises', his death would not go unavenged. Perhaps the senior men of his clan would send word to John's Aboriginal friends in Sydney, or at Yuendumu in central Australia and ask them to visit long distance sorcery on the killers.

Elsewhere in Yirrkala, outside the immediate family, other opinions were being expressed. The leader of the *gutharra* (sisters' daughters' sons) clan was trying to stem other talk of a revenge spearing saying that this would only bring Yirrkala down in the eyes of white Australians and be another reason for them to come and take more land. The main suspects, he suggested, should be exiled from the community. A leader from Elcho Island said John had either died from his drinking, or from sorcery worked by the European and Middle Eastern migrants who came to work at the mine. The brother of the wife of the head of John's clan had divided loyalties. His own wife was from the clan of the main suspect and he almost provoked a family fight when he said the members of his wife's clan were not *galka* and would not have killed John. But the death remained an open wound and, a year later, when John's wife's father died, her family accused his clan of sorcery. Upon hearing these accusations, the head of John's clan collapsed and was taken to hospital where he stayed for a day until assurances were received that his clan was not being blamed.

In very general terms the diffuse and informal inquiry which follows a death such as this has four stages: advancing hypotheses about the cause of death; gathering and sharing evidence; assessing the plausibility of the hypotheses and deciding between them.

Characteristically, several hypotheses or 'stories' are current after a death. The majority of these posit sorcery as the cause but the motivation and identity of the sorcerer vary from story to story. Few people are dogmatic about any particular story. Until all available information is to hand and people have had the opportunity to weigh each critically, their opinions are tentative. As the weeks pass, one or two explanations of the death usually become widespread. This sequence of events is not invariable, but, as the following two cases illustrate, is reasonably typical.

The Death of a Young Boy[2]

An adolescent boy died in a car accident on the road between Yirrkala and Nhulunbuy. In the days which followed, his death was a major topic of conversation. A young woman of the community related the three major versions which she had heard while playing cards ('When you hear most of the stories that are going around'). She related these stories without committing herself to any of them. She merely said that she had heard them, and added that when someone dies, Balanda do not look for a cause they simply accept the concept of an accident, whereas Aborigines do not.

The first story, she said, was that two *galka* had killed the boy. As corroborating evidence, those who propagated this version said that there was a particular bird (possibly a *galka* in bird form) at the scene of the accident which called out or tried to hit the windscreen as the car went past. It was the same kind of bird as the ones which were seen at Yirrkala before the accident.

The second story was that two *galka* from Maningrida had killed the boy by mistake. They thought he was another boy who had been sent there to get some *madayin* (sacred) things for his father. The *galka* were angry that the boy should be in possession of *madayin* things.

The third story attributed the death to the driver, a young man of another clan group. It was said that he had killed the boy himself by driving a stake through his heart and had then put glass on the body to make it appear that the boy had been killed in the accident. The driver's motive was the illegal use of sacred paintings belonging to his own clan by members of the young boy's clan. The driver's father had told him to kill the boy as payback. Three facts

2. This incident occurred after I left the community. I am indebted to Frances and Howard Morphy for the details of the incident. Both knew those affected well and attended the young boy's funeral at the homeland centre of his clan.

were cited as evidence for this version: the driver was unhurt; the two other passengers were knocked unconscious and there were therefore no witnesses; and windscreen glass does not shatter like ordinary glass and could not therefore have inflicted a serious chest wound.

One of the passengers, a young boy, told a different story. The boy said that the deceased had been pestering the driver for a cigarette but eventually gave up and began to talk to the boy with him in the back seat. The driver then took out a cigarette and turned to attract his young passenger's attention. As he did so the car went out of control. If you pass the spot now, he continued, and you are driving too fast, a voice shouts 'Whey!' trying to warn you.

Some people held that the boy's body was dismembered and only blood remained. However, the head of another clan at Yirrkala said this was not true. He had seen the body. There was only a little cut on the forehead which would not have killed anyone. This was proof positive that the boy had been killed by *galka*. He had, in fact, been killed by people from the west. They had attacked him because members of the boy's clan had, the previous year, shot two people from the west who wandered onto their land. (No shootings known to the police had occurred in this area.)

The Death of an Elderly Man

When an elderly man died at a homeland centre there was, within hours of notification of his death, a variety of rumours and stories circulating at Yirrkala about the cause. A notable feature of most of these was that they were based on very little reliable information – a fact which their proponents recognised. People were particularly anxious to know details of the death, especially the findings of the police and medical authorities, but these were not available.

One man said that he had heard that *galka* had come from Maningrida and camped in a sacred place near the homeland centre which Yirrkala people do not know. They came on a horse which had a special song (spell) of its own which blinds people so they cannot see it. Another man repeated this story and added that the tracks of the horse had been found. When the man died, blood had come out of his body which was falling apart because the *galka* had broken his spine. An adolescent boy said that, at midnight, two *galka* had swum to the camp underwater and stabbed the man in the throat. A senior woman related a similar story and said that, after the man became very ill, the clan leader had seen the *galka* swimming in the sea by moonlight. He had shouted into the night, condemning the *galka* loudly and clearly. They were listening and had resolved to return and kill more people there. A warning to this effect had been sent from friendly people at Maningrida. A policeman, she said, had dusted the body with the white powder. When he drew back his hand he was able to see the faces of the three killers. He told the leader that he should shoot them if he saw them. The dead man had spearmarks on his chest and back where a spear had pierced his torso. The leader of the homeland centre mentioned this death to me several months later and said that, although he is not sure that he really believes in *galka*, he patrolled the area with his rifle after the death, intending to shoot any *galka* he saw. 'I didn't see any', he said, 'but I still wonder.'

Shortly after the news reached Yirrkala, an old woman said that the cars of a young Aboriginal community leader and some European men had been involved in an accident and that the Europeans had been killed. (The Europeans were said to be 'Water Resources' men, that is, government employees who were helping homeland centre communities to locate and tap fresh water resources.) She later amended this story when news came that an Aborigine had been killed by two *galka*. She said that the people of the dead man's community (on Groote Eylandt) were blaming the leader of the homeland centre at which he was staying and were sending men in a boat to make trouble for him.

Another expressed great fear that the dead man's relatives would soon arrive at Yirrkala to kill someone there in revenge for the death. She said that the dead man had been out hunting with his wife and children and that they had teased a kangaroo which was, in fact, a *galka*. When they arrived back at camp the man died. This woman maintained that the female *marrnggitj* had gone to the homeland centre and used her *djamarrku_li_* (spirit familiars) to ascertain the cause of death. The *djamarrku_li_* found, upon entering his body, that his organs had been removed and replaced with grass and leaves. The man had been coughing up blood because he was breathing through these. His big heart had been removed and replaced by a little heart. The *galka* attacked him because he had been 'messing around' in ceremonial business. The speaker added that a community leader who visited the man's grave found it empty. He (that is, his ghost or *mokuy*) was wandering around that area and could kill someone.

A clan leader said that the dead man had told him before he died that he became ill after returning from Groote Eylandt, probably because he. was attacked by *manggimanggi*. The people there, the dead man had said, were angry with him because he had taken the possessions of a young woman who had died and brought them back to Yirrkala in order to hold the proper mortuary rites for her. The man had gone down to his clan's homeland centre to die in his own land.

A second hypothesis advanced by this leader was that the man had been killed because of a feud between his people and the people of Maningrida over a ritual string and feather head dress which had not been returned to Maningrida as expected. One or two voices of scepticism were heard. Another man from Groote Eylandt who is living at Yirrkala said that the deceased had died of neglect. Though they knew he had been ill since arriving at Yirrkala, his relatives at the homeland centre had not sent for a doctor. When he died the doctor admonished them severely because they had been derelict in their duty.

A younger man who had undertaken to teach me in some detail about *galka* and *marrnggitj* (and who is also an active church member), said that I should ignore the many stories abroad about the man's death because the police had definitely ascribed it to lung cancer. He said that the man had told the homeland centre leader at least a year before he died that he was very sick and would die soon.

A further example of the proliferation of hypotheses and of the intense desire of the bereaved to find the true story is given in the following case. The sudden death of a woman of the community convinced many people that she had been killed by sorcery. A few, however, including the adult male *marrnggitj*, held that she had sustained internal injuries while throwing herself on the ground and hitting her head in mourning. Members of her family suspected that medical staff at Nhulunbuy Hospital had killed her (deliberately or

otherwise). Whereas in the two cases above people gave the
explanations dispassionately this case illustrates the angry suspicions
harboured by the immediate family when someone dies, as well as
the thoughts on the matter of people outside the family.

The Death of a Woman

Late one night I learned from a mission staff member
that a woman in her fifties was ill. She had, he said, been
hospitalised at Nhulunbuy for a chest complaint earlier in
the day but had absconded from hospital in the late
afternoon and returned to Yirrkala. On the way home I
met a young man, one of the woman's relatives, and
inquired after her. He said, noncommittally, that she was
'home but all right'. I later learned that her condition had
deteriorated that night and that this young man had driven
her back to hospital.

Well after midnight I was awakened by the loud and
persistent blowing of car horns signalling a death in the
community. I left my house and went out to the road.
People were streaming past on their way from their homes
to the camp of the woman's clan. One stopped and told me
that she had died. Within moments I heard the slow beat of
clapsticks preceding the ritual announcement of death
(*bäpurru*). This was followed by cries and wails of grief,
and the dull, distant but distinct thuds as women cut their
heads with knives and other objects and threw themselves
on the ground in the traditional mode of mourning.
Shortly thereafter I heard the *bäpurru* and wailing begin at
another camp.

When I arrived at my sister's house at breakfast time it
was clear that several of the women had been crying. Their
faces were drawn and they looked tired. One of the young
people of the household told me that two of my sisters
cried for me for at least an hour. They feared that I would
be alone and crying in bed close to the deceased woman's camp
where there might be trouble. My sister commented
despairingly that people had been dying one after the other
at Elcho Island and now the same thing was beginning to
happen at Yirrkala.

In the days immediately following the death several
stories circulated about the circumstances and cause of the
death. One of the health workers told me that a flock of
white cockatoos (*nyirrk*) had come to the house where fruit
from the gardens is stored a few days earlier. This was a
sign to all that a death would occur. She also said that the

dead woman had had a low blood cell count and had had a fever all week and inferred that absconding from hospital had caused (or accelerated) her death.

On the evening following the death I visited the family of the dead woman's brother. Both he and his wives had been crying for much of the day. He had then left and gone to the hotel to drink and returned shortly before I arrived. He was somewhat inebriated and, as I approached, welcomed me loudly and began to tell me how preoccupied he was about his sister's death. He explained that she had been sick for only one day and that, after being admitted to hospital and coming home, she was vomiting blood. He felt that something may have been wrong with the two slices of bread she was given to eat in hospital. He paused and then added that he thought she had been killed. This was said in such a way that I assumed he meant she had been killed while in hospital. When I asked him to clarify this statement, he said he did not know. Perhaps, he said, someone had killed her at Yirrkala and she went to hospital and died there. He mentioned that his daughter had been with her aunt at the hospital when a nurse told the woman that nothing was wrong with her and that she could go home. The woman had, however, told her niece that she felt so ill that she was sure she would die that night and therefore wanted to come home and see her children. The dead woman's brother asked me if I would ask the doctors at Nhulunbuy Hospital why she had died. I said I would do my best.

During the day I also saw the health worker from the homeland centre of the dead woman's clan. He said that everyone's head was going round. Many people were saying that the nurses or doctors in the hospital poisoned the woman by putting something in her tea. Later I met the father of Nyurrulnga, the child *marrnggitj*. This man recalled that his son had treated the woman four weeks before while she was in hospital. His son told him, however, that he could only heal the woman a little because she had a crack down the centre of her forehead. Now that she had died he was convinced Nyurrulnga was right.

A senior man of another clan told me that his older sister had seen the woman at her home a week before. The woman told her that she felt so ill she was sure she was going to die and had, accordingly, given all her possessions to her daughters. At that time, this man related, the deceased was spitting up blood and had a cut on her upper back. The dead woman herself had thought it might have been caused maliciously (that is, by *galka*). He himself thought it was probably just a cut from the bush but suspected that she might have been attacked by *galka* two weeks before when she and her family were away camping. Her symptoms before death (coughing up blood and a sore in her chest) were, he said, definitive of a *galka* attack.

In the following days similar stories were advanced to explain the death. One woman who also felt the death might have been caused by *galka* (she was not sure) noted how thin and unwell the woman had been before her death. She was of the opinion that the woman should have sought medical help during the crisis rather than staying at home. The adult male *marrnggitj*, on the other hand, maintained that the deceased had become ill because she had hit herself while grieving and caused an internal sore.

A senior Christian leader and lay pastor told me that he did not think of '*galka* business'. He had visited the woman a few days before she died and she had told him then that she was all right but that a little blood was coming through her mouth. She attributed this to the fact that she had become car sick during a bumpy ride between Yirrkala and a camping spot some distance away. After lunch on the day of her death this leader had visited the woman in hospital and she had told him again she was all right and would return to Yirrkala that day. He said that, since he has no interest in magic, he thought only of sickness – perhaps a sickness of her heart or chest. He maintained that he would not believe in *galka* or *mokuy* (spirits) unless he saw one himself, in the same way as he sees a buffalo or snake. It was difficult, he said, to know what was wrong. He explained that people often damage the insides of their bodies when throwing themselves on the ground during mourning.

The mortuary ceremonies for the dead woman continued for several days and were attended by the members of her own and other related clans. It was suggested to me that I should sit and dance with the members of 'my' clan. During a break in the singing of the sacred songs, a senior man of the dead woman's clan, her son-in-law, took me aside. He said that he wanted to tell a senior medical officer at Nhulunbuy that the doctor at the hospital had treated his mother-in-law roughly. He had poked her body in an extremely painful way. This man also expressed anger at the Yirrkala health centre nursing sister. He maintained that his mother-in-law had gone to the health centre many times asking for medicine and each time the nurse had refused and sent her away saying she was fine. It was his opinion that the nurse was not doing her job properly.

Several months later I was told by a relieving nursing sister, who had been present at the time, that this man had approached the nurse shortly after the death. He blamed her for the death and became so angry that a health worker interposed herself between them to prevent escalation of the conflict. The nurse had been so upset by this incident that she had later contacted this leader to clarify the situation. The relieving nurse who related the incident was, in her own words, disgusted and angered by his behaviour, saying it was unjustifiably rude and that he was 'stirrer'.

Further criticism was subsequently levelled by the dead woman's family at the health workers. They said that the health workers were drawn only from one camp (that is, one group of allied clans) and only treated people there. The health workers, they said, were especially reluctant to go to camps other than their own at night when people were sick. One senior health worker was so angered by this accusation that she offered to live at the health centre as it was much closer to the dead woman's camp than to her own. The health worker said that she herself had, when a position fell vacant, advocated the training of a young woman from the dead woman's clan to ensure more balanced representation of health workers among the various clans.

After expressing his severe doubts about the treatment the woman had received in hospital, her son-in-law, a clan leader, asked me to contact the regional director of the Department of Health in Nhulunbuy. He told me to find out, on his behalf, the cause of death and to ask this doctor to come to Yirrkala and talk about it. Accordingly, I rang the doctor at his home in Nhulunbuy. The doctor told me that he could not, from a medical point of view, be sure of the cause of death. Before her death the patient had had a blood dyscrasia, probably caused by some food or drug she had been given, and leucopenia. Her spleen was enlarged. He asked me to tell her son-in-law that the doctor at the hospital had pressed the patient's abdomen to feel her spleen. This had been the procedure to which the woman had objected. The hospital staff had contacted Darwin for tests during her hospital stay a month before but as yet had not received the results. The doctor pointed out that the woman was a chronic chest patient. He asked me to explain to her son-in-law the process by which a cavity had formed in her lungs and ruptured the blood vessels. When the woman had been brought to hospital the last time, he said, the staff had tried to aspirate the blood. It was too late, and she died shortly after.

I returned to the funeral ceremonies and relayed this information to the leader (the patient's son-in-law) who had asked for it. He listened without comment and returned to the singing. He did not respond to the doctor's comment that a postmortem examination could be performed if the family so desired. As requested, I later told the dead woman's brother and his immediate family of my conversation with the doctor. They listened and said that most people suspected the activities of a *galka*. The younger wife of the woman's brother was singularly unimpressed by the suggestion of an autopsy and said that it was not the Aboriginal way to cut into a body after a death. It would upset the family. There is no Aboriginal law, she explained, governing such a thing. Only a *marrnggitj* could be called in to divine the cause of death.

The following day I met the dead woman's son-in-law on the road. He said he was still worried about her death and was upset that the doctor had not yet visited to tell him personally the true story. He recapitulated his understanding of the events which led up to his mother-in-law's death. She had gone to hospital, eaten a lot of food and felt pain inside. The doctor had come and poked her – something doctors and nurses should not do – possibly causing damage inside. After this the blood travelled upwards and came out through her mouth. Perhaps, he mused, the doctor had *buma* (hit, killed) her. Medical staff should, he said, give old people medicines and injections, not poke and hurt them. He asked whether an autopsy had been performed. I repeated that it would not be done unless the family gave explicit permission. He said that the family was not in agreement. I left.

My last discussion about this woman's death was several days later with a young community leader, a *waku* (sister's son) of the dead woman, who was both well travelled and well educated and who was, at the time, engaged in community work. I relayed to him the medical officer's statements, adding that the doctor had said that the cause of death was something of a mystery to medical staff as well. When I said the family could, if they wished, request an autopsy, the young man asked what this might reveal. Would the doctors, he asked, be able to tell who killed her? Would they see an impression of the face of her murderer when they opened her up? I said they would only be able to see what sort of sickness or injury had caused the death. He said he was quite sure the death was not natural because it had been so sudden.

This man was guardedly critical of the treatment of the woman by hospital staff before she died. He said that she had left because the doctor had hurt her, because the nursing sisters had treated her badly, and because it was too cold in the hospital (which is air conditioned). He explained that he was directly involved in the events preceding her death. When she started to bleed through the mouth late in the evening of the night on which she died, he himself called the hospital and spoke to a sister on duty. She contacted the doctor and then told this man that the patient could stay home that night since she was probably suffering from a bad toothache and a burst blood vessel in the gums. The young man wondered, in retrospect, why he, as a community worker responsible for liaison with the hospital, had not been put directly in touch with the doctor. When she became very ill later in the night he drove her into hospital but she died some time after midnight.

After relating this series of events the young man said he was thinking of calling a meeting with the doctor in charge of the dead woman's case and the nurse on duty that night to discuss all that had transpired. He remarked that, when he was working in Darwin, he always had a good relationship with the staff at the hospital and had been given all details of a patient's illness. He emphasised that he most definitely did not want to start a racial issue by accusing hospital staff of treating Aborigines differently from other people. However he felt that the case should be looked into. He added, quietly, 'They probably think that no one cares about her death here'.

The processes of advancing and assessing the stories surrounding a death do not exclude any hypothesis, however ingenious or unusual. But in the final assessment, community opinion tends to cluster around stories derived from the sociomedical theory and consistent with the ideas discussed in Chapter 4 about insiders and outsiders, the known circumstances of the death, the credibility of the story-teller, the nature of the preceding illness (if any), the state of the body, and the relationships between the protagonists (the dead person and family and suspected sorcerer).

The social identity and personal history of the dead person are basic data for inquiries into the cause of his illness or death; so much so that when I conducted a small survey, asking people about the causes of certain hypothetical illnesses, several said they needed to know whom I was talking about before they could answer.

Relationships and Strategies: the Power of Definition

Although logic and reason are, for Yolngu, key elements in the search for a cause, dispassion is not. Statements about the cause of a person's death, like opinions about the identity of a sorcerer are emotional and social, as well as medical statements. Judgments are always influenced by the feelings, viewpoint, social position, interests and relationship of the inquirer. They also have social implications. When an individual advances a hypothesis, he is conscious not only of its plausibility in the light of available facts but of the consequences of voicing it at all. If judiciously advanced it may form an effective strategy for advancing his own interests. If not, it may rebound on him and his family.

A person's relationship to someone who is seriously ill or has died affects his perceptions and hypotheses in two principal ways. First, it determines the amount of relevant and accurate information to which he has access. Close relatives know more about the illness, relationships and troubles of the victim than distant ones. I was constantly surprised in this small, face-to-face community by how restricted was the flow of personal information. I realised how important it was to my family that they could trust me when it became clear to me that I knew more about their pregnancies, deaths, affairs and fights than anyone except the people who ate at the same hearth (that is, a grandmother, mother, sister and her children, son and his family and one or two other close relatives). Everyday information about people and events is guarded and it is considered rude to ask about other people's business (a problem for an anthropologist) let alone to gossip about others. There is a tension between the use of gossip for advancing one's own interests, entertaining others and sanctioning antisocial behaviour, and ensuring that the person who is the target of the gossip is not provoked to violence or the use of sorcery. So, while people attempt, remarkably successfully, to limit and control the flow of information about themselves, they are always keen to have information about others if it can be obtained without inviting their wrath. As a researcher I learned not to pursue a story by telling someone what I had already heard, because the only response to this was, 'Who told you?'

Second, a person's relationship to the victim affects his view of the victim's responsibility for his own death. If the inquirer is a distant or hostile relative he may consider that the deceased (or his relatives) brought it on himself. If he is a family member he will declare the guilt of the assailant and innocence of the victim. When a middle-aged man died at Yirrkala in 1974, a *marrnggitj*, who was also a close affinal relative, divined with the aid of a magical stone that his killers were two men from Groote Eylandt and Rose River respectively – men who had just left Yirrkala. His family, at least publicly, accepted and repeated this explanation. Some months later I was told by a senior man of another clan that the deceased had, while at Elcho Island many years before, taken his wife into a sacred area. The owners of the area had seen their footprints, been incensed by this offence and let it be known that they intended to kill him by sorcery. Relations between the two clans have long been strained and the speaker in this case was involved in the murder of a step-brother of the dead man several years before.

Similarly, it is not uncommon after a death to hear people in the community criticising the family for not caring adequately for the dead person during his illness, and blaming his death on their neglect. They may assert that the dead person himself was to blame since he knew about his condition and failed to tell others soon enough, or he did not take reasonable care of himself while ill. The family, of course, will attribute the death to sorcery and be furious if they hear such rumours (and reasonably so in a community which generally takes diligent care of the old, sick and dying).

As these examples suggest, personal distance strongly influences any judgment about the guilt or innocence of the victim. As the personal distance between individuals decreases, the extent to which they identify with each other's interests increases. For instance, while sisters can and do quarrel, they are also often exceptionally close. When one woman developed an infected sore a sister and sister's daughter angrily agreed that it was the result of sorcery *(burrpuy)* worked by a woman who was pursuing the sufferer's husband. Their indignation about the wrong done their sister was only matched by their hostility towards the presumed sorcerer, whose clan has little social or ceremonial contact with the sufferer's clan.

The victim himself, of course, whatever his private beliefs and fears, will usually declare that he is the innocent victim of the sorcerer's malice, or that the sorcery was justified, but inflicted by mistake on the wrong person. Cases of mistaken identity and botched or misdirected sorcery abound in firsthand accounts.

Sorcery is an extremely powerful concept, explaining as it does both how and why an illness or death occurs. In addition, because it is widely believed, it is a powerful political tool. To accuse someone of sorcery is a serious condemnation. If the accused is a member of a distant group, suspicion that he has worked sorcery is in keeping with the consensus that strangers cannot be trusted. If he is a community member, it singles him out as immoral, antisocial and untrustworthy. It is not anger, hostility, irresponsibility, selfishness or even cruelty which places him outside the pale of human morality (though, of course, all of these qualities are condemned). It is resort to the use of sorcery. When word reached Yirrkala that a young man of Elcho Island who had come to drink at Nhulunbuy hotel had said the men of a Yirrkala clan were *galka*, the young men of the clan immediately took spears and went to town to search for him. Had he not been located by the leader of an allied clan and been given police protection before being put on a plane to Elcho Island, he would probably have been speared or beaten.

The suggestion of sorcery as a way of increasing personal advantage is not common. When such incidents do occur, they tend to reflect the relationships within the society which are chronic sources of strain and conflict. They cluster around disputes over spouses, lovers and 'promises' and dissension between young and old.

One young woman formed a stable relationship with a man of her own choice and refused to join her elder sister as a co-wife of a clan leader, even though she had been promised to him. He was very persistent and she equally determined. She wrote him a letter saying he had bent the marriage system to marry her sister and therefore could not accuse her of being with someone in the wrong relationship for marriage. The woman's father, who was caught in an invidious position between his daughter and an influential son-in-law, finally acquiesced to her wishes. When her father became ill the woman said he suspected his son-in-law of having worked sorcery on him because he would not force her to marry him. Her father may or may not have harboured such suspicions but the statement reflected her own interests: to discredit her sister's husband and cast herself and her father as the injured parties.

The tensions between the young people and their elders which have been created by the attractions of Western society and by the attenuation of the sanctions which once buttressed the authority of senior men and women, are sometimes deplored by the elders in terms of illness and an increase in sorcery. Older people may attribute illnesses which befall the community to the waywardness of the young or their ignorance of the law. One man, who was deeply troubled by the deaths of several men of Yirrkala, even expressed the fear that young men from Yirrkala (and other neighbouring communities) were obtaining objects of sorcery from distant places to use at Yirrkala.

Sorcery can also provide a person with a coping strategy at times of extreme psychological or social stress. Some problems are not socially acceptable reasons for retreating from social obligations. These include marital difficulties, a drinking (and sometimes violent) relative and caring for children with inadequate resources. An illness thought to have been caused by sorcery, however, provides the sufferer with immediate and socially sanctioned respite from personal pressures. Individuals may, consciously or unconsciously, use a suggestion of sorcery as a means of obtaining familial support, recognition of their distress and an escape from their problems. The young woman whose situation is described on page 54, was clearly in a socially and personally disadvantaged position. She had chosen to reject her betrothed in favour of another young man and so invoked the wrath of several people whose interests were directly affected. When she collapsed and her illness was attributed to sorcery she was treated with concern by family members – even by her aunt, the mother of her promised husband. (Interestingly, the girl's jilted 'promise' later married her sister and, in 1981, the two couples and their children were happily sharing a house.)

It is difficult to say in a case such as that above whether the illness was, in fact, a strategy and whether, if so, it was a conscious strategy. A similar interpretation could be offered for the collapse of Mandjinga (p. 70). This woman was convinced that she had been attacked by *galka*. Nevertheless, her collapse was timely. She was suffering from the accumulated stresses of extremely difficult marital circumstances, a chronic illness (pelvic inflammatory disease) and several other problems. Her situation was barely tolerable. There were, at least very likely in her eyes, no socially sanctioned means of dealing with her problems other than forbearance. Her collapse may therefore have been a subconscious *cri de coeur*. (It was interpreted as such by the nursing sister who cared for her in hospital and who had known her previously.) The immediate result of her illness was to mobilise her family in common concern for her wellbeing. The feelings of family members were focused and intensified by the treatment by the *marrnggitj*. Had it not been for her collapse, the support she clearly needed would probably not have been forthcoming. Certainly, when she was hospitalised a year later for injuries received in a beating by her husband she was visited by only one or two close relatives. Her illness may have been, for her, in Kluckhohn's words, a way of 're-establishing the ego of the individual and of providing [her] with a means of escape from the limitations and thwartings which the social system imposed on [her]' (1944:84).

Another strategic use of sorcery which can be identified is, in fact, a deliberate non-use. Since an accusation, or even strong suspicion of sorcery has very serious social ramifications, it is often in the interest of those who are responsible for maintaining social harmony to minimise the possibility of accusations of sorcery. This need has become particularly pressing at Yirrkala where people live in crowded and often stressful circumstances. Several of the leaders of the community, particularly the older men, say that they consider it their responsibility to curtail speculations about sorcery, and, by extension, about revenge. To this end they sometimes publicly endorse the explanation of the doctor, whether or not they believe it. This strategy is quite explicit in the letters from a clan leader to Aboriginal communities and doctors in northern Australia which are reproduced in the next chapter. Similar sentiments were expressed by another clan leader in the following terms:

> I am *djaka'mirri* [the one who cares] for the clan, the law and the people. I have to think carefully about these things. When people die I don't immediately blame someone and create trouble. I think the cause is illness . . . I feel that as long as I am alive I can reason with people, but if I drop dead people will start blaming others and all my work will be spoiled. On the other hand, if someone spears or knifes someone else in the open, it is clear, and the only decision is whether to pay back or not. This is still something I'm thinking about.

Another leader maintained on several occasions that, if a *marrnggitj* could identify the sorcerer after death, he and his relatives would not act unilaterally. They would contact the police. Of a recent death in his extended family he said:

> I think two men are responsible. We should send them to gaol until they die there. This law [referring to sorcery] is a past law but they still use it. We'll get them by government law.

As these examples indicate, sorcery (or, more broadly the sociomedical theory) provides community members with a convincing and flexible set of explanations for illness and death, and at the same time a powerful means of expressing their loyalties and protecting their own interests.

Yolngu interests today, however, are not only affected by other Yolngu. Many of the problems and negotiations which demand their attention are a direct result of the white Australian presence. The Yolngu know too well that their society has been deeply compromised by the seductions and impositions of white Australia. Their control has been undermined and their epistemology challenged. But, as discussed in the first chapter, they enjoy many of the offerings and opportunities of the wider society and do not yearn sorrowfully for a remembered past. The over-riding Yolngu concern is not for cultural purity or economic isolation. It is for an accommodation with the enveloping society which guarantees a measure of autonomy and a secure cultural identity.

The sociomedical theory, as well as providing meaning in the face of affliction and a strategic tool in Yolngu affairs, has a certain tactical value *vis-à-vis* whites which is becoming evident as Yolngu assume greater control of community affairs. To a degree the theory has become one of the foils available to the Yolngu in the thrust and parry of their relationships with white Australians. In the medical arena especially, it provides an idiom in which Yolngu can assert their own authority when whites attempt to control their affairs.

At Yirrkala for instance, there is a deep and collective conviction that very sick people should be cared for at home by relatives. Patients who fear that they may die often abscond (as medical staff put it) from hospital or are taken home by relatives. When an illness becomes serious scores of close and distant relatives gather around the bed to sit, cry, help or just show their concern. To be sick is unfortunate. To be sick and alone is unthinkable. Doctors and nurses, however, will often bring pressure to bear on the family to let the patient go to hospital in Nhulunbuy or Darwin. More often than not Yolngu will concur and let the sick person go. But if they strongly believe he is dying, or if he is very old, they anguish over the decision, canvassing opinion, weighing the risks, and trying to reach a consensus. For the family, torn between a desire to do what is best for the patient and a wish to please those who control vital services (a dilemma for Aborigines everywhere – cf. Tynan 1979), the only way to insist on their own decision may be to explain that this is not an ordinary illness but one caused by *galka* which must be managed at home. That Yolngu deeply believe this to be so and white staff do not is beside the point. Their claims are given legitimacy by their conviction. When Yolngu insist on their way, as did John and his family (described above), most local staff will respect (if not agree with) their decision.

In a similar vein, when someone is sick or has died, relatives frequently phrase their requests for information from the doctor in terms of their fears about sorcery and their wish to know, as they describe it, the true story. Notwithstanding the risk of criticism or even ridicule, Yolngu are increasingly confident of their ability to argue and hold positions against resistance. The sociomedical theory has become one lever in their attempts to gain jurisdiction over critical matters in their community.

The theory also provides satisfaction in medical encounters not only because it offers useful grounds for argument over authority but because it belongs exclusively to the Yolngu. In mission times the disapproval of many staff members of Yolngu medical beliefs made the theory a liability rather than an asset in interactions with the white providers of health care. But today the theory is becoming one of the markers of cultural identity. The consistent agreement among Yolngu whom I asked that this book should be published is evidence of the significance of the theory for Yolngu in helping to mark the boundary between themselves and others which is one facet of the struggle for respect and independence.

The tactical value of the sociomedical theory is one of its strengths but it does not explain why it has survived the assaults of inconsistency and doubt which a half century of change has brought. Why should a theory which has its conception deep in the past have meaning today? How can it incorporate unfamiliar troubles and new sicknesses without becoming riddled by anomalies? These questions are explored in the following and final chapter of this book.

6 A Semblance of Change

Yolngu spend a good deal of time and emotional energy grappling with the troubles and challenges which Western society has brought and trying to find satisfying solutions. While adaptation to new circumstances was undoubtedly characteristic of Yolngu society before the coming of non-Aborigines, the need to find satisfying syntheses of dissonant ideas and experiences has become increasingly pressing as the changes confronting the Yolngu have proliferated. This chapter deals with Yolngu resolutions of apparent inconsistencies between the traditional medical theory and their experience of white Australian society and Western medicine.

Individuals, it will be seen, differ in the extent to which they deliberate on the intellectual puzzles and social problems generated by white Australian society and in the solutions they reach. But, underlying this variation, the structure of the sociomedical theory remains unchanged. Its content – the motivations for sorcery attacks and the illnesses they cause — may be modified, but in its essence, the theory is as Warner found it at Milingimbi 50 years ago. The theory, moreover, remains an important source of comfort, explanation and guidance in times of sickness and death. It does so, as this chapter shows, because it gives meaning. It gives meaning because it is still plausible to the Yolngu. And it is plausible because of their ingenuity in extending old ideas to the solution of new problems.

Medical Beliefs and Practices: A Questionnaire

In 1975, I interviewed 43 people at length about their medical experiences, their contacts with Yolngu and Western medicine and their opinions about the causes and treatments for nine illnesses. The illnesses were not named. Each was described by a set of symptoms. The questionnaire (Appendix) was administered with the help of interpreters who could explain complex ideas and symptoms.

The sample selected for this survey was not random. The respondents were all people whom I knew well and therefore felt I could impose upon. I was also quite sure that they would answer the questions frankly. An effort was made to interview approximately equal numbers of young and old, men and women. While those who agreed to answer the questionnaire were willing and responsive, some older people thought, no matter what I said, that I was gathering information about the old ways and tended to reply accordingly. Some, for instance, said they would use bush medicines when I suspected they would probably go to the health centre for treatment. On the other hand, some of the younger people may have been influenced by the structured interview to give Western rather than Yolngu explanations for the symptoms described to them. (One woman, for example, who had recently told me a sudden death was caused by sorcery, said during the interview that, in her opinion sudden death was the result of a heart attack or stroke.) We were asking each person to answer personal questions and to envisage hypothetical situations: both non-Yolngu things to do. But, given these considerations, most people quicky grasped the nature of the task and generously persevered with a sometimes tedious and apparently useless exercise. The results are illuminating because they illustrate patterns in community thought which had become apparent through the observations and casual conversations of fieldwork.

The survey was based on the assumption that, by comparing the responses of young and old (under 30 and over 30 years of age) it would be possible to gain some idea of the degree to which Yolngu medical beliefs and practices have changed since 1934, when the mission at Yirrkala was founded. Schooling and level of employment were not useful variables since both depend almost exclusively on age. This is because educational, medical and other services were not well established until the 1950s and only people under the age of 30 have had continuous experience of schooling and wage labour.

In the first section of the questionnaire each person was asked to give certain details of his or her medical history as he (or she) remembered them. Several findings are of interest. First, 35 of the 43 respondents said they had been hospitalised at some time. There is no significant difference between the two age groups. Second, though only seven people had ever had surgery, there is again no difference between those under and those over 30 years of age. Third, more than half of the respondents said they had used bush medicines at some time during their lives but, again, age is not a predictor of use. Fourth, approximately half of the respondents had been treated by a *marrnggitj* during their lives but there is again no difference between under thirties and over thirties in this respect. Fifth, of the 43 respondents, 13 said they had become sick as a result of an attack by sorcery at some time. Nine of these were over and four under 30 – a difference which is not significant. (It should, of course, be noted that the older people, having lived longer, have generally been sick more often than the young.)

In the second section of the questionnaire each person was given a set of symptoms exhibited by a hypothetical patient. Each was then asked to say what he thought might have caused the illness and what, ideally, should be done about it. The causes given by respondents for each symptom set have been categorised as 'social or spiritual' (including sorcery, trespass into dangerous areas and other causes of illness discussed in Chapter 2), 'natural'[1] (such as 'just a sickness', 'smoking too much', 'getting old', 'not enough to eat', 'not being looked after' and 'worrying too much'), 'either' and 'no response/don't know'. Recommended treatments were classified as 'Western' (such as going to the health centre or hospital, consulting a doctor or nurse, taking Western medicines), 'Yolngu' (such as consultation with the *marrnggitj*, taking herbal medicines or steam treatment), 'either', 'other' (such as 'don't sleep around', 'don't smoke', 'do nothing', and 'eat good food'), and 'no response/don't know'.

A total of nine illnesses (as symptom sets) were described to respondents. The results are summarised in Tables 1 and 2. As these tables show, the infant illnesses, such as otitis media and subnutrition with diarrhoea and dehydration are almost unanimously considered to result from causes other than sorcery or spirits. In fact, more often than not, they were attributed to poor maternal care. These illnesses are recognised world wide as diseases of crowding, unsanitary conditions, a poor water supply and depressed socio-economic conditions. The tendency for respondents to blame the mother for her child's illness reflects in part the strong social norm that the health and care of close relatives (particularly children) is the responsibility of other close relatives (particularly parents). It is also likely that the idea that the mother is to blame for her child's illness has been conveyed over the years by white nursing and medical staff, and reinforced by the practice of sending infants to hospital (often without their mothers) for 'fattening up'. Young mothers at Yirrkala are often caught in the double bind of being unable to prevent recurrent illnesses in their children, however diligently they care for them, and yet apparently believing these illnesses are their fault.

The symptoms of influenza (or a heavy cold) and the (generally unrecognised) description of a bleeding peptic ulcer were mostly attributed to 'natural' causes. About one-quarter of the respondents attributed pneumonia to sorcery (primarily *galka*). One-third viewed psychiatric illness (insanity) as either the result of sorcery (particularly *galka* and *nyira*) or of encounters with spirits (*ngänuk* or *mokuy*). Approximately one-half of the respondents attributed a sudden and fatal heart attack to sorcery (primarily to *galka* or *manggimanggi*). Almost one-third said nephritis (or cystitis) was caused by sorcery (specifically by *burrpuy* or *barrakbarrak*). One third attributed leprosy to sorcery (most often *burrpuy* or *barrakbarrak*) or to transgression of sacred laws (particularly walking in a dangerous

---

1. It would perhaps be more precise to designate this category 'not social or spiritual'. My use of the labels 'social or spiritual' and 'natural' corresponds closely to Foster's (1976:775) distinction between 'personalistic' causes ('due to the *active, purposeful intervention of an agent*') and 'naturalistic' causes (which are impersonal and due to '*natural forces or conditions*').

Table 1: Causes Suggested for Hypothetical Illnesses

Symptom set	Social or spiritual	Natural	Either	No response/ don't know
1. Pneumonia	10	24	3	6
2. Infant diarrhoea/ subnutrition/ dehydration	0	40	0	3
3. Psychiatric illness[1]	15	14	3	11
4. Fatal heart attack	19	20	3	1
5. Nephritis/cystitis	12	18	5	8
6. Peptic ulcer	5	29	1	8
7. Cold/influenza	3	29	1	10
8. Leprosy	15	12	1	15
9. Otitis media in a child	0	35	0	8

N = 43
[1] The term used to describe the hypothetical patient's condition was *bawa'mirri*, which is a general term meaning 'insane' or 'crazy', and is applied to specific people at Yirrkala who are receiving (intermittent) psychiatric treatment.

Table 2: Suggested Treatments for Hypothetical Illnesses

Symptom set	Yolngu	Western	Either	Other[1]	No response/ Don't know
1. Pneumonia	7	19	6	4	7
2. Infant diarrhoea/ subnutrition/ dehydration	8	28	4	2	1
3. Psychiatric illness	5	12	1	7	18
4. Fatal heart attack	-	-	-	-	-
5. Nephritis/cystitis	3	20	6	7	7
6. Peptic ulcer	3	24	3	5	8
7. Cold/influenza	7	19	2	6	9
8. Leprosy	2	20	4	2	15
9. Otitis media in a child	4	24	2	6	7

N = 43

[1] The category 'other' includes courses of action other than Western medical treatment, consultation with the *marrnggitj* and the use of bush medicine. Responses in this category can generally be classified as preventive behaviour, self-help or inaction; for instance, 'look after the baby and feed it better', 'don't sleep around', 'lie down or sit quietly', 'eat good food', 'pray to God', 'do nothing', 'don't smoke', 'get fresh bush food for the patient'.

area or failing to observe taboos associated with shedding blood in the Gunapipi ceremony).

Regardless of the suspected cause of the illness respondents gave, the majority in every case considered Western medicine (health centre or hospital) the most appropriate source of treatment and relief. As one might expect, the respondents who are more than 30 years old nominated Western treatments consistently (but not statistically significantly) less often than the under 30 respondents. Opinions about cause show quite a different pattern. Although the majority of the respondents said the illnesses indicated were 'just a sickness', or caused by 'natural' factors, there was no significant difference between old and young in the frequency with which social or spiritual causes were cited. The only illness for which a significant difference ($p < 0.01$ $\chi^2 = 5.76$) exists between older (over 30) and younger (under 30) respondents is pneumonia. Contrary to expectations, in this case the under thirties cited sorcery as the cause more often than the over thirties. In general the results are in keeping with other observations that a social or spiritual cause is usually not sought until an illness is serious or the patient has died. The causes of the great majority of illnesses are either ignored or said to be the result of 'natural' causes.

In summary, although there is considerable variation between the responses to the different illnesses, the figures suggest overall that, while opinions about treatment and, with them, medical behaviour have changed considerably over the past 50 or so years, beliefs about cause have been less affected. It is also apparent from a comparison of the descriptions given in Chapters 2 and 3 of sorcery and of the making and powers of the *marrnggitj* with those recorded by Thomson (1961), Warner (1958) and Webb (1936, n.d.), that the content of these beliefs has changed little.

While these broad conclusions give some indication of the nature of change, or lack of change, in the Yolngu medical system, they conceal a wide range of variation in individual convictions and attitudes. In particular they leave unanswered the general question of the way in which individuals adapt intellectually to the experiences and ideas which domination by white Australian society has brought. If, as the survey indicates, young and old continue to espouse social and spiritual explanations with much the same frequency, how do the young assimilate (if at all) the explanations of illness given at school? How do the health workers reconcile the Yolngu sociomedical theory and Western medical theory? How do community members reconcile the conviction that almost all deaths are caused by sorcery with the observation that a number of men, but only those who were chronic drinkers, have died while quite young or middle-aged? These issues are the subject of the remainder of this chapter.

Explanation and Synthesis

Non-Aborigines who have come to north-east Arnhem Land as staff members at Yirrkala (missionaries, teachers, medical staff and so on) and as researchers, visitors or miners, have, wittingly and unwittingly, been the source of a wide range of new ideas for the Yolngu. For convenience, these are divided into knowledge taught in white Australian institutions and knowledge gained by personal experience.

Formal Learning

All people of Yirrkala receive formal and informal instruction throughout their lives from parents and elders. They are taught by example and by word of mouth. They are expected to acquire as they grow and mature the sacred and secular knowledge which is a prerequisite for maturity and, later in life, authority in the society. The children who have grown up since the mission school was formally established in the mid-1950s, however, have been exposed to the knowledge (or perhaps teaching) of Western society. Almost all of those who have completed primary school are under 30 (a very few under 40) years of age. Some of the graduates of the primary school, such as the health workers, have taken further vocational courses. A small number have received between one and three years of high school education. A few (all young men) have spent time at a Bible College or other tertiary insitutions in southern Australia.

Much of the knowledge which individuals gain in the Western and the Aboriginal contexts is compatible. Knowledge from one sector does not challenge or impinge on knowledge from the other. However, when explanations or ideologies are advanced by Western trained (usually white) teachers which are inconsistent with those advanced by parents and elders, people must either ignore the contradictions and live with the cognitive dissonance, or find a satisfying synthesis. For everyone faced with conflicting views there is a problem of resolution, and the intellectual solutions people reach are diverse. It is possible, though, to discern patterns of reflection and change in community thought, particularly among certain groups. Three groups which illustrate these processes well are professed Christians, health workers and the young people in general.

All health workers, generally women in their twenties or early thirties, have been to primary school (some to post-primary school at Yirrkala), received instruction in the course of their duties and attended in-service training courses in Darwin. All with whom I spoke, both in casual conversation, during interviews and in crises, were convinced of the dangers and effects of sorcery. On many occasions they have undertaken to explain to a doctor or nursing sister that a patient's illness is not ordinary but caused by sorcery. Several times women with some medical training (that is, who were or had been health workers) explained to me that it is possible to distinguish between these two types of illness on the basis of presenting symptoms. According to one:

> When I was working at the hospital and someone came in and said she had a headache, was short of breath and had blood in her phlegm, I'd check the temperature, pulse, blood pressure and respiration. If it's *galka* or *nyira* it doesn't show. It's all perfectly normal. I'd just give her an aspro and tell her to go home and lie down in the shade. In the evening she would die.

This woman went on to describe a case history to illustrate the course which an illness due to sorcery often takes:

> When I was working in the hospital a young boy died. He was my age and very intelligent. He was going to Bible College in Brisbane. One night, as he walked across the oval, a snake bit him. He came to the hospital and I got the sister. We put him on the bed and he was unconscious. His body was stiff and he was only breathing a little. We got an injection but it was hard because we didn't know what sort of snake it was. He said black and white, but there's no such snake around here. He was sent next morning to Darwin Hospital but the following day we were told that he had died. When a person dies that quickly – a young person – in the European way I would think of heart attack. But that way of dying is *galka* [that is, a snake sent by a *galka*].

Another health worker told me in conversation that she did not believe in *mokuy*. Missionaries, she said, do not believe in them and neither does she. In fact, she would sleep at the cemetery where a funeral ceremony was in progress to prove it. I said one missionary on Elcho Island had told me he did believe in evil spirits. 'That's different', she replied, 'there's lots of *galka*, *nyira*, and *manggimanggi* there.' She continued,

> Someone pointed the bone at me last year and I nearly died. I was very sick. I was febrile and could see *mokuy* and people in front of my eyes. They took me to

hospital and operated and found I had appendicitis. It
was due to *manggimanggi*. I wasn't afraid, though,
because I was praying. The next day [the adult male
marrnggitj] came to the hospital, found the *manggimanggi*
and took it out. The operation was very successful.
They told me I was swearing at the nurses when I woke
up! Dad knows who did it. The man lives at Yirrkala.
But Dad won't do anything in the legal way
[implication: he will arrange punishment by sorcery].

As with other community members, the health workers look critically at all the relevant circumstances when trying to find out the cause of an illness or death. When Mandjinga became ill, a health worker told me she doubted the cause was *galka*, since the patient had been hit by her husband the day before. On the other hand, when a man in his fifties died unexpectedly near his home two years later, the same woman said quite definitely that he had been killed in 'the secret way' since his death was so sudden.

For some young and older people the sternest challenge to traditional explanations of illness and death comes not from Western medicine but from church teaching. The first missionaries at Yirrkala advocated a syncretic approach to proselytisation, but more recent teaching and preaching has tended to be evangelical. It has emphasised the need for those who wish to be affiliated with the church to discard old beliefs and make a commitment to a fundamentalist interpretation of Christian ideology.

Although attendance at church by Aboriginal worshippers is sparse, several of the most influential young and older people are either active in the youth fellowship or are themselves lay preachers. A small number of young men have attended Bible College in Brisbane. One of these men with whom I spoke had clearly given considerable thought to the problems of serious illness and death.[2] He said that, while some illnesses stem from such causes as trouble over women and sacred matters, they are the result, not of sorcery, but of the individual's emotional state. They have, in his opinion, a psychosomatic origin. When I described to him the symptoms of pneumonia and asked for his opinion about the cause, he replied:

> In a situation like that in a place like this some people
> would think it was his original sickness or it's from *galka*
> or *manggimanggi*. From my point of view I'd say it's his

2. This young man was the only respondent who immediately recognised the description of a bleeding peptic ulcer. He said that he had had similar symptoms when he was studying extremely hard and worrying about his examinations at college. He was so sick that he had to be hospitalised.

own sickness. He thinks and thinks and talks a lot and too many things are in his mind – good and bad. And so he thinks too long and gets sick and gets worse. This is talking from a psychological point of view . . . Probably you'll come across old people who'll say *manggimanggi* because his blood's coming up and he can't breathe well. For myself it's *mari* [fighting or trouble] or *maḏayin* [sacred] things he's concerned and worried about – the most important things in his life. He gets emotional and upset and gets sick in his spirit and mind and it involves his body.

I've talked to a lot of young people in youth fellowship. I put myself in a situation where Christ is there and backing me up and it's easier for me. A person who doesn't believe in Christ ends up in situations he can't cope with. Throughout the world this is so.

When asked if he had ever been attacked by sorcery, this young man said he had not, nor had he ever seen anyone using *galka*. However he does 'get a bit scared' if someone tells him about it. This man was one of several people (of a wide range of ages) who cited worry as a cause of illness. On one occasion another young man said, immediately after his mother's death, that there were 'stories going around' (that is, about sorcery) but he himself considered that her sickness (a chronic condition) was to blame. On another occasion he obliquely suggested that his mother's death may also have been a result of worry about an illicit liaison between one of her daughters and a married man which was causing a lot of ill-feeling. At the same time the father of the married man was ill. Another community leader told me that, in his opinion, the father was worried about his son's relationship with the girl and that this had caused his illness. As these instances suggest, many community members accept that anxiety may cause or exacerbate an illness.

For young people, as others, the conviction on one occasion that an illness is due to worry does not preclude a suspicion of sorcery on another. One young man (p. 110) who had been educated at Bible College and elsewhere after leaving school, asked, when the possibility of an autopsy for a woman who had died was being discussed, whether or not the doctor would be able to see the face of her killer (sorcerer) when they opened her up. Nevertheless, many of these men have (or say they have) reassessed much of what they have learned while growing up at Yirrkala in the light of later education and experience and in view of a felt obligation to bear witness to their Christian beliefs.

An older lay preacher's statement about the aetiology of mental illness was similar to that of the young man above:

Sometimes I heard a story from my mother and father
about people who were *bawa* [insane] because of
magic – like crayfish magic from the Wessel Islands. Still I
don't understand myself about *bawa'mirri* because the Bible
tells us his head is sinful and his heart is in darkness. This is
only the Christian way, but in the *Yolngu* way it was as I
said . . .

This man, who had suffered from a long and chronic illness, hypothesised that perhaps it had resulted from his entering a dangerous area (*Woku̱ti* or *Yingapungapu*).

For some individuals, adhering to Christian teaching and traditional doctrine does not constitute a problem: each is espoused when appropriate. One of the men who spent many hours explaining to me the various modes of sorcery and healing was very active in church affairs, a consistent church attender and a declared Christian. For others, the idea that the two are incompatible can be very troubling. One woman related how, when the female *marrnggitj* had treated her young son for a painful foot, her husband 'was a little worried because he was still a Christian man working for the church'. She reassured him: 'It doesn't matter, because I think our Lord gave her that power. She might make him better through the Lord . . . like a doctor or nurse'. This woman recalled that, when her husband saw the *marrnggitj* draw a stone from their son's foot, he was convinced of the abilities of the *marrnggitj*. A man from Elcho Island, also a professed Christian, reported a similar experience in which he came to believe in the powers of the female *marrnggitj* (p.68). The father of the child *marrnggitj* similarly stated that he is a Christian and believes that Christ has chosen his son as one through whom He can work miracles of healing.

In the late 1970s a Christian revival swept Arnhem Land. The revival was partly inspired by the visit to Arnhem Land of an evangelist and had pentecostal overtones. On Elcho Island in particular, where the mission staff had been divided between pentecostal and conservative beliefs since at least 1974, the revival was said by Yolngu and missionaries to have transformed the community: the boys had stopped sniffing petrol; the men were no longer drinking; the community was mobilised in good works and nightly hymn singing, and many people were being baptised. It had also, though, divided the community between those who joined and those who did not, and ill-feeling arose because the health service was said to be discriminating against people and homeland centres which had not embraced the Christian message. During my first week in Arnhem Land in 1974, spent on Elcho Island, white mission staff insisted on bringing a man who was dying at home to the hospital, locked the windows and doors and sat and prayed with him until he died. A church circular captured the convictions of staff at the time:

> Please pray for all who mourn his death, that they might be comforted and also find faith in Christ. Let us give thanks to God for the transformation that knowing Christ brought about in this man's life and for the example he set in choosing to die in a quiet prayerful atmosphere rather than in the frenzied atmosphere of the traditional Animistic ceremonial. Let us pray especially for those Christians who are being led by the Holy Spirit to re-think the relationship between Christianity and Aboriginal culture, which is so much bound up with their animistic religion.

Despite the strains in the community, the momentum of the movement brought Aborigines from all over Arnhem Land by air charters to religious rallies at Elcho Island and elsewhere. Though the revival had its roots in the mission effort it was in many senses indigenous and it was the force of Yolngu conviction that carried it forward.

At Yirrkala the impact of the revival was less dramatic. It peaked in 1980 and had waned by the end of 1981. Entire families and clans came forward to commit themselves to Christ during the crusade but all continued to observe Yolngu religious law and ceremonies. In 1981 American cassette tape recordings of testimonies of converts (in the emotive tone and accents of Southern revivals) were still circulating in the community. I was told that prayer sessions for healing had been held in the camp. One, for a woman who had cancer, lasted two days. These were not a feature of social life in late 1981 and the influence of non-Aborigines on the Yirrkala church was as strong as it had ever been.

To the extent that Christian doctrine has influenced Yolngu thought it has been selectively absorbed into the indigenous cosmology (a process which started many years ago; see Berndt 1978-9 and Chaseling 1957). People will readily articulate a synthesis of the two doctrines if asked. Two close Yolngu friends who were visiting Sydney told me disapprovingly that an acquaintance of mine had said she did not believe in the Bible. I said, 'Maybe it's not all true'. 'No!', they exclaimed, 'It *is* true. It was given to us by God', and lapsed into a grim silence. After a strained half hour one asked, 'Well, tell us this then. Who made us?' Warming to the intellectual challenge, I replied, 'I don't know, maybe the Djankawu (creator spirits of their moiety)'. They laughed. 'You're talking in the Yolngu way', and then, triumphantly: 'But *who* made the Djankawu!?'.

A third group in the community which faces problems of explanation and synthesis are others of the young – those under the age of 30 years but who are not necessarily health workers or Christians. One young man who has travelled widely in Australia and has worked for several years as a semi-skilled worker at Yirrkala and elsewhere, expressed the following opinions about *galka*:

> I've never been galkerized [sic]. I've travelled a lot in the Northern Territory and never been attacked. It's unlikely because I don't believe in it. *Galka* only attack people with a point. Like if they've stolen something *madayin* [sacred]. If a man's been through initiation . . . the elders keep an eye on him. If he does something wrong then, bang, that's the end of him. If people are attacked it's for a reason. Even *miyalk* [women] business – like the promise system and all that. In the early days, when a couple ran off together – bang – finished – sometimes publicly, sometimes by *nyira* . . . They killed them and they were both in the grave.

Another, slightly older man who had instructed me in the ways of sorcerers and *marrnggitj* said that he was convinced that the chronic chest conditions and coughs of people at Yirrkala were due to heavy smoking. When an elderly man died at an homeland centre he maintained that the cause was lung cancer. He had, he said, seen a film about a man who had died of lung cancer because he smoked. He said that a white man had told him that it is the 'nickety' in the filter of the cigarette which causes young men to die. (He puffed on a long-stemmed pipe as he told me this, saying, 'It's very hard to stop'.)

It is evident from these examples that some individuals are endeavouring to eliminate dissonance between Western explanations of illness which they have learned and those Yolngu explanations taught to them by parents and elders.

Experience

A formal Western teaching situation is not the only way in which new information is conveyed. Many of the most incisive thinkers at Yirrkala have received very few years of Western schooling. Their knowledge stems from childhood socialisation, initiation into the ritual secrets of the society and personal experience, both of things Aboriginal and things non-Aboriginal. Several of the senior men and women have travelled within Australia and are aware of aspects of white society which are not immediately apparent at Yirrkala.

Others, in their positions as clan leaders, feel a responsibility to understand the changes wrought by contact with Western society and to come to terms with the implications of these changes for the community, particularly for the members of their own clans. The deliberations of many of these individuals are characterised by an innovative thoughtfulness.

One man, a clan and homeland centre leader, who has received little formal schooling but has travelled widely in the North and lived and worked in Darwin, says he is sceptical of explanations of illnesses in terms of sorcery. His own observations suggest to him that they may have other, identifiable, causes. When discussing the technique of *burrpuy*, he said:

> I've heard about this but I don't believe. I haven't seen it with my eyes. If I saw this happen to a person's clothes and he started to die, I could say yes or no. We burn septic tanks and burn things [clothes] in the incinerator but nothing happens.[3]

In response to my question about the cause of the symptoms of nephritis and cystitis he replied:

> It's very hard to answer this. I'm just guessing. It might be someone roasting his patch [of urine] in the fire. That's the thinking by Aborigines. Or someone putting a needle in the wet patch. What I think myself is that the part the drink goes into [bladder] must be rotten. Something like a motorcar. When all is connected and strong it goes well. When something is loose it goes badly. Because of too much dancing or fighting with a stick, the blood doesn't come out but goes down into the *dholng* [urogenital region] and goes hard there and makes it bad by blocking or something. That's what I've noticed. Especially in the old people.
>
> I look at trees and fish. When they're young they're strong. When a man or woman starts to go back, go low down and get weaker and weaker, some of the [blood vessels] are cut off or broken and the person feels sick because they're ready to die. Like a tree when it's burnt with the sun and not much water – it's ready to die . . .

---

3. Sorcery is not usually described as a mechanical act as this statement implies. Normally the intent of the sorcerer is as important as the technique itself. He must sing a known spell or will illness upon his victim at the same time as he, for instance, burns his victim's clothes or excreta.

One day I got a dugong with a spear and the next week I
found him alive. That time I understood everything that
happens in Yolngu. After I speared him again I saw that
there was a rottenness spreading from the old spear marks
all through his body and into the *dholng*. Outside,
everything can be good – inside, you don't know.

In recent years there has been a succession of severe illnesses, usually among related groups of people. These episodes have invariably been marked by acute symptoms and, when these abate, weeks or even months of poor health. The severest symptoms are those which, under other circumstances, would be attributed by many people to sorcery. Everyone agrees, however, that the illness is due to fish poisoning.[4] No one, they say, had ever become ill after eating fish caught in the area before the mining company started operations. Several women pointed out that, until ore processing commenced at the plant in 1972, it was completely safe to eat fish caught in the waters off Yirrkala and Nhulunbuy.[5]

An elderly clan leader said that he believes the poisoning has resulted from the emptying of effluent from the plant, caustic waste ponds, sewerage ponds, garbage dump and town into the sea and from the polluting of the air above the sea with smoke and fumes. A variation of this explanation is given as the reason for the appearance of poison fish by many other community members, all of whom have noted its correlation with the commencement of operations at the mine. One young woman asked me whether I could procure medicine for her to administer if anyone at her island homeland centre was poisoned. Ever alert for an ethnographic opportunity I asked whether there were any herbal medicines on the island which could be used instead. She cast me a withering look and said that this

---

4. According to a medical officer formerly stationed in north-east Arnhem Land (Quinn 1973:1), these cases of fish poisoning have been diagnosed as ciguatera. Although well known in Queensland, ciguatera had not (before its appearance in this area) been described in the Northern Territory. Ciguatera generally refers to poisoning from scale fish. Symptoms appear within a few hours of eating affected fish, usually with a feeling of lassitude and aching in the joints. This is frequently followed by gastro-intestinal symptoms of vomiting, diarrhoea and abdominal cramps. More specific symptoms are tingling or numbness about the lips, hands or feet and bizarre alterations of sensation, particularly the reversal of temperature association.

5. A former medical officer observed that there were 3000 construction workers living and fishing in the area from 1969-72, but that the first case of fish poisoning did not occur until December 1972. (The plant opened in May 1972.) In June and July of 1975 alone there were 23 recorded cases of fish poisoning among Yirrkala residents.

is a 'Balanda (white) sickness' caused by pollution from the plant and therefore needs 'Balanda medicine'.

The incidence of fish poisoning is not the only consequence of the mining venture which troubles the community. As discussed in Chapter 1, the presence of Nhulunbuy hotel has caused considerable social disruption. It has also posed a number of vexing questions and challenges to the traditional world view with which relatives of chronic drinkers and community leaders have recently had to grapple. These questions arose following the unexpected deaths of three men who had frequented the hotel regularly for several years.

In 1974, the first, a middle-aged man who was known as a heavy drinker, died in Nhulunbuy Hospital. He was the father of several children. His doctors told his family he died of pneumonia and a stroke. In 1975 another middle-aged man, also a regular drinker, died at Nhulunbuy Hospital. In 1976 another, somewhat younger family man died, reportedly of pneumonia. He also drank heavily. In the years which followed, fights, road accidents and illnesses linked with drink claimed other victims. Following these deaths, grieving relatives of the men spoke, and clearly thought, often about their causes.

First death

Many people thought the death of the man who died in 1974 was the work of *galka*. The adult male *marrnggitj* saw and identified the images of two men from elsewhere on the corners of one of his *milirrk* when he held it against the body of the dying man. Others were not convinced by this explanation. One man said that 'poison', perhaps battery acid, had been put in his drink at the hotel by people from elsewhere. Others said aspirin was used as the 'poison'. One man believed he had been killed for trespassing with his wife in a sacred place. Several other people said they believed he had been killed by the alcohol. One young woman, for instance, told me that a missionary at Yirrkala had had a dream that twelve young men would die from the effects of consuming alcohol. One had already died (the man in question), leaving just eleven more. Her brother, she said, had been frightened by this dream for he also drank a lot. Several people recalled that the visiting psychiatrist from Darwin and a former director of medical services in north-east Arnhem Land had told community members previously that if this man and others who were drinking heavily did not stop they would not survive more than one or two years. The partial fulfilment of this prophecy was taken by many people to be convincing evidence of the accuracy of the doctor's predictions.

The problem of deciding which of the current explanations was the most plausible was particularly worrying and pressing for those most closely related to the deceased. If the use of sorcery could be established, action (possibly retaliation) would be called for. At least one accusation of sorcery was levelled publicly at the members of another Yirrkala clan during the mortuary rites for the dead man.

A prominent clan leader strongly suspected that the dead man's long sojourns at the hotel were implicated in his death. He said he considered that men from Yirrkala who drank at the hotel were exposed to the malicious magic worked by men from other places, such as Groote Eylandt and Maningrida, who also drank there. Soon after the man died this senior man (referred to here as the clan leader or leader) took time from a heavy load of administrative, political, ceremonial and other official duties to teach me the various causes of death. He explained:

> I'm worried about our people who have died here before and about what's happening. Some are young. Some are small. Some are strong and middle-aged. I'm telling these dangerous laws [ways of performing sorcery] because many people have died from unknown causes. That's why I'm putting them in a book. Nobody, no doctors or nurses, have been taught this way before. These are new things we'd like to teach to help European and Aboriginal people – our people. This is for people who are interested in these things. So many people talk if a person dies. If it's a young or a middle-aged man we think straight away about these dangerous laws.

Second death

In 1975, shortly after the clan leader had explained the techniques of sorcery and dangers of certain areas to me, his own brother died suddenly in hospital. He was the second of the middle-aged drinkers to die. For a community still mourning the loss of a kinsman some nine months earlier, this death was appalling. For the clan leader it was tragic confirmation of his fears for the drinkers of the community. The members of the dead man's family and allied clans were deeply grieved and angered and many, again, suspected sorcery.

After the mortuary ceremonies ended and his brother was buried, the clan leader sent open letters to the leaders of twenty-three Aboriginal communities in northern and central Australia and to doctors working among Aboriginal people in the North. In the first, that to other communities, the leader proclaimed the peaceable intentions of Yirrkala people, and asked what, if anything, they knew about sorcery or objects of sorcery which might be implicated in his brother's death:

> *Letter to Aboriginal Councils in the Northern Territory*
> Yirrkala via Darwin
>
> Dear Friends, Representatives from Every Clan Living in Towns or on Aboriginal Reserves:
>
> I am writing to you on behalf of my people in Arnhem Land about what you can do to help me about some thoughts I have. I live in Yirrkala mission on the Gove Peninsula in the Northern Territory. I have been establishing outstations in different areas since 1971 and we have been doing good work and getting help from the government and from our staff. The work is going all right because we want our land to be used for work, things like craft. Our clan hasn't done any special things; we have just helped many people in every clan who are living in the outstations or in the mission. Our school will be in Yirrkala or in Nhulunbuy, and this school will be helping us with teaching the children in the outstations.
>
> We don't know much about the Aboriginal rules for causing sickness and death because we have been living in one place; we didn't move from place to place or go to your town. I'd like to tell you some thoughts and ask you to help my community in the outstations, because two people from the outstations have died, one last year and one this year. And this makes us worry and wonder. I'd like to ask you how many Yirrkala people or Elcho and Milingimbi people have gone to visit your people in your town and learned about something that causes death. We have our own madayin, singing and sacred dreaming in our country. We didn't take yours. Can you tell me how many people have got from you bone pointer and things and mangimangi, lawayin and singing that can cause a person's death?
>
> We lost my brother, who was still a young man and strong, and we just wonder like that and whether you are going to help me on this. That's why I write you about this, on settlements or missions, to let me know. We don't want to fight or make trouble with other people; we just only want to know how many people in Arnhem Land have dangerous things, how many people know galka rules and a sneaking person will be coming in the night and kill the person – he will live a short time and then he will die. That's what happened to my brother, and I can't trust drinking

liquor but I can trust another way around from yulngu [sic] rules that might do it – or murder my brother just for fun, no reason.

My name is ——, I represent the —— tribes, my clan is —— and my country is ——. And all my people are very sad because we lost our brother badly.

That's why I write to you, friends, because I would like to know and find out who are the people who don't like us, which people, which station, which settlement. We are not really important people for the money side, we only get help from the government. We ask the government for money for our land. That's how we have got money and how we are building houses and schools for the outstations. We don't like to harm people, we don't like to destroy people; we like to be kind to and help people, make good relationship with one another. We never have known how to use your things – your singing, your dangerous things; we only know how to throw spears, how to fight in the outside, not in the sneaking way. We can't use bone pointing, singing, lightning, big rain, storms, or drawing people on the sacred place to destroy them, and we haven't got any wives from your country.

So we would like to know from every councillor in all that area – it must be talked over and you must find out for me and let me know, because I am your friend, my brother and my father are your friends – if there is something wrong in your country. If there is something in your country, I will be talking from here and I will help you. I will write to you again if I lose my people. Now we are missing my brother; he was a very young man and wasn't sick for a long time. He just suddenly died. His sickness started Friday night and he died at 6 o'clock Saturday night in Nhulunbuy Hospital. I noticed that sickness two ways: maybe that sickness was caused by liquor because he drank a lot, or maybe someone murdered him in yulngu way. This is only my guessing, my friends, and I would only like to know. Because Yirrkala people have not learned to use things from your country that would make it become a bad place, destroy many of us. I want you to tell me so I can help my brothers who are still alive. I didn't put the blame through your people; I just want help from your council. You must call your own meeting and talk about what I am saying in this letter.

My märi, my real grandfather, belonged to Yirrkala and is [name of clan]. And my mother side is [name of clan]. And that is all that I know: these two people's sacred things, big rules, big laws. There could be someone against us some way that we don't know. I am the only person who is very strong in the Northern Territory, who is helping all the Aboriginal people in the outstations, or even in this town, in Arnhem Land, or even the people in the Centre. Why do people want to destroy my people, my clan? If someone would do bad things for us, we will still be working helping people. I don't want to give it away because I like to work with the community, no matter what clan you are, what language you have, because we are still human beings, and this is my thinking. That is why I push through the government very hard to make your country free so you don't worry about it now. You are free now, not to worry so much like you did before. I can't hate your people, because your people are just the same like me, as the yulngu people, Aboriginal. We are not unkind or unfriendly to your people. We are thinking your people are as the yulngu. We should be working together, not sending my people to kill or murder in the mission or settlement. That is bad. We don't want to lose our people, Aboriginal people, in the future. We should be growing up people, more population, like they do in other countries. Will you ask you own tribes, your people, who did this, who did that, which people have hated us, from which country? We don't know the sneaking rules, how you kill people . . . sometimes you send an enemy (that's what we call galka, the sneaking people in the night). Sometimes you send a buffalo – it becomes a buffalo first, then changes into a human being. There are many buffalo here and birds that make us frightened in the night. Sometimes we think they are people, sometimes we think they are animals (or reptiles) to eat. Some people use these rules in Arnhem Land maybe – this is only my guessing. I write to you because we have not got enough people here now since so many died last year and are continuing to die this year — some in Elcho Island, some in Milingimbi, some in Yirrkala, some in Groote Eylandt – some people have died who were very strong people, a lot of young men and women. Why is this, I wonder? It could be something, some sort of things that somebody here has been using from your people. How did they get it? Did they buy it from you? Or did you just give a present to them to destroy people by their friends or relatives?

The thing that is in my mind I think about one way only: people are people who are living in the world today; only the balanda people are strange and that we need liquor from them. Pubs are all around Australia now, and this is the thing that will destroy us. You must keep your things that are dangerous things in your country because your troubles are there, you must not sell them to Arnhem Land people or give them away. If people come to your country and ask for your things to destroy people in our country, you will say 'No', please. Don't sell them, don't give them to our people. If our people will take those things back to our country, they will use them to kill our people secretly. That's why we are missing our people now. I'd like the answer from your council, and that will be a great help for my people. We don't like to be sad or annoyed if you tell us.

I must close this little note.

               Yours sincerely
               [Signature]

In the second letter, the leader acknowledged, as suggested by a trusted doctor some time before, that the death could have been due to alcohol. However, he expressed some reservations about this hypothesis since 'so many people, Aboriginal people, love to drink and they haven't died like that, very quickly'.

Letter to Doctors Working with Aboriginal People in Northern Australia

                                 Yirrkala via Darwin

Dear Doctors in Arnhem Land in the Northern Territory Who are Working Amongst the Aboriginal People:

You remember me. I am writing to you on behalf of my people in Yirrkala town and in the outstations. I need help from you people about my brother who died in Nhulunbuy Hospital: he died very quickly; what was happening?

I known the full story from Dr [Raven] about his sickness from last year to this year, and that man was finished dead. How we were sad and how we worry because the doctor hasn't told us the full story like Dr [Raven] was telling us: 'He's got a very bad head'. Can you tell me the full story, what was happening to him before he died? Was anything caused by the yulngu way of doing things that you didn't know? Any damage that you saw inside his lungs or heart that you know but didn't tell us?

Our rules are very difficult for all the doctors in Australia to understand, and that's why I'm working with some anthropologists like Jan Reid – she was working with me for quite a while about Aboriginal rules for murdering each other (and freely, instead of policemen coming and picking up people). We can't spear somebody now; so some people just use another way, yulngu rules: pointing people dead, singing people making them sick, poisoning people (yulngu poison, not balanda poison) to kill them. There are some new tricks that I know, like they are using liquor and battery water. Yes, I think you do not understand this, doctors, some sort of tricks to kill persons, murder by this way.

I'd like to ask you some questions: did you find any damage in my brother's body, inside or outside? Why I ask you this is because I know only that he was sick for quite a while because he didn't stop drinking. But there are so many people who drink the same way my brother had been drinking and getting drunk. My brother was sick no time at all; he just suddenly died in hospital. When he came back from the pub he started to be sick – that was Friday, and that sickness was gone in the morning. He was good, all right in the morning until the sun was coming up very high and very hot and then he started to get sick again. He was having a hard time breathing, he couldn't talk, his tongue was going upside down, his teeth were tight together; then there was white stuff like soap bubbles coming out of his mouth; and his eyes stayed in one position, not moving, before he went to Nhulunbuy hospital. Then we took that man to [the doctor on duty] and [he] was doing good work. He tried to make my brother live and he couldn't. He tried and tried and then he stopped (my brother) his breathing straightaway. That was the first one. Then my brother was still because his heart stopped, it wasn't working. Then the doctor gave him an injection. I was there, watching over him and what he was doing, giving him medicine to help him breathe again. He waited for half an hour, then he was breathing again. He couldn't talk, his tongue couldn't move, and he was thinking only of one bunggul [sacred dance]: he tried to tell me something as he passed over; then three times he bit his wrist at the base of his thumb. Then he said – just only little bits of words inside his mouth – 'Where's -----?' He was asking for -----; he wanted to see him. But ---- was not there; another member of his family was there, his brother. Then he finished his breathing and died straightaway. Then the doctor tried and tried to get that person alive again, but he couldn't. Then the doctor told me like this: 'He's all right. See what we did? Our best'. But that wasn't a true story. Then after that he sent another doctor, a lady doctor, with a little torch, and she tried and tried with injections. Then [the doctor] told me not a true story: he should have told me, 'Your brother is dead'. And I want to know why he told me an untrue story;

he should have told me a true story, because he's a doctor, he knows all about it. Why did he hide it from me? I think the doctor knew already that my brother was dead.

Yes, I can trust one doctor, like Dr [Raven] to tell us the whole story. I would like to know all the story about my brother, the doctors to tell me what was happening. How much do you doctors know about this sickness? I'd like to ask some questions. Did his brain get bad? Is that the true story? Did he drink a lot? Was his blood all gone? What was the matter with him? Something cause him to worry, make him die? Any problems in the camp that you know about? Or just only drink? I don't think I believe drink a lot because so many people, Aboriginal people, love to drink and they haven't died like that, very quickly.

Well, doctors, I want to know from you the full story; and I want to ask Dr [Raven] to come back to Yirrkala just for a little while and answer what's happened to my brother, because I believe his story from last year when my brother nearly shot himself with the .22. That's what will help me, and also help my people, too, Dr [Raven]. I write to you because I know the story from you last year, and that is the story I explained to my people from [my outstation] (some of them are still here; they haven't all gone back yet). I can trust your promise from last year to this year because you told us that if he drinks a lot he will be dead. And that's the story that I passed through the wireless to the outstations, to Elcho Island, to Milingimbi, so those people won't want to fight – because I knew the story from Dr [Raven] – I just called the people to come for manikay and bunggul. I told them that, and said, 'Then you will be going back'.

Yes, Dr [Raven], I don't want something to come like blaming from the Aboriginal people here. They think someone was murdering through Aboriginal rules. That's why I want to help my people again when I receive your full story. There's a bit of fuss about it; they want to stir up trouble, want to blame the other tribes, but I don't want that. That's why I write to you to ask for the full story: I want to send it back to my people at [my] outstation . . . Yes, you know me, Dr [Raven], very well, and I know you very well, and that's why I ask you for the full story. I will be here all the time until the next Dhanbul Association election comes. I know myself very well that my brother was a sick man. When he was at [our outstation] he couldn't work very well: he would work for one minute, then sit down. He couldn't carry heavy things (like the posts we were digging holes for). He was too fussy in the evenings, then I had to go and settle him down – his head was going round and round.

I must close this letter, doctors, and I look forward to hearing from you.

> Yours sincerely,
> [Signature]

Following the dissemination of these letters the leader did, as he intended, send a message to the homeland centres that alcohol was the cause of death. He felt that it was his responsibility as a clan leader to quash talk of revenge and open hostilities. This tactic was at least partially effective for a wife of the dead man's father's brother (that is, a wife of the deceased's classificatory father) later told me:

> If someone dies very quickly, they only think about *galka*. They don't think about other sickness. For [the clan leader's brother] we all know about alcohol. His brother [the clan leader] explained to us that it was not from *galka* or other people from Elcho Island. It was only alcohol. He explained to all the relatives because the doctor had told him about what had happened and we all believed.

The clan leader's search for the true story is typical of the critical approach of many Yolngu to problematic situations. The leader recognises that the hotel has had a disruptive influence on Yirrkala, as do many non-Aborigines. He is, however, not convinced by the explanation that it is alcohol *per se* that has caused the illnesses and deaths of the drinkers. For him alcohol is only half an explanation. Intellectually and emotionally he finds sorcery the only satisfying explanation for these tragedies.

As far as I know the leader did not receive any replies from Aboriginal Councils. But the letter to the doctors provoked an interesting response. The leader received two replies, one from the doctor who attended his brother just before he died, and one from his trusted friend, Dr Raven, who had previously worked in the region but had transferred to another area. The attending doctor, perhaps upset by the suggestions of bad faith contained in the leader's letter, replied curtly:

> Dear Sir,
> ... As far as I am concerned I have never lied or intended to lie to you, or anyone for that matter. Your brother has been a heavy drinker and has been sick for quite some time. You yourself mentioned it in your letter. I cannot answer your

question why lots of people like to drink and not all die very quickly. There are so many things that could contribute to the drinking that could cause sudden acute illness.

You are aware that your brother was very sick when he was admitted to Gove Hospital on [date], and suddenly he had a cardiac arrest (heart stopped) but I was able to revive him. He later had another arrest and that was the time [the other doctor] attended to him, but unfortunately he did not survive the 2nd episode.

I have told, and I would like to tell you again in case you have forgotten that your brother had a heart attack and that was confirmed at the post mortem examination. He had a myocardial infarction and his liver had been affected adversely by alcohol. It showed fatty degeneration. His brain was normal.

In short, he died of heart attacks and bad liver.

                    Respectfully yours,
                    [Signature]

Dr [Raven's] reply reflected the helplessness Westerners who subscribe to no ultimate truths feel when faced with heartfelt ultimate questions. He knew that the leader was not going to receive answers of the order he wanted and was at pains to explain why:

Dear [name of clan leader],

. . . I remember you talking with me last year about the problems of aboriginal sickness and death.

. . . I can also remember your brother very well and how worried I was about him. I understand why you are now worried. Why did he die while other people drink and don't die? This is the same question people [here] ask me when their young people die. It seems that Aboriginal people everywhere are asking the same question. They are all worried about poisons and killers.

It seems to me that your people want to make sure that young people who die have not been killed (either our way or your yolngu way). In our culture we have a special lawman called a *coroner* whose job it is to find out the truth when people are worried about how someone has died. His job is to find out the truth and stop crooked stories about people. *The problem is that your people ask different questions to what my people ask, so that my people cannot understand why you are worried about things that do not worry us.* This is why the coroner is not called in for many of the deaths that worry your people – our people do not see any need, and your people have not enough power to make him come.

I shall try to explain with a story that my people and your

people can understand. Suppose a crocodile catches and eats a young man. Unless someone threw the young man into the sea, people in my culture would not ask any more questions. My people would never ask questions that your people might ask and that many people in Africa and other countries would ask:

– Why did the crocodile eat this man and not his friend?

If someone asked my people this question, they would just say 'bad luck' or 'It was the will of God', and would then forget about it. But many other people in the world might think that the man or his tribe did some wrong and the crocodile was sent to punish them or that some other tribe could control the crocodile so as to kill this man. *Please understand that our people would never ask these questions, so they cannot understand why you ask them or why you are so worried about them.*

I can see why you ask them, but I also cannot answer them. I cannot tell you why the crocodile ate this man and not his brother. I cannot tell you why drink killed your brother and not some other man . . .

Yours sincerely,
[Signature]

Third death

The death of the third of the heavy drinkers in 1976 also caused great grief and anger. Not only was he a husband and father but he was an eldest son and, had he lived, he would have succeeded his father as head of his clan. In 1974, more than a year before his death, the clan of the dead man had established a homeland centre south of Yirrkala close to one of the most sacred sites of the Yirritja moiety. Although he was in his fifties, the head of the clan had not been in the area since he was a child. Nevertheless, his father had taught him each feature of the land, its history and mythology and he had long wanted to go home. The clan head and his family were delighted to be living on their own territory. Their joy was unbounded and their health, by their own report, rapidly improved. The clan head attributed this in part to the excellent diet and in part to the supernatural power inherent in the area. Because of its Dreaming associations the billabong, he said, is a 'clever' place ('like a *marrnggitj*') and washing in the billabong confers good health.

For all this, the head's classificatory daughter was concerned, for their camp was not far from a sacred and dangerous area. She said she was 'worried about what will happen if he [the head, her classificatory father] passes away, because he knows everything. His children haven't learned which part is good and which is dangerous . . . If people go into [the dangerous area] they'll break their arms and legs and the strength will go from them'.

Her fears were confirmed when the infant son of the head's daughter became ill. This was the only illness which had occurred in the eight months they had lived at the homeland centre. The head thought this illness was due to the fact that the child's mother had absentmindedly scratched her ringworm with a bone. The bone was similar to that which the female ancestral spirit associated with the dangerous area had used to hit her head while mourning in mythical times. The spirit, offended by this woman's sacrilege, had made the child sick. Such dangers are ever-present. Even the head said he was not entirely sure of the locations of all the dangerous areas near the homeland centre. When they were thinking of moving camp he proposed to camp alone for a week at the new site to make sure it was safe. If he stayed well the rest of the family would follow.

Following his grandchild's sickness, the head himself became ill. His illness occurred while he and his family were visiting Yirrkala. He told me that his head was 'bad' – it was dark inside. He seemed depressed and spoke unhappily of his son's drinking. He spoke fervently also of his wish to have the hotel closed to Aborigines and of the weakness and illness among the young. This, he explained, was due to their ignorance of the traditional law and preference for gambling and going to the hotel.

A doctor who examined this man suggested he was suffering a reaction to leaving his homeland which would probably pass. The head himself was undecided about the cause of his illness and hypothesised that, since his homeland was a *mokuy wanga* (home of spirits), the spirits may have been jealous of human beings taking up residence there and attacked him. Alternatively, he thought he might have fallen ill as the result of passing too close to a dangerous area on another clan's land on his way back to Yirrkala. It was several weeks before he seemed to have recovered from his illness.

About four months later, after I had left Yirrkala, I received a message that the head's eldest son had died. (He was, as mentioned, the third of the drinkers of the community to die within 18 months.) A little more than a month later the head's eldest daughter, the mother of several children, died suddenly and unexpectedly. She had several times spoken of her great fear of sorcery – in particular of her fear that strangers who visited Yirrkala would attempt to harm her. After his daughter's death the head resolved not to return to his homeland centre. He said it was too dangerous a place at which to live, as shown by the tragic and premature deaths of his two eldest children. In late 1976 he told me that he planned to go home but that he would move the camp to a nearby but less hazardous area. However, he never returned to live on his land and, in 1980, he collapsed and died in Yirrkala while being harrassed by his drunken sons.

Categories of Cause

It is evident that, even in the face of competing ideas and the challenging experience of Western society, Yolngu at Yirrkala continue to rely heavily on the sociomedical theory to explain illness and death. It is not, though, the exclusive source of understanding. Some explanations which do not presuppose the activation of supernatural power were described above in the discussion of the results of the questionnaire on illness-related beliefs and practices. Still others have emerged in recent times to explain unaccustomed illnesses and events.

Table 3 is a representation of the contemporary aetiological domain of the people of Yirrkala. Within this domain I classify explanations under three broad headings: social and spiritual, natural and emergent. Emergent causes are those linked to the social and epidemiological changes which have followed the coming of white Australians. Social and spiritual causes are described in Chapter 2 and other causes at the beginning of this chapter. This diagram is an observer's abstraction. It is presented not as a faithful representation of Yolngu categories, for these are shifting and each person has his or her own ideas, but as a means of summarising the changes and continuities in belief. The table includes, in general terms, all recorded causes of illness and death given by individuals during the study. Those in Category 1 consist of causes subsumed by the sociomedical theory which are characteristically invoked only when a person is very ill or has died. Category 2 consists of a set of discrete causes which are not linked by an over-arching theory and which are usually (but not always) given as explanations of illnesses and injuries which do not constitute a threat to life. Unlike the elements of the sociomedical theory, which people will describe in the abstract if asked, these causes depend on the context and are usually only mentioned in response to specific conditions.

The main causes in Category 2 are: contagion (contracting an illness – psychiatric or physical – as a result of close association with others); emotional state (such as worry, anxiety, grief, fright or jealousy, sometimes expressed as 'worrying' or 'thinking too much'); excessive exposure to the elements (such as cold, wind, rain, sun, sea, fire); food ('too much', 'not enough', 'bad'); heredity (the passing of an illness from parent to child); neglect by responsible others (neglect of a child by his or her mother, of a wife by her husband, of a sick relative by other kin); old age (and associated degenerative conditions); other (such as 'eating too much clay', 'sleeping around', 'swallowing a bone', careless handling of poisonous substances, such as the nut of the cycad palm); physical assault and injury; predation (such as snake bite, sea wasp sting,

Table 3 – The Contemporary Aetiological Domain

Category 1	Category 2	Category 3
Social and spiritual causes	Natural causes	Emergent causes
1. Sorcery (all illness attributed to sorcery is understood ultimately to be the result of social or religious offences, intergroup or intragroup conflict)
2. Transgression of laws governing sacred areas
3. Transgression of laws governing ceremonial activities and sacred objects
4. Failure to observe food restrictions
5. Breaches of social norms	1. Contagion
2. Emotional state
3. Excessive exposure to the elements
4. Food
5. Heredity
6. Neglect by responsible others
7. Old age
8. Other
9. Physical assault and injury
10. Predation
11. Pregnancy
12. Neglect of self
13. Suicide or attempted suicide
14. No attributable cause	1. Alcohol
2. Assault or mistreatment by medical or nursing staff
3. Illness defined in Western medical terms
4. Motor vehicle accident
5. Sin
6. Smoking
7. Unsanitary or unhealthy living conditions on the settlement

shark attack); pregnancy (nausea and vomiting early in pregnancy, conceiving at too young an age, conceiving too soon after last child); neglect of self (failing to take adequate care of oneself, to seek medical care when sick or to tell others of one's illness); suicide or attempted suicide (as the result of extreme grief, unhappiness or provocation, or as a strategy); no attributable cause (often expressed as 'it's just a sickness [*rerri*]').

The supposed effects on health of the weather, food, neglect by relatives, injury, predation, pregnancy and other 'natural' causes have, if not self-evident, been discussed previously. The Yolngu view of the physiological effects of contagion, emotions, heredity, old age, self-neglect and of suicide are discussed briefly below.

Contagion is only occasionally given as the cause of an illness. Several informants stated that emotional illness can be contracted by association with those who are *bawa'mirri* or can be transmitted from parent to child. Similarly, the transmission of physical illness is considered possible. One woman told me that she was afraid she would catch her husband's illness (diagnosed as pneumonia) while sleeping with him. A man expressed concern about a painful finger. He recalled shaking hands with a seriously ill man shortly before the man died and wondered whether this could have caused the pain in his finger. Another man said he was extremely worried by the delay in a funeral because, according the doctor, the dead woman had suffered from a serious sickness and should be buried with dispatch. He feared that her sickness might spread to others and that everyone in Yirrkala would die.

Emotions such as grief at the death of a relative, worry about personal, familial or ritual problems, and fear are all said to cause illness. When an elderly and much respected clan head died at Yirrkala one of his granddaughters said he had 'fainted' with grief after the deaths of three of his wives within weeks of each other, and 'died thinking of them'. When I was ill my condition was attributed by a senior man to the fright I had received when a man who was drunk burst into my house. The former child *marrnggitj* told me his mother had asked him to cease his work (particularly the use of his clairvoyant powers in relation to death) because the worry made her ill. She also begged him to bring his young son back from Elcho Island where the child was staying with his mother because her grandchild's absence made her ill. Several other people said that worry can cause emotional illness. One woman said that a wife could become *bawa'mirri* if her husband left her and she thought about him all the time.

Heredity is an accepted mode of illness transmission. It has escaped no-one's attention that some illnesses at Yirrkala run in families. Two explanations are possible: that the entire family is the target of sorcery, or that it has been passed down (by birth or contagion). Of a mother and three daughters who are *bawa'mirri* and of a man, his father, two of his sisters and a son who have a degenerative neuromuscular disease (probably a localised syndrome and as yet unidentified) people often say 'She got it from her mother', or 'He got it from his father'. (Eastwell (1976) and Reser and Eastwell (1981) give psychiatric perspective on the clustering of emotional disturbances in Arnhem Land Aboriginal families.)

Old age is usually considered sufficient cause for a death but at least a few close and grieving relatives will murmur about sorcery when an old person has died. When an elderly woman from Balnguma Road camp died, one daughter said it was the result of sorcery worked by a Top Camp clan because one of her classificatory sons had partly erased a ceremonial sand sculpture of that clan when dancing. Another daughter said the doctor had told them she was old and died of hepatitis (she hesitated), or was it cancer? She said she believed the doctor's explanation. A man of another camp was unsure: 'Perhaps heart; perhaps *galka*'. Said one health worker after her death, 'If anyone dies here it's almost always *galka* or *manggimanggi* except if that person is very old and we expect her to die'.

Neglect of self is not commonly cited as a cause of illness. Individuals are usually blamed for their own illnesses or deaths only by distant kin. One man said that a woman may have died as a result of continually hitting herself on the head while mourning her deceased brother. He also considered that this woman's brother may have died because he drank alcohol continually and neglected to take the medicine the doctor had prescribed. The chronic ill-health of an old man and highly respected clan head was attributed by his classificatory son's wife to his smoking and failing to take the medicine prescribed by the doctor.

Worry, grief, anger and anxiety may precipitate a suicide or attempted suicide. One woman said she almost threw herself under a car in Darwin when she received news of the death of a close relative at Yirrkala. A young man recalled that he had thought about killing himself when he heard of his mother's death. When I asked a health worker why a woman (who is commonly described as *bawa'mirri*) and her child were wet and covered with sand, the health worker said that the woman had tried to drown both herself and the child. Another man (thought to have been drunk at the time) cut his own throat with a razor blade (a non-fatal injury). One of the reasons given for the death of a man in the community was that he was so upset by the recent death of his infant child that he deliberately and grievously provoked two men in the knowledge (or hope) that they would retaliate and kill him. These men, it was said, assaulted this man and placed him on the road where a car hit him. (It must be noted, however, that a *galka* is commonly said to cause the death of a victim by causing him to seek out the means of his own death. The victim may provoke a fight, swim in shark- or crocodile-infested waters, allow a snake to bite him or otherwise commit a suicidal act. Thus, apparent suicide may be interpreted by Yolngu as the result of a *galka* attack.)

The third category of causes given in Table 3 consists of explanations of illness or death which have identifiably arisen in response to the changes brought by contact with non-Aborigines: alcohol (excessive drinking); assault or mistreatment by medical or nursing staff (usually 'stranger' health personnel in regional hospitals); illnesses defined in Western medical terms and probably considered non-indigenous (such as 'bad brain', 'bad heart', 'cancer', 'cold', 'fish poisoning', 'flu', 'germs', 'heart attack', 'hookworm', 'infected sore', 'leprosy (*burrpuy*)', 'malaria', 'measles', 'mumps', 'stroke', 'TB', 'VD'); motor vehicle accidents; sin; smoking pipes or cigarettes; unsanitary or unhealthy living conditions on the settlement ('camping in one place all the time', 'dirty clothes', 'dirty cups and plates', 'dirty water', 'dogs licking bowls', 'eating store food', 'flies', 'gambling', [losing money for subsistence needs and neglecting dependent kin], 'no bush [or sea] food', 'not washing [oneself]').

These three categories are not mutually exclusive. An emergent cause (Category 3) may also be a social cause (Category 1), as may such causes as 'suicide', 'physical assault' and 'predation' (Category 2). Car accidents, fights, shark attacks and snake bite, as mentioned, are often considered the means chosen by *galka* to kill their victims. Similarly, conditions which some individuals call 'heart attack', 'TB' and 'leprosy (*burrpuy*)' may also be attributed to sorcery. It should be noted that knowledge of these diagnostic labels does not necessarily imply knowledge of their medical meanings. The adult male *marrnggitj* told me that what he calls TB, a disease which the doctor (not he) could cure, is caused by a snake (*bapi*, also used to refer to hookworm) which attaches to the inner walls of a person's stomach and sucks his blood. Similarly, a senior man who expressed scepticism about the hypothesis that a man's death was caused by sorcery, said he believed the drinking had caused a 'very black lung cancer'.

The classification of causes given in Table 3 is not a classification into traditional and non-traditional. Those in Category 1 are defined by the people of Yirrkala as Yolngu in origin and effect. The causes in Category 2 may well have been influenced by Western education and medicine. It is highly likely, however, that they constituted an important source of explanations for illness before white conquest and that their importance in Yolngu thought has hitherto been underestimated. They are advanced as hypotheses by both younger and older people. The causes in Category 3 may have a conceptual basis which predates conquest. They relate, though, to innovations in lifestyle and to disruptive social changes which are relatively recent.

The existence of a large set of possible explanations gives individuals wide latitude in their deliberations about the causes of illness and death. It enables them to select critically among these options without necessarily embracing exclusively one or other category. The young man who attributed a variety of conditions to worry ('a psychological point of view') was clearly influenced by Western beliefs. He was not, however, stepping outside the accepted Yolngu causal field. He was shifting illnesses which he acknowledged most other people would attribute to sorcery from Category 1 to Category 2. In his search for a reason for his brother's death, the clan leader oscillated between Categories 1 (sorcery) and 3 (alcohol). Health workers hold that some symptoms are definitive of sorcery (1) while others are the result of ordinary sickness (2 or 3). By categorising sicknesses in this way (rather as Melanesians distinguish between 'sik nating' and 'sik bilong ples': Hamnett and Connell, 1981), they do not have to choose between rival explanations.

It is not uncommon for people to give two or more reasons for a death in quick and apparently comfortable succession. Some individuals say they have not decided between them and others that both are true but at different levels (symptomatic or aetiological, proximate or ultimate). A death, for instance, may be attributed to sorcery (Category 1) and to the neglect of the patient by his relatives (Category 2). The aunt of a boy who died explained that he had a hole in his heart like his mother and sister ('it's in the family'), *and* that he had been attacked by a sorcerer who put the 'eyes' of a Yirritja moiety serpent in his beer. A clan leader said an elderly man had died because he hit his head in his grief when his two children were lost in the bush and the blood flowed down into his heart and spoiled it. His relatives, he also said, found a pool of blood on the beach left by a *galka* who had attacked him.

Even the health workers are unperturbed by dual explanations of what ails or kills a patient. For instance, when a young man was found dead near the hotel, apparently from a blow to the head, and a community meeting was called to discuss the death, the health workers addressed the meeting. Recounting the occasion one said:

> Everyone was present at the meeting – the doctor, the district medical officer, the health workers, the nursing sister and all the people. The doctor told us what had happened so we could explain it to the meeting. We brought our teaching dummy, took him apart, showed everyone the anatomy of the brain and explained that he had died from bleeding in the

brain – a subdural haemorrhage (her words). So, we said, it must have been *galka* from other places that did it.

Finally, as described in Chapter 5, different people may hold different points of view. When an old man died at a homeland centre, the explanations given included sorcery (in association with a variety of ultimate causes), neglect by relatives and lung cancer (that is, causes from all three categories). The aetiological domain provides a rich and varied source of explanations which can be invoked singly or in combination and modified to provide plausible and satisfying explanations. Its breadth gives doubters, thinkers and innovators room for manoeuvre.

Change in Yolngu illness-related beliefs cannot be represented by a unidirectional arrow running from Yolngu to Western. Change is characterised, first, by the gradual addition of causes and elaboration of existing causes. The aetiological domain of the Yolngu has probably always provided a variety of explanations for a variety of conditions and shed or absorbed causes as required. These days this process takes place in response both to individual acquisition of new knowledge, experiences and ideas, and to the difficulties of explaining unfamiliar illnesses or illnesses linked to unfamiliar occurrences.

Second, change is characterised by the critical and thoughtful use of existing causal possibilities. There is a strong commitment at Yirrkala to the principle of individual thought, consideration and judgment (albeit, as in any society, within socially prescribed limits) and to the obligation of each person to think about an issue and make up his own mind. When a decision must be made and a consensus is required, those with vested interests may attempt to persuade an individual to view a matter in a particular way. Ultimately, however, the choice about what he will think and the position he will take is his own. The young health workers and those with Christian convictions appear to be choosing explanations from Categories 2 and 3 somewhat more frequently than others, but almost all draw on Category 1 in a crisis. When a death occurs, there is a striking consensus within the community that the cause is sorcery.

The third characteristic of change in illness-related beliefs – in particular, in the sociomedical theory – is that it has taken place much more slowly than change in medical practice. Whereas Western medical care is sought for all manner of illnesses and injuries, in critical situations the explanations of Western medicine are rarely considered more convincing than those offered by the sociomedical theory. This is partly because, even if Western medicine had answers of meaning which would satisfy a layman, most Yolngu are not conversant enough with its dogmas to consider it a viable alternative. A very few people, such as health workers, have been tutored in Western medical practice and theory. The children receive a little instruction in health and hygiene at school, but often not enough to constitute for them a coherent explanatory framework. Others have been given disjointed information by busy nursing staff, normally under conditions in which comprehension and effective learning are impossible. For almost everyone at Yirrkala there is effectively no competing explanation for acute illness and death. Both because of the lack of competition and because of their internal logic, the beliefs which constitute the Yolngu sociomedical theory have been transmitted in much the same form as early authors described them and continue to command the intellectual loyalty of the community.

This pattern of medical behaviour – the resort to Western medicine while embracing indigenous explanations – is not, of course, unique to Yolngu society. Studies the world over have shown that people are conservative in their medical beliefs but flexible in their therapeutic choices. Beliefs about illness are much less readily abandoned than indigenous treatments. People of all societies, including the industrial West, are skilful in reconciling new medical knowledge with their own ideas or simply ignoring logical inconsistencies. By means of various mechanisms – secondary elaboration (Evans-Pritchard 1937), assimilation and particularisation (Young 1976) and other (Gellner 1974:158-67; Polanyi 1958) – their beliefs are insulated from the winds of contradiction and doubt. Even a Western tertiary education (Erinosho 1977; Jahoda 1968) will not necessarily bring about a change in a person's theoretical allegiances. Ultimately the overthrow of cherished beliefs is probably less a matter of critical reflection than it is of radical change in the social and economic structures of a society (see Comaroff 1981; Feierman 1979; Thomas 1971).

New Puzzles, Old Understandings

In this and previous chapters it has been argued that the sociomedical theory continues to provide explanations of suffering which Yolngu find relevant and reasonable. Specifically, the theory provides ultimate explanations for sickness and death with which Western medicine cannot compete. It is, further, internally logical, self-validating, strategically useful and, in the face of new ideas and events, flexible.

But perhaps the greatest strength of the theory in contemporary life is that it has proved, in the eyes of its adherents, devastatingly true. The events of recent times confirm that vulnerability and trouble lead to sickness and death. Relations in the community have intensified since settlement and social boundaries have become changeable and ill-defined. Men and women whose families and clans are only distantly related are marrying. 'Stranger Yolngu' are coming to stay at Yirrkala and drink at the hotel. People of clans which own widely separated territories now live round the corner from each other. Young people are defying their elders. Men get drunk and say things which enrage others. They beat their wives. Some, it is said, are obtaining objects of sorcery from other places to use at Yirrkala. The enemy, in various guises, is now within. Worse, the hands of the traditional peace-makers and judges are effectively tied. The *makarrata* or ritualised ordeal – a confrontation which, once blood was drawn, ended a feud – has long since been stopped. A beating or spearing is a risky punishment. The authorities have made it forcibly clear that violence will not be tolerated and that the Australian legal system will oversee the dispensation of justice to those who assault or kill others. Under these circumstances, it seems to many Yolngu that the only available redress for an insult or injury is a covert attack by sorcery.[6]

Occasionally contacts with outsiders are seen to have their advantages. Links of marriage can provide a bridge between Yirrkala people and Aborigines elsewhere and transform them conceptually, if not geographically, from distant, dangerous people to distant, useful people. When a woman married a man from Maningrida, her relatives at Yirrkala were quick to seize upon the implications of having reputed *galka* for in-laws. After a boy of their family drowned they talked about whether their Maningrida in-laws might be willing to exact revenge on their behalf. Similarly, some years before the man, John, died, the welfare officer at Nhulunbuy had devised a plan to bring juvenile offenders from other parts of the Northern Territory to live at a homeland centre affiliated with John's clan instead of sending them to a corrective institution in Darwin. The scheme had a short life, but for a while boys from as far away as Yuendumu, a desert town, were cared for by Yolngu women at the homeland centre. When John died (p. 100) his family mused that perhaps their distant Yuendumu friends (the parents of the boys they had looked after) would reciprocate by visiting long distance sorcery (described as 'like a shooting star') on the killers.

Frequently, though, the perceived benefits of the new-found mobility of Yolngu and their enemies are outweighed in their minds by the dangers. Middleton's (1960) description of the increase in accusations and suspicions of sorcery which have accompanied

---

6. This is a fear which rapid and deleterious social changes engender all over the world: see Guenther (1976:127) on the consequences of farm living for the nomadic San of the Kalahari Desert, and Colson (1971:244–50) on the fears generated by forced resettlement among the Gwembe Tonga.

social change among the Lugbara of Africa might have been written of Yirrkala in the 1970s and, for that reason, is well worth quoting here:

> Traditionally the use of sorcery is said to have been away on the horizon and never among 'us here' (p. 246) . . .
> Today, however, sorcery is entering into relations between men within this field: the sorcerers are among 'us here'. The appearance of *elojua* [sorcerers] is an expression of the fear and resentment of the changes taking place in Lugbara society, changes such as those implied in labour migration, in a cash economy and a market system, and secular *walangaa* dances. Lugbara have no control over these changes, which have no obvious cause other than the Europeans and the many 'strangers' who today wander about the country. *Elojua* is a symbol of all that is unusual and uncanny and is a response to social change (p. 247) . . . Traditionally the significance of sorcery seems to have been that it marked, conceptually, the limit of a group's field of social relations, and its significance today is consistent with this. The increase in social mobility, both within and beyond the borders of Lugbara, has introduced new relationships which did not exist before. All these, together with the prohibition on fighting, on killing witches, severely beating one's wife and children, and so on, have led to new stresses and conflicts in the society (p. 248).

The antithesis of living in Yirrkala, of course, is life far removed from its perils among people who are moral and caring – one's own extended family. One of the many reasons people value life at homeland centres is the protection and security they provide. Theoretically *galka* can ride horses, drive cars or walk overland long distances in search of victims. However, since deaths are unusual in these small communities people are rarely confronted with the possibility of sorcery. Visitors to homeland centres throughout Australia have remarked on the dignity and industry of residents (Morice 1976, 1978). The depression and anxieties generated by living in the big and crowded communities (well described for the North by Reser and Eastwell [1981]), lift when people go home. With fewer worries and fewer reasons for fear, the 'darkness' which people feel at Yirrkala dissipates.

Deaths are rare at homeland centres partly because very sick people are evacuated to hospital, partly because there are only one or two old people in any one community and partly because residents are in better health. There is no reliable epidemiological data comparing Yolngu health at homeland centres and the large communities (to collect it would be an intrusion of the very sort

Yolngu have gone home to avoid) but the Yolngu themselves are in no doubt about the physical and psychological benefits of life on their land. Even in 1975, when the movement was less than two years old, the changes were evident. In the words of a ritual leader:

> When the old men living at the outstations come to Yirrkala they get sickness every time. When they go back to their homeland and taste many different foods they die at the right time [that is, not prematurely]. The young people always change when they go to the outstations and become strong. But even when people go to the outstations, tobacco, sugar and tea will follow the people and make them sick in their land. But we get hunted food, bush honey, wild meat and many other foods. When I go there I have oysters, crabs, fish, turtle eggs and stingray and it makes me happy and strong and opens my life.

The leader of one homeland centre told me that, when his family first went to live there, they were skinny. After some time, though, they had shiny hair and round faces. This, he maintained, was due to the supernatural power inherent in the area and in some of the foods, such as the rock oysters. Another leader remarked in 1977, shortly after his homeland centre had been established, that the young children used to be constantly in and out of hospital when they lived at Yirrkala. At the homeland centre, however, the honey, fish, shellfish and other fresh land and sea foods 'cure' them. He also observed that the young who used to break into buildings and steal money, drink and sniff petrol, are happy and constantly learning new things about their culture and about life on the land at the homeland centre. He laughed and said that, when he is leaving to drive back to Yirrkala and asks the children if they want to come, they usually say, vehemently 'No!'.

Whether Yolngu look to homeland centre life, where harmony and good health prevail, or to Yirrkala, beset with troubles and sicknesses, the sociomedical theory is confirmed. It is not because Yolngu are 'closed' in their attitudes towards received truths that the theory endures as the core of the medical belief system, but because the relationships between human affairs and individual wellbeing which it assumes are supported by the events of recent decades. Its scope and logic are compelling. There is no area of life at Yirrkala which it leaves untouched and few values which it does not uphold. Community members have a strong social, ideological and emotional investment in the theory. To abandon it would be to abandon a means of imposing order on a shifting world, of giving meaning to pain and suffering and of retaining a sense of mastery over the people and powers of the Yolngu cosmos.

Appendix

Questionnaire: Medical Experience and Attitudes to Illness

Name: Date:
Age:
Male or Female:

A. Contacts with Western and Traditional Medicine

1. How many years did you spend in school? Which school(s)? What post-primary training?
2. What jobs have you had?
3. Have you ever been hospitalised down south (i.e. Adelaide, Sydney, etc.)?
4. Have you ever been a patient in Darwin Hospital?
5. Have you ever been in Nhulunbuy Hospital?
6. Have you ever been hospitalised at Yirrkala (when the health centre was still a hospital)? (for Questions 3-6 ask for the *dawu* [story])
7. Have you ever had an operation? (If yes, ask for story.)
8. Have you ever used bush medicines yourself or did your mother or any other relatives give them to you when you were young?
9. Have you ever been treated by a *marrnggitj*? (If yes, ask for story.)
10. Have you ever been attacked by a *galka* or a Yolngu using *manggimanggi, nyira, burrpuy, biyi'* or anything else, or have you ever been made sick by a spirit or by going into a sacred place? (If yes, ask for story).

B. Suggested Causes and Treatments of Preference for Nine Sets of Symptoms

Tell respondent: 'I've thought of some things that could be wrong with a person at Yirrkala. This could be anybody (*birrka'mirri* Yolngu). I'll tell you what might be wrong with the person. Please give it some thought and tell me what you think might have caused it and, if that was you or a member of your family, what you would do about it.'

1. This man or woman is very sick, and needs to lie down all the time. He's feeling very hot and has a headache. He's feeling sick

all over his body. He's breathing like this (rapid, shallow – demonstrate). When he breathes he has a bad pain in his chest here (indicate lower right hand rib cage) inside. He is coughing up phlegm with blood in it. (For this and all subsequent questions: 'What do you think would cause this?' and 'What would you do about it?')

2. This little child – a baby or a toddler – is crying all the time and is hot to touch. He is vomiting and has diarrhoea. He's getting thinner and his skin is dry to touch. It's like an old person's skin.

3. This person, man or woman, most of the time acts like other people and leads a normal life, talking to people, sitting in the camp, going to the store, cooking the food, looking after the children, going to work and so on. But suddenly the person becomes crazy (*bawa'mirri*). He or she runs around, says and does strange things, doesn't look after the children or carry out his/her usual tasks.

4. This person, man or woman, when working or walking fast, is often short of breath and feels a pain in the centre of his/her chest (indicate). One day this person is running or dancing or working very hard and suddenly feels a very bad pain in the chest, shoulders, arms and head, falls over unconscious and dies very quickly. (What do you think would cause that?)

5. This man or woman has a *dholng rerritthun* (painful/sick lower abdomen implicating urogenital system). He/she also feels hot and shivery and has a pain in here (indicate position of kidneys, both sides). He/she feels a bad burning pain when passing urine.

6. This person often has a bad pain in the stomach here (indicate stomach — up and under rib cage) especially after he/she has eaten food. Sometimes he/she vomits and brings up blood as well. When he/she defecates there may be (occult) old, black blood in the stool.

7. Imagine a person who wakes up one morning and feels rather ill all over. His/her muscles and joints ache and he/she has a headache, feels hot and has a sore throat.

8. This description is of leprosy. It starts with sores on the arms and legs and the person develops white spots on the skin. The hands and feet lose feeling and the fingers and toes may develop sores and eventually fall away.

9. This baby or child cries a lot and feels hot. He/she can't hear very well and has a sore ear (or ears) which is discharging (pus coming out).

References

Ardener, E. 1970. Witchcraft, Economics, and the Continuity of Belief. In M. Douglas (ed.). *Witchcraft Confessions and Accusations*. London: Tavistock.

Australia, Parliament. 1974a. House of Representatives Standing Committee on Aboriginal Affairs. Transcripts of Evidence of Enquiry into Present Conditions of the Yirrkala People taken at Yirrkala 9 February 1974.

— 1974b. *Present Conditions of Yirrkala People*. House of Representatives Standing Committee on Aboriginal Affairs. Canberra: Australian Government Publishing Service.

— 1979. *Aboriginal Health*. House of Representatives Standing Committee on Aboriginal Affairs. Canberra: Australian Government Publishing Service.

Barnes, B. 1969. Paradigms – Scientific and Social. *Man* **4**(1):98-102.

— 1973. The Comparison of Belief-systems: Anomaly Versus Falsehood. In R. Horton and R. Finnegan (eds.). *Modes of Thought*. London: Faber and Faber.

Bauer, D.F. and J. Hinnant. 1980. Normal and Revolutionary Divination: A Kuhnian Approach to African Traditional Thought. In I. Karp and C.S. Bird (eds.). *Explorations in African Systems of Thought*. Bloomington: Indiana University Press.

Bell, D. 1980. Daughters of the Dreaming. Ph.D. thesis, Department of Prehistory and Anthropology. Canberra: Australian National University.

— 1982. Women's Changing Role in Health Maintenance in a Central Australian Community. In J.C. Reid (ed.). *Body, Land and Spirit*. St Lucia: University of Queensland Press.

Berndt, C.H. 1964. The Role of Native Doctors in Aboriginal Australia. In A. Kiev (ed.). *Magic, Faith, and Healing*. New York: The Free Press of Glencoe.

— 1971. Prolegomena to a Study of Genealogies in North-eastern Arnhem Land. In R.M. Berndt (ed.). *Australian Aboriginal Anthropology*. Perth: University of Western Australia Press.

Berndt, R.M. 1947. Wuradjeri Magic and 'Clever Men'. *Oceania* **17**(4):327-65 and **18**(1):60-86.

— 1955. Murngin (Wulamba) Social Organization. *American Anthropoligist* **57**(1):84-106.

— 1964. The Gove Dispute: The Question of Australian Aboriginal Land and the Preservation of Sacred Sites. *Anthropological Forum* **1**(2):258-95.

— 1965a. Marriage and the Family in North-eastern Arnhem Land. In M.F. Nimkoff (ed.). *Comparative Family Systems.* Boston: Houghton Mifflin.

— 1965b. Law and Order in Aboriginal Australia. In R.M. and C.H. Berndt (eds.). *Aboriginal Man in Australia.* Sydney: Angus and Robertson.

— 1978-9. Looking Back into the Present: A Changing Panorama in Eastern Arnhem Land. *Anthropological Forum.* **(3-4):**281-96. (Journal date 1978-79. Published in 1980.)

Berndt, R.M. and C.H. 1951. The Concept of Abnormality in an Australian Aboriginal Society. In G.B. Wilbur and W. Muensterburger (eds.). *Psychoanalysis and Culture.* New York: International Universities Press.

— 1954. *Arnhem Land: Its History and Its People.* Melbourne: F.W. Cheshire.

— 1977. *The World of the First Australians.* Sydney: Ure Smith.

Biernoff, D.C. 1978. Safe and Dangerous Places. In L. Hiatt (ed.). *Australian Aboriginal Concepts.* Canberra: Australian Institute of Aboriginal Studies.

— 1982. Psychiatric and Anthropological Interpretations of 'Aberrant' Behaviour in an Aboriginal Community. In J.C. Reid (ed.). *Body, Land and Spirit.* St Lucia: University of Queensland Press.

Buxton, J. 1973. *Religion and Healing in Mandari.* Oxford: Clarendon Press.

Calley, M. 1955. Aboriginal Pentecostalism. M.A. Thesis, Department of Anthropology. Sydney: University of Sydney.

Cannon, W.B. 1942. Voodoo Death. *American Anthropologist* **44**:169-81.

Cawte, J. 1974. *Medicine is the Law*. Honolulu: The University Press of Hawaii.

Chaseling, W. 1957. *Yulengor: Nomads of Arnhem Land*. London: The Epworth Press.

Cole, K. 1979. *The Aborigines of Arnhem Land*. Sydney: Rigby.

Colson, E. 1971. *The Social Consequences of Resettlement: The Impact of the Kariba Resettlement Upon the Gwembe Tonga*. Manchester: Manchester University Press.

— 1974. *Tradition and Contract: The Problem of Order*. Chicago: Aldine Publishing Company.

Comaroff, J. 1981. Healing and Cultural Transformation: The Tswana of Southern Africa [1]. *Social Science and Medicine*. **15**B:367-78.

Cook, C.E. 1970. Notable Changes in the Incidence of Disease in Northern Territory Aborigines. In A.R. Pilling and R.A. Waterman (eds.). *Diprotodon to Detribalization: Studies of Change Among Australian Aborigines*. East Lansing: Michigan State University Press.

Coombs, H.C. 1981. Yirrkala Law Council. *Social Alternatives* **2**(2):36 and 60.

Cooper, D.E. 1975. Alternative Logic in 'Primitive Thought'. *Man* (N.S.) **10**:238-56.

Douglas, M. 1970. Introduction: Thirty years after *Witchcraft, Oracles and Magic*. In M. Douglas (ed.). *Witchcraft Confessions and Accusations*. London: Tavistock Publications.

Eastwell, H. 1973. The Traditional Healer in Modern Arnhem Land. *Med. J. Aust.* **2**:1011-17.

— 1974. Dilemmas of Aboriginal Marriage in East Arnhem Land, North Australia. *Australian and New Zealand Journal of Psychiatry* **8**:49-53.

— 1976. Associative Illness Among Aboriginals. *Australian and New Zealand Journal of Psychiatry* **10**:89-94.

Eliade, M. 1973. *Australian Religions: An Introduction*. Ithaca: Cornell University Press.

Elkin, A.P. 1935a. Primitive Medicine Men. *Med. J. Aust.* **2**(22):750-7.

— 1935b. Civilized Aborigines and Native Culture. *Oceania* **6**(2): 117-46.

— 1975. *The Australian Aborigines*. Sydney: Angus and Robertson (first edition 1938).

— 1977. *Aboriginal Men of High Degree*. St Lucia: University of Queensland Press (first edition 1945).

Epstein, S. 1967. A Sociological Analysis of Witch Beliefs in a Mysore Village. In J. Middleton (ed.). *Magic, Witchcraft, and Curing*. New York: The Natural History Press.

Erinosho, O.A. 1977. Belief-system and the Concept of Mental Illness among Medical Students in a Developing Country. *J. Anthrop. Research* **33**:158-66.

Evans-Pritchard, E.E. 1937. *Witchcraft, Oracles and Magic Among the Azande*. Oxford: Clarendon Press.

Feierman, S. 1979. Change in African Therapeutic Systems. *Social Science and Medicine* **13B**:277-84.

— 1981. Therapy as a System-in-Action in Northeastern Tanzania. *Social Science and Medicine* **15B**:353-60.

Flinders, Matthew. 1814. *A Voyage to Terra Australis*. London: G. and W. Nicol.

Foster, G.M. 1976. Disease Etiologies in Non-western Medical Systems. *American Anthropologist* **78**:773-82.

Frankenberg, R., and J. Leeson. 1976. Disease, Illness and Sickness: Social Aspects of the Choice of Healer in a Lusaka Suburb. In J.B. Loudon (ed.). *Social Anthropology and Medicine*. London: Academic Press.

Frazer, Sir J. 1922. *The Golden Bough*. London: Macmillan (first edition 1890).

Geertz, C. 1960. *The Religion of Java*. London: The Free Press of Glencoe.

Gellner, E. 1974. *Legitimation of Belief*. Cambridge: Cambridge University Press.

Gillies, E. 1976. Causal Criteria in African Classifications of Disease. In J. Loudon (ed.). *Social Anthropology and Medicine*. London: Academic Press.

Glick, L.B. 1967. Medicine as an Ethnographic Category: The Gimi of the New Guinea Highlands. *Ethnology* **6**:31-56.

Gluckman, M. 1968. Social Beliefs and Individual Thinking in Tribal Society. In R.A. Manners and D. Kaplan (eds.). *Theory in Anthropology: A Sourcebook*. London: Routledge and Kegan Paul.

Gray, D. 1976. Aboriginal Mortuary Practices in Carnarvon. *Oceania* **47**(2):144-50.

— 1979. Traditional Medicine on the Carnarvon Reserve. In R.M. and C.H. Berndt (eds.). *Aborigines of the West: Their Past and Present*. Perth: University of Western Australia Press.

Guenther, M.G. 1976. From Hunters to Squatters: Social and Cultural Change among the Farm San of Ghanzi, Botswana. In R.B. Lee and I. DeVore (eds.). *Kalahari Hunter-Gatherers*. Cambridge: Harvard University Press.

Hallpike, C.R. 1976. Is There A Primitive Mentality? *Man* (NS) **11**:253-70.

Hammond-Tooke, W.D. 1970. Urbanization and the Interpretation of Misfortune: A Quantitative Analysis. *Africa* **40**(1):25-39.

Hamnett, M.P. and J. Connell. 1981. Diagnosis and Cure: The Resort to Traditional and Modern Medical Practitioners in the North Solomons, Papua New Guinea. *Social Science and Medicine* **15B**:489-98.

Harris, S. 1977. Milingimbi Aboriginal Learning Contexts. Ph.D. thesis. Department of Education. Albuquerque: University of New Mexico.

Hiatt, L.R. 1965. *Kinship and Conflict: A Study of an Aboriginal Community in Northern Arnhem Land*. Canberra: Australian National University Press.

Horton, R. 1962. The Kalabari World-View: An Outline and Interpretation. *Africa* **32**(3):197-219.

— 1964. Ritual Man in Africa. *Africa* **34**(2):85-104.

— 1968. Neo-Tylorianism: Sound Sense or Sinister Prejudice? *Man* **3**(4):625-34.

— 1970. African Traditional Thought and Western Science. In B.R. Wilson (ed.), *Rationality*. Oxford: Basil Blackwell.

Horton, R. and R. Finnegan (eds.). 1973. *Modes of Thought: Essays on Thinking in Western and Non-Western Societies*. London: Faber and Faber.

Howitt, A.W. 1886. *On* Australian Medicine Men; *or,* Doctors and Wizards of Some Australian Tribes. *J. Anth Inst. of Great Britain and Ireland* **16**(1):23-59.

Hughes, C.C. and J.M. Hunter. 1970. Disease and 'Development' in Africa. *Social Science and Medicine* **3**:443-93.

Jahoda, G. 1968. Scientific Training and the Persistence of Traditional Beliefs among West African University Students. *Nature* **220**:1356.

Janzen, J.M. 1981. The Need for a Taxonomy of Health in the Study of African Therapeutics. *Social Science and Medicine* **15B**:185-94.

Jay, R.R. 1969. *Javanese Villagers: Social Relations in Rural Modjokuto*. Massachusetts: MIT Press.

Keen, I. 1977a. One Ceremony, One Song: An Economy of Religious Knowledge Among the Yolngu of North-east Arnhem Land. Ph.D. thesis. Department of Prehistory and Anthropology. Canberra: Australian National University.

— 1977b. Yolngu Sand Sculptures in Context. In P. Ucko (ed.). *Form in Indigenous Art: Schematisation in the Art of Aboriginal Australia and Prehistoric Europe*. Canberra: Australian Institute of Aboriginal Studies.

Kluckhohn, C. 1944. *Navaho Witchcraft*. Boston: Beacon Press.

Kuhn, T.S. 1970. *The Structure of Scientific Revolutions*. Chicago: University of Chicago Press.

Law Reform Commission. 1980. *Aboriginal Customary Law – Recognition?* Discussion Paper No. 17. Sydney.

Lévy-Bruhl. L. 1922. La mentalité primitive. Paris: Alcan (Eng. translation. *Primitive Mentality.* New York: Beacon Press. 1966).

Lewis, Gilbert. 1975. *Knowledge of Illness in a Sepik Society: A Study of the Gnau, New Guinea.* London School of Economics Monographs on Social Anthropology *52.* London: Athlone Press.

Lindenbaum, S. 1971. Sorcery and Structure in Fore Society. *Oceania* **41**(4):277-87.

Lockwood, D. 1962. *I, the Aboriginal.* Adelaide: Rigby.

Lowe, B. n.d. Gupapuyngu Alphabet and Pronounciation. Unpublished manuscript. Milingimbi, Northern Territory.

Macfarlane, A. 1970. Witchcraft in Tudor and Stuart Essex. In M. Douglas (ed.). *Witchcraft Confessions and Accusations.* London: Tavistock Publications.

Macknight, C.C. 1972. Macassans and Aborigines. *Oceania* **42**(4):283-321.

— 1976. *The Voyage to Marege': Macassan Trepangers in Northern Australia.* Melbourne: Melbourne University Press.

— 1982. Journal of a Voyage Around Arnhem Land in 1875. *Aboriginal History* **5**(2):135-45.

Marwick, M. 1964. Witchcraft as a Social Strain-Gauge. *Aust. J. Science* **26**:263-8.

— 1965. Some Problems in the Sociology of Sorcery and Witchcraft. In M. Fortes and G. Dieterlen (eds.). *African Systems of Thought.* London: Oxford University Press.

— 1970. Introduction. In M. Marwick (ed.). *Witchcraft and Sorcery.* Middlesex: Penguin Books.

— 1973. How Real is the Charmed Circle in African and Western Thought? *Africa* **43**(1):59-71.

— 1974. Is Science a Form of Witchcraft? *New Scientist* **63**(913):578-81.

McArthur, M. 1960. Food Consumption and Dietary Levels of Groups of Aborigines Living on Naturally Occurring Foods. In C.P. Mountford (ed.). *Records of the American-Australian Scientific Expedition to Arnhem Land*. Melbourne: Melbourne University Press.

McKnight, D. 1981. Sorcery in an Australian Tribe. *Ethnology* **20**:31-44.

Middleton, J. 1960. *Lugbara Religion: Ritual and Authority Among an East African People*. London: Oxford University Press.

Milliken, E.P. 1974. The Aboriginal Population Based on Yirrkala. Unpub. paper. Darwin: Dept Aboriginal Affairs files.

Mitchell, J.C. 1965. The Meaning of Misfortune for Urban Africans. In M. Fortes and G. Dieterlen (eds.). *African Systems of Thought*. London: Oxford University Press.

Moodie, P.M. 1973. *Aboriginal Health*. Canberra: Australian National University Press.

Morice, R.D. 1976. Women Dancing Dreaming: Psychosocial Benefits of the Aboriginal Outstation Movement. *Medical Journal of Australia* **2**:939-42.

— 1978. Central Australian Aborigines: Changes in Lifestyle and Their Effect on Health. *New Doctor* **8**:24-6.

Morphy, H. 1977a. 'Too Many Meanings': An Analysis of the Artistic System of the Yolngu of Northeast Arnhem Land. Ph. D. Thesis. Department of Prehistory and Anthropology. Canberra: Australian National University.

— 1977b. Yingapungapu – Ground Sculpture as Bark Painting. In P.J. Ucko (ed.). *Form in Indigenous Art*. Canberra: Australian Institute of Aboriginal Studies.

— Forthcoming. 'Now You Understand': An Analysis of the Way Yolngu have used Sacred Knowledge to Retain Their Autonomy. In N. Peterson and M. Langton (eds.). *Aborigines, Land and Land Rights*. Canberra: Australian Institute of Aboriginal Studies.

Morphy, F. 1977. Language and Moiety: Sociolectal Variation in the Yu:lngu Language of North-east Arnhem Land. *Canberra Anthropology* **1**(1):51-60.

Myers, F. 1980. A Broken Code: Pintupi Political Theory and Contemporary Social Life. *Mankind* **12**(4):311-26.

Nadel, S.F. 1952. Witchcraft in Four African Societies. *American Anthropologist* **54**:18-29.

Northern Territory Department of Health. 1977-8. *An Environmental Survey of Aboriginal Communities*. Darwin: Government Printer of the Northern Territory.

NTEHP. 1977 Interim Report on Yirrkala. Department of Ophthalmology. Sydney: University of New South Wales. Unpub. ms.

— 1980. *Report of the National Trachoma and Eye Health Program*. Sydney: Royal Australian College of Ophthalmologists.

Packard, R.M. 1980. Social Change and the History of Misfortune among the Bashu of Eastern Zaïre. In I. Karp and C.S. Bird (eds.). *Explorations in African Systems of Thought*. Bloomington: Indiana University Press.

Peterson, N. 1971. The Structure of Two Australian Aboriginal Ecosystems. Ph.D. thesis. Department of Anthropology. Sydney: University of Sydney.

Polanyi, M. 1958. *Personal Knowledge*. Chicago: University of Chicago Press.

Quinn, J.V. 1973. Ichthyosarcotoxism. In *Northern Territory Medical Service Bulletin,* Australian Department of Health **1**(1):1.

Radin, P. 1927. *Primitive Man as Philosopher*. New York: D. Appleton and Co.

Reay, M. 1949. Native Thought in Rural New South Wales. *Oceania* **20**(2):89-118.

Reid, J.C. 1978. Sorcery and Healing: The Meaning of Illness and Death to an Australian Aboriginal Community. Ph.D. thesis. Department of Anthropology, Stanford University, California.

— 1979a 'Women's Business': Cultural Factors Affecting the Use of Family Planning Services in an Aboriginal Community. *Med. J. Aust.* Special Supplement **1**:1-4.

— 1979b. A Time to Live, A Time to Grieve: Patterns and Processes of Mourning Among the Yolngu of Australia. *Culture, Medicine and Psychiatry* **3**:319-46.

— (ed.). 1982. *Body, Land and Spirit: Health and Healing in Aboriginal Society*. St Lucia: University of Queensland Press.

Reid, J.C., and B. Dhamarrandji. 1978. Curing, not Caring: Why Aboriginal Patients 'Abscond'. *New Doctor* **8**:27-32.

Reid, J.C. and M. Gurruwiwi. 1979. Attitudes Towards Family Planning Among the Women of a Northern Australian Aboriginal Community. *Med. J. Aust.* Special Supplement **1**:5-7.

Reid, J.C., and D. Mununggurr. 1977. 'We Are Losing Our Brothers': Sorcery and Alcohol in an Aboriginal Community. *Med. J. Aust.* Special Supplement **2**:1-5.

Reid, J., Yunupingu, L. and D. Yunupingu. 1978. Caring for the Aged and Dying in an Aboriginal Community. *Australasian Nurses Journal* **7**(12):22-6.

Reser, J.P. and H.D. Eastwell. 1981. Labeling and Cultural Expectations: The Shaping of a Sorcery Syndrome in Aboriginal Australia. *Journal of Nervous and Mental Disease* **169**(5):303-10.

Reynolds, H. 1981. *The Other Side of the Frontier*. Townsville: James Cook University of North Queensland.

Scarlett, N., White, N. and J. Reid. 1982. 'Bush Medicines'. The Pharmacopeia of the Yolngu of Arnhem Land. In J. Reid (ed.). *Body, Land and Spirit,* St Lucia: University of Queensland Press.

Schwartz, L.R. 1969. The Hierarchy of Resort in Curative Practices: The Admiralty Islands, Melanesia. *Journal of Health and Social Behaviour* **10**(3):201-9.

Shapiro, W. 1969. Miwuyt Marriage. Ph.D. thesis. Canberra: Australian National University.

— 1973. Residential Grouping in Northeast Arnhem Land. *Man* (NS) **8**:365-83.

— 1977. Structure, Variation, and Change in 'Balamumu' Social Classification. *J. Anth. Research* **33**:16-49.

Skorupski, J. 1973. *Symbol and Theory: A Philosophical Study of Theories of Religion in Social Anthropology.* Cambridge: Cambridge University Press.

Spencer, B., and F.J. Gillen. 1899. *The Native Tribes of Central Australia.* London: Macmillan and Company. (Reprinted 1968, New York: Dover Publications.)

Stanner, W.E.H. 1979a. Continuity and Change. In W.E.H. Stanner. *White Man Got No Dreaming: Essays 1938-1973.* Canberra: Australian National University Press.

— 1979b. Religion, Totemism and Symbolism(1962). In *White Man Got No Dreaming: Essays 1938-1973.* Canberra: Australian National University Press.

Thomas, A.E. 1970. Adaptation to Modern Medicine in Lowland Machakos, Kenya: A Controlled Comparison of Two Kenya Communities. Ph.D. thesis. Department of Anthropology, California: Stanford University.

Thomas, K. 1971. *Religion and the Decline of Magic.* London: Weidenfeld and Nicolson.

Thomson, D.F. 1939. *Report on Expedition to Arnhem Land, 1936-37.* Canberra: Commonwealth Government Printer.

— 1961. *Marrngitmirri* and *Kalka* – Medicineman and Sorcerer – in Arnhem Land. *Man* **61**(131):97-102.

— 1975. The Concept of 'Marr' in Arnhem Land. *Mankind* **10**(1):1-10.

Tonkinson, M. 1982. The *Mabarn* and The Hospital: The Selection of Treatment in a Remote Aboriginal Community. In J.C. Reid (ed.). *Body, Land and Spirit.* St Lucia: University of Queensland Press.

Tonkinson, R. 1974. *The Jigalong Mob: Aboriginal Victors of the Desert Crusade.* Menlo Park: Cummings Publishing Company.

Turner, V. 1964. Witchcraft and Sorcery: Taxonomy Versus Dynamics. *Africa* **34**(4):314-24.

Tynan, B.J. 1979. Medical Systems in Conflict: A Study of Power. Dip. Anth. thesis, University of Sydney. (Subsequently published in limited edition by the Government Printer of the Northern Territory for the Department of Health.)

Warner, W.L. 1958. *A Black Civilization: A Social Study of an Australian Tribe.* New York: Harper and Brothers (first edition 1937).

Webb. T.T. 1936. The Making of a Marrngit. *Oceania* **6**(3):336-41.

— n.d. Aboriginals and Adventure in Arnhem Land. Unpublished manuscript. Australian Institute of Aboriginal Studies Library, Canberra.

White, N. 1979. Tribes, Genes and Habitats: Genetic Diversity Among Aboriginal Populations in the Northern Territory of Australia. Ph.D. thesis. Department of Genetics and Human Variation. Melbourne: La Trobe University.

Williams, N.M. 1973. Northern Territory Aborigines Under Australian Law. Ph.D. thesis. Department of Anthropology. Berkeley: University of California.

— n.d. Black Earth: The Yolngu and Their Land – A System of Land Tenure. Unpublished manuscript. Canberra: Australian Insititute of Aboriginal Studies.

— 1982. A Boundary is to Cross: Observations on Yolngu Boundaries and Permission. In N.M. Williams and E.S. Hunn (eds.). *Resource Managers: North American and Australian Hunter-Gatherers.* AAAS Selected Symposium 67. Boulder: Westview Press.

Wilson, B.R. (ed.). 1970. *Rationality.* New York: Harper and Row.

Wiminydji and A.R. Peile. 1978. A Desert Aborigine's View of Health and Nutrition. *Journal of Anthrop. Research* **34**(4):497-523.

World Health Organization. 1978. *Report of the International Conference on Primary Health Care, Alma-Ata, USSR.* 6-12 September 1978. Geneva.

Yirrkala Health Workers. 1982. Do Aboriginal Health Centres Need Nurses? *The Aboriginal Health Worker.* **6**(1):14-19.

Young, A. 1976. Some Implications of Medical Beliefs and Practices for Social Anthropology. *American Anthropologist* **78**(1):5-24.

Young. E. 1981. *Tribal Communities in Rural Areas.* Canberra: Development Studies Centre, Australian National Universtity.

Index

Aboriginal health workers, 70, 106-7; attitudes towards, 70, 109; explaining illness in Yolngu terms, 71, 80, 84, 100, 126-7, 149, 151-2; mediating between Western and Yolngu illness explanations, 75, 84, 109, 126, 151-2; role in illness management, 71, 95, 100; training of, 21-2, 125; Yolngu treatment used by, 63, 67

Aboriginal strangers (*see also* Social distance): conflict with, 48-9; drinking at Nhulunbuy, 25, 48-9, 135; *galka* as, 37, 49, 84, 113-14, 134; from other communities as *galka*, 37, 39, 48, 84, 101, 104, 113, 135; *see also* Elcho Island; Maningrida; sorcery techniques obtained from, 84, 136-9; Yolngu fear of, 48, 87, 145; Yolngu relations with, 86, 87, 135-9, 154; Yolngu suspicion of, 25, 48, 82, 88-9, 113-14, 135

Accusations of sorcery: against non-Aborigines, 101, 107; causing conflict, *see* Conflict; reactions to, 35, 49, 84, 85, 89, 90, 101, 114; social structure and, 49, 79, 82, 84, 87, 113-14; strategic uses of, 112-16, 135; *see also* Yolngu sociomedical theory; suppression of, 49, 84, 101, 115-16, 141-2; *see also* Explanations of illness

Alcohol: Australian laws on, 25, 27; as cause of death, 80, 101, 134-5, 142-3, 145, 149, 150; conflict caused by, 25-7, 48-9, 114, 135, 145; implicated in death, 84, 89, 99, 145, 150; implicated in illness, 80, 145; introduction of, 25; mission control of, 25; social problems caused by, 25-7, 70, 84, 89, 134-9; Yolngu control of, 25-7; Yolngu criticism of, 15, 25-6, 66, 68, 83, 138-9, 145

Ardener, E., xxiv

Autopsy, 80, 100, 110-11, 128

Barnes, B., xxii, 55
Barrakbarrak, 43, 82-3, 84, 121, 132-3
Bauer, D.F., xxiv
Bell, D., xiv, 30, 87
Berndt, C.H., xiv, 5, 57
Berndt, R.M., xiv, 3, 5, 29, 57, 81, 130
Biernoff, D.C., 5, 50, 87, 92
Birrimbirr, 32-3, 51, 79, 97
Biyi', 42, 44, 84
Blood: absence of, 54, 80, 82; bad, 61, 71, 105, 132-3, 151; dangers of shedding, 79, 80-1; extracted by *galka*, *see* Wulạ̈; menstrual, 79, 80; prohibitions relating to, *see* Taboos; ritual letting of, 52-3, 80; significance of, 79; in sorcery, *see* Wulä; as source of power, 33, 41, 42, 79, 80, 83; transfusions, 80

Bukulup, 81

Bunggul, 5, 34, 51, 108, 140
Burrpuy: as illness, 43; as leprosy, 50, 51, 52-3, 80, 121-4; scepticism over, 132; as sorcery technique, 42-3, 49, 82-3, 84, 113, 121-4
Buxton, J., xxiv

Caledon bay massacre, 10-11, 27-8
Calley, M., xiv
Cannon, W.B., xix
Causal categories (*see also* Yolngu sociomedical theory): emergent, 146-7, 150; 'natural', 121, 146-50; proximate *v.* ultimate, xix, 32, 36, 52, 53, 54-6, 99, 151-2; social, 47-8, 53-4, 120-1, 146-7; spiritual, 44-7, 50-3, 120-1, 146-7
Cause of death (*see also* Causal categories; Cause of illness; Sorcery; Yolngu sociomedical theory): alcohol and, *see* Alcohol; assault (physical) as, 102, 108-10, 150; assault (physical) implicated in, 84, 89-90, 145; breach of law as, 44-6, 51-2, 102, 113, 134; breach of marriage system as, *see* Marriage system; *burrpuy (q.v.)* as, 43; dangerous places as, 52; disagreement over, 101-11; factors influencing search for, *see* Explanations of illness; *galka* attack as, 45-6, 69, 99-111 *passim,* 121, 126, 134, 151-2; *manggimanggii (q.v.)* as, 85, 121, 149; mistreatment by hospital staff as, 107-11, 150; motor vehicle accident as, 46, 102-3, 150; murder as, 47, 86; neglect by others as, 105, 113; neglect of self as, 105, 108, 113, 149, 151; *nyira (q.v.)* as, 131; old age as, 36, 149; poison as, 107, 134; power (unrestrained) as, 51-2; predation as, 36, 38, 126, 146-8; smoking as, 105, 150; sorcery (technique unspecified) as, 45-7 *passim,* 53, 84, 88-90, 116, 149, 151; spirits as, 52; suicide as, 149-50
Cause of illness (*see also* Causal categories; Cause of death; Sorcery; Yolngu sociomedical theory): alcohol and, *see* Alcohol; anxiety as, 127-9, 146, 148; assault (physical) as, 70, 146, 150; *barrakbarrak (q.v.)* as, 121; breach of law as, 51-3, 121-4, 145; breach of marriage system as, *see* Marriage system; *burrpuy (q.v.)* as, 49, 113, 121; contagion as, 146, 148; dangerous places as, 50-1, 52, 121-4, 129, 144-5; factors influencing search for, *see* Explanations of illness; fish poisoning as, 133-4; food as, 52-3, 96, 121-4, 146; *galka* attack as, 36-7, 39-40, 60-1, 70-6, 82, 121; grief as, 148; heredity as, 66, 146, 148-9, 151; *manggimanggi* as, *see Manggimanggi;* neglect by others as, 96, 121, 146; neglect of self as, 95, 96, 148, 149; not sought, 94, 96, 98, 124, 148; *nyira (q.v.)* as, 121; old age as, 146; predation as, 146-8; pregnancy as, 148; power (unrestrained) as, 51; sacred objects as, 51; smoking as, 96, 131, 150; sorcery (technique unspecified) as, 47, 48, 54, 86, 120, 121; spirits as, 51, 52, 144-5; *see also Mokuy*
Cawte, J., xiv, 65, 86
Ceremonies, *see* Rituals

INDEX 173

Change: caused by white domination, 2, 13, 15, 20, 22, 24, 117, 121-4; education as agent of, 14, 15, 120, 125; in incidence of sorcery, 37, 84-5, 114, 136-9, 139-40, 154; in law, 114; *see also* Legal systems; in lifestyle, 11, 14, 22-4, 114, 121, 153-4; *see also* Alcohol; in marriage system, 46; in sorcery techniques, 43, 44, 134, 140; in Yolngu health status, *see* Yolngu; missions as agents of, *see* Missions; resistance to, *see* Alcohol; Yolngu sociomedical theory; technology as factor in, 14-16, 22-4; through Christian influence, 126, 127-30; Yolngu strategies for dealing with, 2-3, 24-5, 29-30, 116-18

Chaseling, Rev. W., 5, 11, 20, 51, 130

Christianity: compatible with Yolngu beliefs, 64, 129-30; conflict caused by, 129-30; evangelical, 127, 129-30; incompatible with Yolngu beliefs, 73, 74, 129; influences Yolngu beliefs, 126, 127-30; interference of, *see* Missions

Clairvoyance, 62, 63-4, 68, 85

Clans: corporate nature of, 5, 33, 40, 45-6, 48, 88, 102, 103; and land, 1-2, 5-6, 15-16, 17, 33; leadership of, 5, 26, 52, 116, 132, 144-5; origins of, 1-2, 5-6; patrifiliation in, 5; relations between, *see* Social distance; Conflict; relations within, *see* Kin

Cole, K., 29

Colson, E., 9, 84, 154

Comaroff, J., 153

Conflict (*see also* Gossip, Jealousy): alcohol and, *see* Alcohol; between clans, 7, 45-6, 48-9, 102, 105, 109, 114; between clans at Yirrkala, 8, 27, 84, 85, 89-90, 109; evangelical movement causes, 129-30; from sorcery accusations, 84, 89, 101, 109, 114; increased incidence of, 46, 153-4; *see also* Alcohol; leading to sorcery, ·37, 45-6, 47, 85, 100-5 *passim,* 113; management of, 7, 8-9, 87-8, 135-9; over land, 45, 89; over marriage, *see* Marriage system; over ritual matters, 45-6, 102, 105; sanctions against, 8-9, 47, 101, 116; within clans, *see* Kin; with non-Aborigines, 10-11, 108-9, 129-30

Connell, J., 151

Cook, C.E., 20

Coombs, H.C., 5

Cooper, D.E., xxi

Dangerous laws, *see* Sorcery

Dangerous places, 121-4, 144-5; *wänung,* 50-1; *wärral,* 51; *wokuti,* 51, 29; Yingapungapu, 50, 51, 52, 129

Department of Aboriginal Affairs, xiii, 18

Department of Health (NT), xii-xiii, 19, 21-2, 85-6, 109

Dhäkiyarr, 11

Dhamarrandji, B., xii

Dillybag, used in magic, 41-2, 60; *see also Galka, Marrnggitj*

Djamarrkuli, 33, 34, 37, 58n., 59, 62, 104-5; *see also Manggata*

Djanggitj, see *Galka*
Djerrkura, Gatjil, 18
Doctors: attitude of, 100, 105, 142-4; *marrnggitj* and, 47-8, 63, 75-6, 97, 99; respect for, 63, 82, 100, 134, 141-2; role in explanation, 84, 90, 105, 109-11, 117, 142-4, 151-2; role in illness management, 82, 97, 99, 117, 149, 150; suspicion towards, 82, 107-11, 140-1; Yolngu, see *Marrnggitj;*Yolngu reactions to explanations by, 51, 90, 110, 142, 149
Douglas, M., xx
Dreamtime, see *Wangarr*

Eastwell, H.D., 46, 57, 149, 155
Education: Western, 14, 15, 18, 120, 125, 128; Yolngu, see Knowledge
Elcho Island, 59, 64, 86, 106; conflict at, 47; conflict between Yirrkala and, 113, 114; evangelical movement at, 129-30; *marrnggitj* from, 68; mission at, 14, 129-30; sorcerers from, 39, 84, 126; sorcery at, 47, 77-8; spirits at, 52
Eliade, M., xiv
Elkin, A.P., xiv, 78
Epstein, S., xx
Erinosho, O.A., 153
Europeans, see Non-Aborigines
Evans-Pritchard, E.E., xx, xxi, xxiv, 55, 153
Explanations of illness (see also Cause of death; Cause of illness): confined to serious cases, 92, 94, 96, 98; function of, 98, 135, 152; see also Yolngu sociomedical theory; non-Aboriginal influence on, 127-9, 131-2, 142, 146, 150-1, 152-3; in Papua New Guinea, xi, 87; search for, 99, 101-2, 105-6, 111-12, 135-42, 150-2; see also Causal categories; social factors influencing, xvii-xviii, 89-90, 99, 112-14, 152-3; Western medical diagnosis aids, 84, 90, 105, 116, 126-7, 131, 142, 149, 150-2; Western medical diagnosis *v.*, 45, 47, 48, 54, 75, 99-100, 109-11, 145, 152-3

Feierman, S., xx, xxiv, 153
Fieldwork: approach to, xvii-xix; difficulties of, xiv-xvii, 84-5, 112; methodology, xix-xxv, 112; survey as part of, 119-24, 146-51, 157-8; Yolngu attitude to, xvi, 118, 135
Finnegan, R., xxi
Flinders, Matthew, 9-10
Foster, G.M., 121
Frankenberg, R., xx
Frazer, Sir J., xi, xxi

INDEX   175

Galiwin'ku, *see* Elcho Island
Galka (*see also* Sorcery): as agents of retribution, 40, 44–5, 47, 102; attacks by, 37–40 *passim*, 45–6, 60–1, 70–1, 99–108 *passim*, 126; attack turned back on, 83; blood used by, *see Wulä;* the dead associated with, 41; dillybags used by, 39–40, 41, 45–6; fear of, 35, 36, 40–1; making of, 41–2, 49; malice of, 48, 113; non–Aborigines and, 41; practices of, 33, 35, 37–9, 69, 81–3, 88, 103–4, 126; as scapegoats, 88; source of power of, 33–5, 41–2; strangers as, *see* Aboriginal strangers; techniques of, 37–40
Gangan: homeland centre, 15–16; massacre at, 10
Geertz, C., 67
Gellner, E., xxii, xxiii, 153
Gillen, F.J., xiv
Gillies, E., 92
Glick, L.B., 32
Gluckman, M., xxiv, 67
Gossip (*see also* Jealousy): as cause for sorcery attack, 47, 49; frowned upon, 49, 112
Gove, *see* Nhulunbuy
'Gove case', *see* 'Yirrkala case'
Gray, D., xiv
Guenther, M.G., 154
Gumana, Gawirrin, 14–15
Gunapipi, 52–3, 80, 121–4
Gurruwiwi, M., xii, 20, 54

Hallpike, C.R., xxi
Hammond-Tooke, W.D., xx
Hamnett, M.P., 15.1
Harris, S., xviii, 5
Healers, *see Marrnggitj*
Health centre (*see also* Aboriginal health workers), xvi, 17; established, 21; staffing of, 21–2; use of, 19, 70, 80, 95, 108–9; Yolngu attitudes to, 70, 108–9
Health workers, *see* Aboriginal health workers
Hiatt, L.R., 8, 46, 87
Hinnant, J., xxiv
Homeland centres: activities of, 15, 22–4; breach of law at, 52, 145; establishment of, 12–16, 136, 144–5; exile to, 26, 27, 154; health status at, 15, 51, 76, 144–5, 155–6; *marrnggitj* at, 37, 40, 48, 58, 63, 64–5, 86; non–Aboriginal attitude to, 13, 14; reasons for, 13–16, 155–6; sorcery at, 36–7, 86, 103–5; technology at, 15–16, 22–4, 52; also mentioned, 75, 76, 95, 101, 129
Horton, R., xxi, xxii, 55
Hospital: admission of sorcery victims to, 40, 71–2, 89–90, 106–11, 126, 127; admissions (other) to, 54, 63–4, 70, 76, 80, 82, 106, 134;

discrimination (alleged) at, 111; *marrnggitj* at, 64, 65, 72; at Nhulunbuy, 12, 21; recommended use of, 99, 121; use of, 120, 121, 155; at Yirrkala, 20-1; Yolngu attitudes towards use of, 40, 82, 107, 117

House of Representatives Standing Committee on Aboriginal Affairs, xiii, xvi, xvii, 19

Howitt, A.W., xiv

Hughes, C.C., xx

Hunter, J.M., xx

Illness: kin's responsibilities during, 72-3, 94-5, 97, 105, 113, 117, 121; management of, 94-7, 124; patient's responsibilities during, 95; perceptions of, 70-3, 76, 92, 94, 96, 115; *see also* Cause of illness; treatment of, *see* Medical treatment (Western); Yolngu treatment

Indonesians, *see* Macassans

Jahoda, G., 153

Janzen, J.M., 92

Jay, R.R., xviii

Jealousy, 47-8, 64, 65, 82, 138; *see also* Gossip

Keen, I., 5, 6, 33, 81

Kin: author as, xiv-xv, xviii, 108, 112; conflict between, 8, 46-7, 87-8, 89-90, 114, 145; co-operation between, 7-8, 49, 88; prohibitions affecting, xviii, 53, 79, 80-1; responsibilities of, 6, 7-8, 47, 49, 88; *see also* Illness; social distance between, 86, 89; sorcery between, 39-40, 49, 81, 85, 90, 114

Kinship, *see* Clans; Kin; Marriage system

Kluckhohn, C., 84, 115

Knowledge: access to, xviii, 6-7, 44-5; acquisition of, 7, 125, 131, 137-8; non-Aboriginal influence on, 125, 130; Yolngu conception of, xviii

Kroeber, Alfred, 2

Kuhn, T.S., xxii

Land (*see also* Dangerous places): conflict over, 45, 89; *see also* Land rights; importance of, 1-2, 6, 13, 15, 29; ownership of, 1-2, 5-6, 15-16, 17, 33; trespass on, 103, 113, 134

Land rights (*see also* Land): Act of Parliament on, 2; bark petition for, 1, 12; 'Yirrkala case', 1-2, 12, 15, 24-5

Law (*see also* Knowledge; Ritual; Taboos): bestowed by *wangarr*, 5; conflicting with Australian law, *see* Legal systems; death caused by breach of, 46, 51-2, 102, 113, 134; illness caused by breach of, 49-53, 121-4, 145; land ownership based on, 1-2, 6; sanctions

against breach of, 8-9, 44-5; sorcery avenging breaches of, 44-5, 52, 116
Law Reform Commission, 28-9
Leeson, J., xx
Legal systems (for Yolngu, *see* Law): and Australian Law Reform Commission, 28-9; conflicting jursidictions of, 1-2, 8-9, 24-30, 78, 116, 139-40, 154; *see also* Land rights and Garma Council, 28-9; reconciliation of, 27, 29-30, 154
Leprosy, *see Burrpuy*
Lévy-Bruhl, L., xxi
Lewis, G., 92
Lindenbaum, S., 87
Liquor Commission (N.T.), 27
Lockwood, D., 82
Lowe, B., ix

McArthur, M., 20
Macassans: contact with, 9, 10; influence of, 9-10, 25
Macfarlane, A., xx
Macknight, C., 5, 10, 25
McKnight, D., 46, 49
Magicians, Black, *see Galka*
Magicians, White, *see Marrnggitj*
Manggata (see also Djamarrkuli): communication with, 34, 63, 73; as protectors of *marrnggitj,* 47, 61; as source of power, 33-4, 59, 65; as spirit familiars of *marrnggitj,* 33-4, 41, 59, 61, 73, 83
Manggimanggi: as sorcery technique, 42, 83, 84; suspected use of, 44, 60-1, 62, 85, 105, 121, 126-7
Manikay: bestowed by *wangarr,* 5; sung during illness, 72-3, 74, 97, 100; theft of, 45
Maningrida, 25; conflict with people from, 45, 48, 105; sorcerers from, 37, 45, 48, 102, 103-4, 135; sorcery at, 43
Marriage system: adultery and, 7, 46, 49, 70, 88-9, 99-101, 113, 128; betrothals in, 6, 46, 47, 54, 70, 88-9, 114, 131; conflict over, 8, 46-7, 90, 114; death caused by breach of, 53, 88-9, 99-101; exogamy in, 6, 88; illness caused by breach of, 53-4, 128; manipulation of, 6-7, 114; marital problems and, 8, 47, 70, 76, 115; monogamy in, 46; non-Aboriginal interference in, 46; polygyny in, 6-7, 8, 46; sanctions against breach of, 6, 8-9, 90; sorcery and, 47, 49, 53-4, 99-101, 113, 114, 131; sorcery avenging breaches of, 46, 53-4, 131
Marrnggitj (see also Clairvoyance; Jealousy; Power; Yolngu treatment): alcohol and, 66, 68, 73, 83; dillybags used by, 41-2, 61, 69; as diviner, 62-3, 73, 77-8, 99, 104-5, 113, 134; fraudulent practices by, 68; functions of, 32, 56, 75-7, 78, 116; *galka v.,* 33-5, 41-2, 57, 65, 83-4; heat harmful to, 64, 83; limitations of, 43, 51,

68, 69, 81, 97, 101, 107, 150; making of, 41-2, 58-65; massage used by, 37, 40, 66, 77, 100; non-Aboriginal attitudes towards, xiii, xvi, 47-8, 64, 65, 72-6 *passim;* objects used by, 34, 60-4 *passim,* 73, 77, 83, 113, 134; other treatment by, 50-1, 62, 63-4, 68, 77, 107, 120; payment of, 40, 64-5; personality of, xvi, 57-8, 65-6, 85-6; role of, 57, 65-6, 69-70, 78, 97; sorcery and, 85-6; source of power of, 33-5, 41-2, 59-61; *see also Manggatta;* spirit familiars of, 58n., 59-60, 64, 83; *see also Djamarrkuli; Manggatta;* techniques of, 61, 64, 69, 83, 85; treating effects of sorcery, 37, 40, 60-1, 62, 72-4, 100-1, 127; Western doctor *v.,* 47-8, 64, 75-6, 82, 97, 99-100; Western medicine used by, 63, 85-6; Yolngu attitudes towards, 58, 66-9, 74, 76, 78, 85-6, 97, 129

Marwick, M., xx, xxii, xxiii, 55

Massacres: of Japanese, 10-11; of Yolngu, 10, 14

Mawiya, 44

Medical treatment (Western): appropriateness of, 97, 133-4; availability of, 20, 72, 94-5, 96-7; *see also* Health centre; blood-transfusions in, 80; hospitalisation as, *see* Hospital; lack of confidence in, 40, 70, 72, 75, 107-11, 140-1; limitations of, 54, 75, 82, 97, 99, 100, 126; medicines used in, 80, 99; preferred, 20, 68, 96, 97, 123-4, 152; *see also* Doctors; of sorcery attack, 40, 71-2, 89-90, 99-100, 106-11, 126-7; surgery in, 82, 120; suspicion of, 82, 107-11, 140-1; Yolngu treatment conflicts with, 40, 71-4, 99-100, 117-18, 126; Yolngu treatment used with, 63, 64, 67, 94-6, 97, 126-7

Medicine men, *see Marrnggitj*

Medicine, Western, *see* Medical treatment (Western)

Middleton, J., xx, 154

'Milirrpum case', *see* 'Yirrkala case'

Milliken, E.P., 20

Mining (*see also* Nhulunbuy): employment of Aborigines through, 12; establishment of, 1-2, 11-12; fish poisoning and, 133-4; impact of, 24-5; *see also* Land rights; royalties from, 2, 14, 17, 45; Yolngu attitude to, 1-2; *see also* Land

Miny'tji: bestowed by *wangarr,* 5; as source of power, 34; theft of, 45-6, 102

Missions (*see also* Christianity; Yirrkala): as agents of social change, 11, 20, 46, 125; conflict with, 129; impact of, 13, 20; influence of, 1, 14, 17, 126; interference by, 25, 46, 62, 65, 73-6 *passim,* 129-30; medical services of, 11, 20-1, 51

Mitchell, J.C., xx

Moieties, 6, 39, 47; *see also* Social distance

Mokuy: as cause of illness, 33, 52, 68, 121, 145; danger of, 33, 105; described, 33; scepticism about, 108, 126; as source of power, 32-3, 60-1

Moodie, P.M., 19

Morice, R.D., 155
Morphy, F., ix, 5
Morphy, H., 5, 29, 33, 34, 50
Mununggurr, D., xiii
Murngin, xii, xv, 7, 37; *see also* Yolngu
Myers, F., 30

Nabalco Pty Ltd, 1-2, 12, 17; *see also* Mining; Nhulunbuy
Nadel, S.F., xx
National Trachoma and Eye Health Program, 19-20
Ngänuk, see Mokuy
Nhulunbuy (*see also* Mining; Hospital): Aboriginal strangers at, *see* Aboriginal strangers; airport, 11, 12; establishment of, 12; hotel at, 12, 25-6, 27, 134, 142; sorcery at, 44, 84, 134-5; Yirrkala people drinking at, 12, 25-7, 68, 73, 84, 114, 134; Yolngu attitudes to, 15, 48-9, 135, 145; Yolngu employed at, 12, 17; Yolngu use of, 12
Non-Aboriginal society (*see also* Christianity; Mining; Missions): criticised, xvi, 16, 29, 138-9; change and, *see* Change; domination by, 1-3, 13, 15, 29-30, 46, 116-18, 121, 154; influences of, 116, 121, 125, 127, 129, 130-2; *see also* Legal systems; Explanations of illness; relations with, 16, 25-6, 27-30; *see also* Conflict; Yolngu use of products of, 11, 14-16, 22-4; *see also* Alcohol
Non-Aborigines (*see also* Doctors; Nursing sisters): attitudes to Yolngu beliefs and practices, 13, 65, 73-6 *passim*, 117-18, 126-7, 130; conflict with, *see* Conflict; relations with, 9-10, 16, 47-8, 65, 73, 111; sorcery or poisoning by, 82, 101, 107; Yolngu response to, xvii, 2-3, 10-11, 36, 48, 135; *see also* Non-Aboriginal society
Nursing sisters, 40, 85-6; attitudes of, xvi, 71-2, 75, 109; criticised, 70, 72, 107, 108-9; employed by mission, 21; *marrnggitj* and, 72; withdrawn from health centre, 21
Nyira, 43-4, 84, 97n., 121, 126, 131

Outstations, *see* Homeland centres

Packard, R.M., xx, xxiv
Peile, A.R., 83, 92
Peterson, N., 5
Polanyi, M., xxii, 153
Power (*see also* Clairvoyance): benevolent use of, 34, 35; *see also Marrnggitj;* control of, 51-2; from dead bodies, 34, 41; from rituals, 34, 51-2; from sacred places, 34, 144; *see also* Dangerous places; from spirits, 32-4, 41-2, 63-4; *see also Mokuy; Wangarr;* heat harmful to, 64, 83; invoked unintentionally, 34, 51-2; malevolent use of, 33-4, 35, 85-6; *see also Galka;* Sorcery; names, 5; nature of, 35, 41-2, 51, 56; other sources of, 33-4, 41, 79, 80; *see*

also Blood; personal, 34-5, 66-7; potential access to, 32, 34-5; sacred objects possessing, 34, 51
Psychiatric illness, 66, 71, 148-9; attributed to sorcery, 121, 129; attributed to spirits, 33, 52, 121-2

Quinn, J.V., 133

Radin, P., xxiv
Ragalk, see Galka
Rangga: bestowed by *wangarr,* 5; cause of illness as, 51; source of power as, 34; theft of, 45
Reay, M., xiv
Reid, J., xii, xiii, xx, 20, 23, 54, 99
Reser, J.P., 149, 155
Reynolds, H., 43
Rites, *see* Rituals
Rituals (*see also* Knowledge; Law): alcohol at, 26; birth, 79; bloodletting involved in, 52-3, 80; circumcision, 7, 79; conflict resolved at, 7, 87; at death, 51, 52, 80-1, 99, 100, 105, 106, 108; at first menstruation, 79; healing, 81n.; prohibitions relating to, *see* Taboos; purification, 79, 81; revelatory, 7
Roberts, Philip, 82

Scarlett, N., 92, 95
Schwartz, L.R., 97
Shapiro, W., 3, 5
Shepherdson, Rev. H., 14
Skorupski, J., xxi
Social change, *see* Change
Social distance (*see also* Aboriginal strangers), xviii, 20, 82, 86-7, 112-13; sorcery accusations and, 49, 79, 82, 84, 87, 113-14
Social structure, *see* Clans; Kin; Marriage system; Social distance
Sociomedical theory, *see* Yolngu sociomedical theory
Sorcerers, *see Galka;* Sorcery
Sorcery (*see also* Accusations of sorcery); assault, *see Galka;* blood used in, *see Wulä;* breaches of law punished by, 44-5, 52, 116, 131; cases of, *see* Cause of death; Cause of illness; as cultural motif, *see* Yolngu sociomedical theory; dillybags used in, 39-40, 41, 42, 45-6; excrement used in, *see burrpuy;* heat in, 42, 43, 83; image magic as technique of, *see Biyi';* increased incidence of, 37, 84-5, 114, 136-9, 139-40, 154; non-Aboriginal artefacts used in, 43, 44, 134, 140; non-Aborigines and, 41, 82, 101, 107; in Papua New Guinea, xi-xvi; pointed objects used in, *see Manggimanggi;* poison used in, 44, 50, 107, 134; practised by ordinary people, 42, 47, 49, 82, 113, 114; revenge by, 47, 84, 86, 90, 101, 103, 105, 127; *see also Galka;* social breaches punished by, 45, 53-4, 105; social distance

and, 49, 79, 82, 84, 87, 113–14; soiled clothes used in, *see Burrpuy;* spell-singing used in, *see Nyira;* symptoms of attack by, 71–2, 103, 108, 126; techniques causing illness and death, 42–4, 82–3, 121–2; *see also Galka;* theft as reason for, 45–6, 131; threatened use of, 47, 101; urine used in, *see Barrakbarrak;* Yolngu scepticism about, 104, 116, 127–8, 131–3

Soul, *see Birrimbirr*

Spencer, B., xiv

Spirits: benign, *see Birrimbirr;* as causes of illness, 33, 50–1, 52, 68, 121, 145; communication with 34, 41–2, 58, 60–1, 62, 64; *see also Manggata;* Dreamtime, *see Wangarr;* hostile, 50–1, 68, 145; human, *see Mokuy;* as protectors, 34, 47, 61, 62; as sources of power, 32–4, 41–2, 50–1, 60–1, 63–4; *see also Wangarr;* totemic, *see Wangarr;* used in healing, 34, 63–4; *see also Djamarrkuli; Manggata;*

Stanner, W.E.H., xi, 3

Suicide: attempted, 148, 149; as cause of death, 149–50; provoked by sorcery, 39, 88, 149–50

Swantz, xx

Taboos (*see also* Knowledge; Law; Rituals): during circumcision, 53, 79; during menstruation, 53, 79; during pregnancy, 53; post-partum, 53, 79; relating to blood-letting, 52–3, 80, 121–4; relating to food, 52–3, 80–1; relating to polluting substances, 80–1; relating to sacred objects, 44–5, 50–1, 145; relating to sacred places, 44–5, 50–1, 145; ritual, 6–7, 45, 51–2, 52–3

Thomas, K., 153

Thomson, D.F., 28, 34, 36, 37, 57, 58, 66, 124

Tonkinson, M., xiv

Tonkinson, R., xiv

Traditional medicine, *see Marrnggitj;* Yolngu treatment

Treatment, for Western, *see* Doctors; Medical treatment; for Yolngu, *see Marrnggitj;* Yolngu treatment

Turner, V., xx

Tynan, B.J., xiv, 117

Wangarr: as endowers of clans, 5–6, 33; implicated in illness, 50, 52, 145; places dangerous *per se, see* Dangerous places; places used in sorcery, 33–4, 50–1; as sources of power, 33–4, 50–1, 52, 62, 67, 144

Warner, W.L., xii, 3, 5, 7, 32, 34, 35, 37, 41, 57, 58, 65, 81, 119, 124

Webb, T.T., 36, 37, 50, 57, 58, 65, 124

White Australians, *see* Non-Aborigines

White Australian Society, *see* Non-Aboriginal Society

White, N., 5, 81

Williams, N.M., 5,6, 8, 28, 33, 47

Wilson, B.R., xxi

Wiminydji, 83, 92
Witchcraft: in African societies, xx–xxii, xxiv, 55, 84, 154–5; in Australia, *see* Sorcery; in Papua New Guinea, *see* Sorcery
Wongar, see Wangarr
World Health Organisation, xiii
Wulä: extracted by *galka,* 37–8, 39, 69, 78, 81–2, 101; *marrnggitj* uses, 41, 69; other uses of, 38, 40, 42; as source of power, 33, 41, 42, 83

Yirrkala: administrative services of, 14, 17; alcohol at, 25–7, 89, 145; commercial enterprise at, 12, 14, 17–18; conflict within, 84, 85, 114; Dhanbul Council/Association, 17, 25–6; evangelical movement at, 127, 130; history of, 1, 11–12; housing at, 18–19, 86–7; income of, 2, 17–18; Methodist mission at, 11, 20–1, 127; mission influence at, 1, 17, 20, 130; population at, 16–17;
schools at, 17, 18; sorcery within, 84, 85, 114, 127, 138–9; Village Council, 14; Yolngu health status at, *see* Yolngu
'Yirrkala case', 1–2, 12, 15, 24–5
Yolngu: and non-Yolngu Aborigines, *see* Aboriginal strangers; attitude to children, 53, 54, 70, 121; and employment, 11, 12, 15–17, 21–2, 70; health status at homeland centres, 15, 51, 76, 144–5, 155–6; health status at Yirrkala, 13, 14, 19–20, 93–4, 120, 121, 133–4, 156; men's role, xviii, 5, 6–8, 47; non-Aborigines and, *see* Non-Aborigines; origin of name, 3n.; pre-mission lifestyle, 5, 7–8, 20, 46; self-determination, xiii, 13, 17, 21, 24–31, 116–18; *see also* Homeland centres; settlement of, 11; social structure, *see* Clans; Kin; Marriage system; women's role, xviii, 5, 6–7, 8, 30, 44–5, 53, 54, 79, 95
Yolngu sociomedical theory (*see also* Cause of death; Cause of illness; Sorcery); continuing validity of, xxiv xxv, 30–1, 116, 119, 121–4, 146, 156; development of, 152; flexibility of, 150–2; function of, 55, 99, 111–12, 116, 153–4, 156; *see also* Explanations of illness; sorcery's centre role in, xix, xxv, 90–1, 116, 152; *see also* Accusations of sorcery; structure of, 54–5, 90; *see also* Causal categories; tactical value of, xx, 117–18; *see also* Aboriginal health workers; under challenge, 125, 127, 129, 133–4; *see also* Alcohol
Yolngu treatment: appropriateness of, 74–6, 97, 133–4; bush medicine in, 92, 96, 120, 133–4; lack of confidence in, 68, 85; limitations of, *see Marrnggitj;* massage in, 37, 40, 66, 67, 72, 77, 94, 100; objects used in, 67; *see also Marrnggitj;* by ordinary people, 34, 67, 72, 94–5; of sorcery-induced illness, *see Marrnggitj;* spirit familiars in, *see Djamarrkuli; Manggata;* Western treatment used with, 63, 64, 67, 94–6, 97, 126–7; Western treatment *V,* 40, 63–4, 71–4, 76, 99–100, 117
Young, A., 153
Young, E., 87
Yunupingu, D., xiii
Yunupingu, Galarrwuy, 18, 29
Yunupingu, L., xiii

Dr Janice Reid graduated in science from the University of Adelaide before being awarded a scholarship in 1969 to study anthropology at the University of Hawaii. In 1972 she commenced a doctorate in medical anthropology at Stanford University and in 1974–5 lived at Yirrkala in the Northern Territory carrying out field research on the Yolngu theory of illness, the use of indigenous therapies and the relationship between the community and its Western health services. She has held positions at the University of New South Wales and Cumberland College of Health Sciences and since 1979 has been senior lecturer in medical anthropology at the Commonwealth Institute of Health, Sydney University.

Text set in 10/11 pt Bembo by Eastern Type Setters.
Printed on 80 gsm semi matt by Globe Press Pty Ltd, Brunswick, Victoria.